Confronting Environmental Racism

Voices from the Grassroots

Edited by
Robert D. Bullard

Foreword by
Benjamin F. Chavis, Jr.

South End Press
Boston, Massachusetts

Library of Congress Cataloging-in-Publication Data

Confronting environmental racism: voices from the grassroots /
edited by Robert D. Bullard.
p. cm.
Includes bibliographical references.
1. Environmental policy—United States. 2. Hazardous waste sites—United States. 3. Afro-Americans—Politics and government. 4. Racism—United States. 5. Minorities—United States—Political activity. 6. Environmental policy—Unites States—Case studies. 7. Hazardous waste sites—United States—Case studies. 8. Afro-Americans—Politics and government—Case studies. 9. Racism—United States—Case studies. 10. Minorities—United States—Political activity—Case studies.
I. Bullard, Robert D. (Robert Doyle), 1946-
HC110.E5C665 1993   92-28125
363.7'008'693—dc20   CIP
ISBN 0-89608-447-7 (cloth) : $40.00
ISBN 0-89608-446-9 (paper) : $16.00

South End Press, 116 Saint Botolph Street, Boston, MA 02115
99 98 97 96 95 94 93   1 2 3 4 5 6 7 8 9

Acknowledgments

It has been two years since I began this anthology. During this time I received valuable assistance, comments, and suggestions from numerous individuals, groups, and organizations. This book addresses topics that touch the lives of millions of individuals who are affected by environmental problems. I am especially grateful to the contributors who conducted research and prepared essays for this project. Their persistence, patience, and goodwill were key to bringing this book to fruition. Without the help of these friends and others who shared their stories with us, this project would have been impossible.

I offer special appreciation to the Charles Stewart Mott Foundation, the Fund for Research for Dispute Resolution, and the Ford Foundation for their financial support. The Ford grant was critical in commissioning papers from leading environmental justice scholars and activists.

I am also grateful for the support we received from Robin Whittington and the staff in the Department of Sociology at the University of California, Riverside, for wordprocessing assistance, editing, indexing, and other work to keep the project on schedule. Conrad Miller's copyediting also proved invaluable. Finally, thanks go out to Steve Chase, my able editor at South End Press, whose enthusiasim and labor led to the final publication of this book.

—RDB

Foreword

Rev. Benjamin F. Chavis, Jr.

Millions of African Americans, Latinos, Asians, Pacific Islanders, and Native Americans are trapped in polluted environments because of their race and color. Inhabitants of these communities are exposed to greater health and environmental risks than is the general population. Clearly, all Americans do not have the same opportunities to breathe clean air, drink clean water, enjoy clean parks and playgrounds, or work in a clean, safe environment.

People of color bear the brunt of the nation's pollution problem. This was the case, for example, in Warren County, North Carolina, in 1982. It is still true today. Warren County is important because activities there set off the national environmental justice movement. The rural, poor, and mostly African-American county was selected for a PCB landfill not because it was an environmentally sound choice, but because it seemed powerless to resist. During the subsequent protests and demonstrations against the landfill, the term "environmental racism" was coined. For the more than 500 protesters who were arrested, the behavior of county authorities was seen as an extension of the institutional racism many of them had encountered in the past—including discrimination in housing, employment, education, municipal services, and law enforcement.

Environmental racism is racial discrimination in environmental policymaking. It is racial discrimination in the enforcement of regulations and laws. It is racial discrimination in the deliberate targeting of communities of color for toxic waste disposal and the siting of polluting industries. It is racial discrimination in the official sanctioning of the life-threatening presence of poisons and pollutants in communities of color. And, it is racial discrimination in the history of excluding people of color from the mainstream environmental groups, decisionmaking boards, commissions, and regulatory bodies.

The United Church of Christ Commission for Racial Justice was among the first national civil rights organizations to raise the question of environmental racism. The Commission's 1987 groundbreaking study *Toxic Wastes and Race* brought national attention to this problem. In preparing the study, the Commission was moving into a new arena—research on environmental injustice. But we already knew then what we know now—injustice must be fought wherever and whenever it is found. The environmental arena is no exception.

Robert D. Bullard's important 1990 book *Dumping in Dixie* examined this type of racism in our nation's own underdeveloped "Third World" region, African-American communities in the South. However, no one segment of the population and no one region has a monopoly on this problem. It is national and international in scope.

Environmental racism does not only involve the siting of toxic waste facilities. This insightful new book, *Confronting Environmental Racism,* extends the analysis and coverage even further to explore the problems of lead, pesticides, and petrochemical plants that have a disproportionately large impact on communities of color. This book also examines sustainable development, job blackmail, discriminatory public policy, and dispute resolution strategies.

As is typical of the environmental justice movement, *Confronting Environmental Racism* has brought together a diverse group of academicians and activists from all across the country to write about these life-and-death environmental justice issues. Many were active participants at the First National People of Color Environmental Leadership Summit. Held in Washington, D.C., in October 1991, this Summit brought together more than 650 grassroots and national leaders from all 50 states, the District of Columbia, Puerto Rico, Mexico, and the Marshall Islands. The delegates adopted the "Principles of Environmental Justice," which have since been disseminated throughout the United States and were taken to the 1992 United Nation's Commission on Environment and Development (UNCED) and to parallel Global Forum meetings in Rio de Janeiro. The goal is to have these principles resonate throughout the globe wherever unjust, racist, and nonsustainable environmental and development policies exist.

The struggle for environmental justice has intensified in communities that have become "sacrifice zones." Chicago's southeast neighborhood of Altgeld Gardens has been described as a "toxic doughnut" because it is surrounded by polluting industries. Similar threats exist in East St. Louis, in Louisiana's "Cancer Alley," on Navaho lands where uranium is mined, and in farmworker communities where laborers and their families are routinely poisoned by pesticides.

Environmental justice struggles have now been extended beyond U.S. borders, as threats multiply in the Third World. Many of these threats are beyond the control of the world's poor nations. Toxic wastes, banned pesticides, "recycled" batteries, and scrap metals are routinely shipped to Third World nations by multinational corporations. Further, the atrocious environmental policies of these firms, when operating in the Third World, are well documented. One only needs to look at the environmental record of the nearly 2,000 *maquiladoras* plants that operate on the Mexican side of the U.S.-Mexican border to see the pattern. Environmental justice activists are challenging policies and practices that target wastes and polluting industries for the Third World as well. After all, the international waste and pollution practices of U.S.-based corporations merely reflect the U.S. domestic policy of targeting low-income, disenfranchised communities of color.

The contributors to *Confronting Environmental Racism* make it clear that the environmental justice movement is not an anti-white movement. They document the stories of grassroots leaders who are struggling against unjust, unfair, unethical, and sometimes illegal practices of industry and government. Environmental justice advocates are not saying, "Take the poisons out of our community and put them in a white community." They are saying that *no* community should have to live with these poisons. They have thus taken the moral high road and are building a multiracial and inclusive movement that has the potential of transforming the political landscape of this nation.

Introduction

Robert D. Bullard

An environmental revolution is taking shape in the United States. This revolution has touched communities of color from New York to California and from Florida to Alaska—anywhere where African Americans, Latinos, Asians, Pacific Islanders, and Native Americans live and comprise a majority of the population. Collectively, these Americans represent the fastest growing segment of the population in the United States. They are also the groups most at risk from environmental problems.

At the heart of the problem is the fact that the United States is a racially divided nation where extreme racial inequalities continue to persist (Kozol 1991). Because racial segregation continues to be the dominant residential pattern, people of color are clustered in urban ghettos, barrios, reservations, and rural "poverty pockets." This pattern is created by boundaries and restrictions set by the dominant white society. Racism created and perpetuates separate and unequal communities where people of color and whites live apart (Feagin & Feagin 1986). In other words, "America's *apartheid,* while lacking overt legal sanction, comes closest to the system even now being reformed in the land of its invention" (Hacker 1992).

This book focuses on people of color because their struggles unite environmentalism and social justice into one framework: the environmental justice movement. Their struggles emphasize justice, fairness, and equity. Grassroots groups challenge the "business-as-usual" environmentalism that is generally practiced by the more privileged wildlife- and conservation-oriented groups. The focus of activists of color and their constituents reflects their life experiences of social, economic, and political disenfranchisement.

After writing *Dumping in Dixie,* I came to see that environmental justice issues were top concerns among African Americans. Clearly, the research in that book dispelled the myth that environmental activism was solely the domain of whites (Bullard 1990). Moreover, subsequent research reinforced what many of us already knew: environmental racism is not confined to African-American communities or to the southern United States (Grossman 1991, 1992; Bullard 1991a, 1991b).

A broader analysis is needed on the environmental problems faced by communities of color in the United States. Thus, this book is a follow-up to *Dumping in Dixie*. This anthology was two years in the making. I used a multidisciplinary approach in selecting the individual contributors. These individuals come from a wide range of backgrounds and professions including sociology, political science, urban planning, law, and medicine. I also made a conscious effort to include both academicians and activists. The perspectives both groups bring to the work are valuable complements to the overall analysis. In keeping with the theme of "we speak for ourselves," the vast majority of essays were written by persons of color who are active in or have worked with grassroots groups around environmental justice issues. It is also worth noting that six of the thirteen essays were written by women.

It is no mystery that the environmental justice groups discussed in this volume are attacking the institutions they see providing advantages and privileges to whites while perpetrating segregation, underdevelopment, disenfranchisement, and the poisoning (some people would use the term genocide) of their constituents. The analysis documents struggles for environmental justice, many of which are embedded in the larger struggle against oppression and dehumanization that exists in the larger society (Bullard 1990).

The quest for environmental justice is a dynamic social movement. In many respects, it parallels the mainstream environmental movement. Perhaps its most unique aspect is its leadership. The movement is led, planned, and to a large extent funded by individuals who are not part of the established environmental community: namely, national environmental and conservation groups such as the National Wildlife Federation, Sierra Club, and the Audubon Society. Few of the environmental justice groups organized by people of color receive government or foundation funding. Most of them are small and operate with resources generated from the local community (Bullard 1992).

The actions of grassroots groups defy the social movement and collective behavior theories marshaled to explain their longevity and success. In many instances, grassroots leaders emerged from groups of concerned citizens (many of them women) who see their families, homes, and communities threatened by some type of polluting industry or governmental policy (Gibbs 1982; Shiva 1988; Bullard 1990; Hamilton 1990; Pardo 1990). For too long these groups and their leaders have been "invisible" and their stories muted. This is changing. Grassroots groups are beginning to appear in government reports, the mass media, and public forums. They have forced their issues onto the nation's environmental agenda.

The thirteen chapters in this volume all address some aspect of environmental racism and the unjust treatment of people of color. The major issues and disputes examined include toxics, waste facility siting, urban industrial pollution, childhood lead poisoning, pesticides and farmworkers, land rights, sustainable development, and the export of toxics and "risky" technology. From Native-American lands to urban ghettos and barrios, environmental problems are taking a heavy toll in these communities. Residents of places like West Dallas, West Harlem, East St. Louis, East and South Central Los Angeles, Emelle, Richmond, and the Rosebud Reservation see their struggle as a life-and-death matter. Grassroots leaders are demanding action. They are tired of promises.

Many of the environmental problems chronicled in this book did not appear overnight; some have been around for centuries. Moreover, the root cause of many of them can be traced to the imperial ethics and values surrounding the "conquest" of the land and its people and the glorification of the colonization process in our literature. Rather than listening to and learning from Native Americans, who cared for the land for centuries, European colonists chose to control, dominate, tame, and develop the "wilderness" for their material comfort and profit (Limerick 1987; Jaimes 1992). Generally, disputes over use of public lands, water rights, and alternative development projects in heavily Latino places, like southern Colorado and northern New Mexico, stem from the conflict of values surrounding stewardship.

The struggle for environmental justice was not invented in the 1990s. People of color, individually and collectively, have waged a frontal assault against environmental injustices that predate the first Earth Day in 1970. Many of these struggles, however, were not framed as "environmental" problems—rather they were seen as addressing "social" problems. For example, the U.S. National Advisory Commission on Civil Disorders (1968) discovered that systematic neglect of garbage collection and sanitation services in African-American neighborhoods contributed to the urban disturbances in the 1960s. Inadequate services, unpaved streets, lack of sewers and indoor plumbing were environmental problems in the 1960s and are environmental problems in the 1990s.

The 1967 riot at predominately black Texas Southern University in Houston was precipitated by two separate demonstrations against what was perceived as institutional racism. One group was protesting the death of an eight-year-old black girl who drowned at a city-owned garbage dump. The second protest was sparked by individuals who were challenging the way black and white students were disciplined in the Houston Independent School District. Needless to say, black students were disciplined more harshly than white students. The two protest groups combined forces against what they saw were unjust and unacceptable conditions (U.S. Commission on Civil Disorders 1968; Bullard 1987).

Civil rights leader Martin Luther King, Jr. came to Memphis in 1968 to resolve an economic and environmental justice dispute. African-American sanitation workers were striking for better wages, improved work conditions, and equity with other municipal employees. King was assassinated before he could complete his mission. Nevertheless, the issues raised by the sanitation workers were placed on the national civil rights agenda.

A growing body of evidence reveals that people of color are subjected to a disproportionately large number of health and environmental risks in their neighborhoods (e.g., childhood lead poisoning); and on their jobs (e.g., pesticide poisoning of farm workers) (Bryant & Mohai 1992). Various levels of government have done little to correct the environmental imbalances that exist in this country. Even worse, governmental action has in fact exacerbated many of the environmental threats to communities of color.

Some institutional arrangements between government and industry have placed communities of color at greater risk than the general population. For example, one unanticipated result of more stringent federal environmental regulations has been the increased vulnerability of communities of color to the siting of unpopular industrial facilities such as municipal landfills, toxic waste dumps, lead smelters, and incinerators. NIMBY (not in my backyard) actions have also intensified the pressure on poor communities and communities of color from the dumping groups for polluting industries and other locally unwanted land uses (LULUs).

Given the political and economic climate of the time, unpopular polluting facilities such as hazardous waste landfills, incinerators, garbage dumps, lead smelters, and paper mills are likely to end up in somebody's backyard. But whose? More often than not, polluting industries end up in communities color, rather than in the affluent white suburbs.

How have some white communities kept out unwanted facilities? First of all, some communities escape by virtue of where they are located and who lives there. Few dirty industries are proposed for wealthy areas such as Beverly Hills or Kennebunkport. Zoning is the chief device for regulating land use. However, exclusionary zoning practices have provided benefits for whites at the expense of people of color.

This in no way means that some white communities have not been adversely affected by industrial pollution. Very few Americans have not heard of Love Canal and Times Beach (Levine 1982; Edelstein 1987).

However, the poisoning of African-American communities such as those in Triana, West Dallas, Reveilletown, and Texarkana are not as well known to the public. Environmental and health risks are not randomly distributed throughout the population. On close examination of the costs and benefits derived from unpopular environmental decisions, communities of color have borne and continue to bear a disproportionate share of the burden of the nation's pollution problems.

Environmental inequities cannot be reduced solely to class factors or the economic ability of some people to "vote with their feet" and escape polluted environments. Race and class are intricately linked in our society. However, race continues to be a potent predictor of where people live, which communities get dumped on, and which are spared. Racial bias creates and perpetuates unequal environmental quality in communities of color and white communities.

The practice of targeting communities of color for the siting of unpopular industrial facilities is a form of environmental racism. Government has been slow to address environmental and other forms racism. Part of the problem lies in the continued denial of the existence of racism by government officials and policymakers.

Who benefits from and who pays for our modern industrial society? Environmental and health costs are localized: risks increase with proximity to the source and are borne by those living nearby, while the benefits are dispersed throughout the larger society. Communities that host hazardous waste disposal facilities (importers) receive fewer economic benefits (jobs) than do communities that generate the waste (exporters). The people who benefit the most bear the least burden.

Persons of color who live in contaminated areas are often victims of a "double whammy" in that they are exposed to elevated risks, while at the same time they often have problems getting access to health and medical facilities. East St. Louis, Illinois, typifies this (Kozol 1991). In general, inner-city hospitals are closing in record numbers, while environmental and health problems in these areas are on the rise. The federal government has made only minimal attempts to level the playing field. Communities of color are still confronted with rules, regulations, and policies governing them that are not applied uniformly across the board.

A case in point is the conditions under which farmworkers must labor. Thousands of migrant farmworkers (over 90 percent of whom are person of color) and their children are poisoned by pesticides sprayed on crops. These individuals are "second-class" workers and are considered expendable. Of course, there is no uniform set of standards specifying "acceptable" levels of pesticide exposure for plant workers who manufacture the pesticides, nearby community residents who are exposed to plant emissions, farmworkers who apply the pesticides, and consumers who eat the food on which pesticide residue may be found. Yet, the health and safety of farmworkers and their families receive the least amount of consideration and protection (Moses 1989).

Millions of inner-city children (many of whom are African-American and Latino) are poisoned by lead-based paint from old houses, drinking water from lead-soldered pipes and old water mains, soil contaminated by industry, and air pollutants from smelters. Lead poisoning is considered the number one environmental health problem facing children in the United States (Agency for Toxic Substances and Disease Registry 1988). Yet, little has been done over the past 20 years to rid the nation of this preventable childhood disease.

The nation is also now faced with a garbage and hazardous waste crisis. States are grappling with the question of what to do with their mounting wastes and the federal government is confronted with mounting nuclear and toxic wastes from its weapons and military installations. Tougher environmental regulations and increased public opposition have made it difficult to site any new waste management facilities, ranging from recycling centers and garbage incinerators to radioactive storage dumps. Communities of color have become prime targets as a solution to the facility siting gridlock (Angel 1992).

Some communities have been turned into "human sacrifice zones." Places like Chicago's South Side, Louisiana's "Cancer Alley," and East Los Angeles share two common characteristics: 1) they already have more than their share of environmental problems and polluting industries, and 2) they are still attracting new polluters. Past discriminatory facility-siting and land-use practices appear to guide future public policy decisions. Site selection is rationalized by arguing that an area already has multiple facilities. Of course, any saturation policy derived from past siting practices perpetuates and worsens environmental inequities (Bullard 1990).

Communities saturated with polluting industries may have become less sensitive to the impact of a proposed new facility than those having few facilities (Edelstein 1987). Yet, siting hazardous waste incinerators in the same community where there is an operating hazardous waste landfill may make economic and political sense, but may create an environmental and public health nightmare for impacted residents.

Chronic unemployment, poverty, and the lack of a sound economic infrastructure all place communities of color at risk from polluting industries which exploit this economic vulnerability. African-American communities in Louisiana's "Cancer Alley" (those communities along the 85-mile stretch of the Mississippi River from Baton Rouge to New Orleans) have long suffered economic blackmail and environmental racism (Beasley 1990a; Bullard 1990; Grossman 1992). The plantation owner in the rural parishes was replaced by the petrochemical industry executive as the new "master" and "overseer."

Petrochemical colonialism mirrors the system of domination typical of the Old South. In addition to poisoning the people, this new master is robbing many of the local residents (many of whom are descendants of slaves) of their ancestral homes. Environmental racism is now turning century-old African-American communities into ghost towns. One need only visit communities like Alsen, Sunrise, St. Gabriel, and Lions to understand the ultimate price of petrochemical colonialism along the winding Mississippi River in southeast Louisiana (Anderson 1992).

Social critique is not sufficient, however. This book also addresses the question of vision: Where is the environmental justice movement headed? What mechanisms are being used to strengthen regional and national networks among environmental activists of color? What is their relationship to the mainstream environmental movement? Will inclusion of persons of color on decisionmaking boards make a difference? It is clear that people of color will no longer stand by while their communities are assaulted and their families poisoned. As this book makes abundantly clear, people of color are using their own organizations and, where necessary, forming alliances with outside environmental, legal, and civil rights groups to fight for environmental and economic justice.

The nation has a long way to go before it achieves environmental quality and equity. Many of the decisionmaking boards and commissions still do not reflect the racial, ethnic, and cultural diversity of the country. The exclusion of significant segments of the population has biased environmental decisionmaking in favor of white middle-class communities. However, tokenism is not the answer. Inclusion of persons of color on boards and commissions does not necessarily mean that their voices will be heard or their cultures respected. Nevertheless, the ultimate goal of any inclusion strategy should be to democratize environmental decisionmaking and empower disenfranchised people to speak and act for themselves. This commitment is at the heart and soul of our book.

CHAPTER 1

Anatomy of Environmental Racism and the Environmental Justice Movement

Robert D. Bullard

Communities are not all created equal. In the United States, for example, some communities are routinely poisoned while the government looks the other way. Environmental regulations have not uniformly benefited all segments of society. People of color (African Americans, Latinos, Asians, Pacific Islanders, and Native Americans) are disproportionately harmed by industrial toxins on their jobs and in their neighborhoods. These groups must contend with dirty air and drinking water—the byproducts of municipal landfills, incinerators, polluting industries, and hazardous waste treatment, storage, and disposal facilities.

Why do some communities get "dumped on" while others escape? Why are environmental regulations vigorously enforced in some communities and not in others? Why are some workers protected from environmental threats to their health while others (such as migrant farmworkers) are still being poisoned? How can environmental justice be incorporated into the campaign for environmental protection? What institutional changes would enable the United States to become a just and sustainable society? What community organizing strategies are effective against environmental racism? These are some of the many questions addressed in this book.

This chapter sketches out the basic environmental problems communities of color face, discusses how the mainstream environmental movement does not provide an adequate organizational base, analysis, vision, or strategy to address these problems, and, finally, provides a glimpse of several representative struggles within the grassroots environmental justice movement. For these purposes, the pervasive reality of racism is placed at the very center of the analysis.

Internal Colonialism and White Racism

The history of the United States has long been grounded in white racism. The nation was founded on the principles of "free land" (stolen from Native Americans and Mexicans), "free labor" (cruelly extracted from African slaves), and "free men" (white men with property). From the outset, institutional racism shaped the economic, political, and ecological landscape, and buttressed the exploitation of both land and people. Indeed, it has allowed communities of color to exist as internal colonies characterized by dependent (and unequal) relationships with the dominant white society or "Mother Country." In their 1967 book, *Black Power,* Carmichael and Hamilton were among the first to explore the "internal" colonial model as a way to explain the racial inequality, political exploitation, and social isolation of African Americans. As Carmichael and Hamilton write:

> The economic relationship of America's black communities [to white society]...reflects their colonial status. The political power exercised over those communities goes hand in glove with the economic deprivation experienced by the black citizens.
>
> Historically, colonies have existed for the sole purpose of enriching, in one form or another, the "colonizer"; the consequence is to maintain the economic dependency of the "colonized" (pp. 16-17).

Generally, people of color in the United States—like their counterparts in formerly colonized lands of Africa, Asia, and Latin America—have not had the same opportunities as whites. The social forces that have organized oppressed colonies internationally still operate in the "heart of the colonizer's mother country" (Blauner 1972, p. 26). For Blauner, people of color are subjected to five principal colonizing processes: they enter the "host" society and economy involuntarily; their native culture is destroyed; white-dominated bureaucracies impose restrictions from which whites are exempt; the dominant group uses institutionalized racism to justify its actions; and a dual or "split labor market" emerges based on ethnicity and race. Such domination is also buttressed by state institutions. Social scientists Omi and Winant (1986, pp. 76-78) go so far as to insist that "every state institution is a racial institution." Clearly, whites receive benefits from racism, while people of color bear most of the cost.

Environmental Racism

Racism plays a key factor in environmental planning and decisionmaking. Indeed, environmental racism is reinforced by government, legal, economic, political, and military institutions. It is a fact of life in the United States that the mainstream environmental movement is only beginning to wake up to. Yet, without a doubt, racism influences the likelihood of exposure to environmental and health risks and the accessibility to health care. Racism provides whites of all class levels with an "edge" in gaining access to a healthy physical environment. This has been documented again and again.

Whether by conscious design or institutional neglect, communities of color in urban ghettos, in rural "poverty pockets," or on economically impoverished Native-American reservations face some of the worst environmental devastation in the nation. Clearly, racial discrimination was not legislated out of existence in the 1960s. While some significant progress was made during this decade, people of color continue to struggle for equal treatment in many areas, including environmental justice. Agencies at all levels of government, including the federal EPA, have done a poor job protecting people of color from the ravages of pollution and industrial encroachment. It has thus been an up-hill battle convincing white judges, juries, government officials, and policymakers that racism exists in environmental protection, enforcement, and policy formulation.

The most polluted urban communities are those with crumbling infrastructure, ongoing economic disinvestment, deteriorating housing, inadequate schools, chronic unemployment, a high poverty rate, and an overloaded health-care system. Riot-torn South Central Los Angeles typifies this urban neglect. It is not surprising that the "dirtiest" zip code in California belongs to the mostly African-American and Latino neighborhood in that part of the city (Kay 1991a). In the Los Angeles basin, over 71 percent of the African Americans and 50 percent of the Latinos live in areas with the most polluted air, while only 34 percent of the white population does (Ong and Blumenberg 1990; Mann 1991). This pattern exists nationally as well. As researchers Wernette and Nieves note:

> In 1990, 437 of the 3,109 counties and independent cities failed to meet at least one of the EPA ambient air quality standards...57 percent of whites, 65 percent of African Americans, and 80 percent of Hispanics live in 437 counties with substandard air quality. Out of the whole population, a total of 33 percent of whites, 50 percent of African Americans, and 60 percent of Hispanics live in the 136 counties in

which two or more air pollutants exceed standards. The percentage living in the 29 counties designated as nonattainment areas for three or more pollutants are 12 percent of whites, 20 percent of African Americans, and 31 percent of Hispanics (pp. 16-17).

Income alone does not account for these above-average percentages. Housing segregation and development patterns play a key role in determining where people live. Moreover, urban development and the "spatial configuration" of communities flow from the forces and relationships of industrial production which, in turn, are influenced and subsidized by government policy (Feagin 1988; Gottdiener 1988). There is widespread agreement that vestiges of race-based decisionmaking still influence housing, education, employment, and criminal justice. The same is true for municipal services such as garbage pickup and disposal, nieghborhood sanitation, fire and police protection, and library services. Institutional racism influences decisions on local land use, enforcement of environmental regulations, industrial facility siting, management of economic vulnerability, and the paths of freeways and highways.

People skeptical of the assertion that poor people and people of color are targeted for waste-disposal sites should consider the report the Cerrell Associates provided the California Waste Management Board. In their 1984 report, *Political Difficulties Facing Waste-to-Energy Conversion Plant Siting,* they offered a detailed profile of those neighborhoods most likely to organize effective resistance against incinerators. The policy conclusion based on this analysis is clear. As the report states:

> All socioeconomic groupings tend to resent the nearby siting of major facilities, but middle and upper socioeconomic strata possess better resources to effectuate their opposition. Middle and higher socioeconomic strata neighborhoods should not fall within the one-mile and five-mile radius of the proposed site (p. 43).

Where then will incinerators or other polluting facilities be sited? For Cerrell Associates, the answer is low-income, disempowered neighborhoods with a high concentration of nonvoters. The ideal site, according their report, has nothing to do with environmental soundness but everything to do with lack of social power. Communities of color in California are far more likely to fit this profile than are their white counterparts.

Those still skeptical of the existence of environmental racism should also consider the fact that zoning boards and planning commissions are typically stacked with white developers. Generally, the decisions of these bodies reflect the special interests of the individuals who sit on these boards. People of color have been systematically excluded from these decisionmaking boards, commissions, and governmental agencies (or allowed only token representation). Grassroots leaders are now demanding a shared role in all the decisions that shape their communities. They are challenging the intended or unintended racist assumptions underlying environmental and industrial policies.

Toxic Colonialism Abroad

To understand the global ecological crisis, it is important to understand that the poisoning of African Americans in South Central Los Angeles and of Mexicans in border *maquiladoras* have their roots in the same system of economic exploitation, racial oppression, and devaluation of human life. The quest for solutions to environmental problems and for ways to acheive sustainable development in the United States has considerable implications for the global environmental movement.

Today, more than 1,900 *maquiladoras,* assembly plants operated by American, Japanese, and other foreign countries, are located along the 2,000-mile U.S.-Mexico border (Center for Investigative Reporting 1990; Sanchez 1990; Zuniga 1992, p. 22A). These plants use cheap Mexican labor to assemble products from imported components and raw materials, and then ship them back to the United States (Witt 1991). Nearly half a million Mexicans work in the *maquiladoras.* They earn an average of $3.75 a day. While these plants bring jobs, albeit low-paying ones, they exacerbate local pollution by overcrowding the border towns, straining sewage and water systems, and reducing air quality. All this compromises the health of workers and nearby community residents. The Mexican environmental regulatory agency is understaffed and ill-equipped to adequately enforce the country's laws (Working Group on Canada-Mexico Free Trade 1991).

The practice of targeting poor communities of color in the Third World for waste disposal and the introduction of risky technologies from industrialized countries are forms of "toxic colonialism," what some activists have dubbed the "subjugation of people to an ecologically-destructive economic order by entities over which the people have no control" (Greenpeace 1992, p. 3). The industrialized world's controversial Third World dumping policy was made public by the release of an internal, December 12, 1991, memorandum authored by Lawrence Summers, chief economist of the World Bank. It shocked the world and touched off a global scandal. Here are the highlights:

"Dirty" Industries: Just between you and me, shouldn't the World Bank be encouraging MORE migration of the dirty industries to the LDCs [Less Developed Countries]? I can think of three reasons:

1) The measurement of the costs of health impairing pollution depends on the foregone earnings from increased morbidity and mortality. From this point of view a given amount of health impairing pollution should be done in the country with the lowest cost, which will be the country with the lowest wages. I think the economic logic behind dumping a load of toxic waste in the lowest wage country is impeccable and we should face up to that.

2) The costs of pollution are likely to be non-linear as the initial increments of pollution probably have very low cost. I've always thought that under-polluted areas in Africa are vastly UNDER-polluted; their air quality is probably vastly inefficiently low compared to Los Angeles or Mexico City. Only the lamentable facts that so much pollution is generated by non-tradable industries (transport, electrical generation) and that the unit transport costs of solid waste are so high prevent world welfare-enhancing trade in air pollution and waste.

3) The demand for a clean environment for aesthetic and health reasons is likely to have very high income elasticity. The concern over an agent that causes a one in a million change in the odds of prostate cancer is obviously going to be much higher in a country where people survive to get prostate cancer than in a country where under 5 [year-old] mortality is 200 per thousand. Also, much of the concern over industrial atmosphere discharge is about visibility impairing particulates. These discharges may have very little direct health impact. Clearly trade in goods that embody aesthetic pollution concerns could be welfare enhancing. While production is mobile the consumption of pretty air is a non-tradable.

The problem with the arguments against all of these proposals for more pollution in LDCs (intrinsic rights to certain goods, moral reasons, social concerns, lack of adequate markets, etc.) could be turned around and used more or less effectively against every Bank proposal...

Beyond the Race vs. Class Trap

Whether at home or abroad, the question of who *pays* and who *benefits* from current industrial and development policies is central to any analysis of environmental racism. In the United States, race interacts with class to create special environmental and health vulnerabilities. People of color, however, face elevated toxic exposure levels even when social class variables (income, education, and occupational status) are held constant (Bryant and Mohai 1992). Race has been found to be an independent factor, not reducible to class, in predicting the distribution of 1) air pollution in our society (Freeman 1972; Gianessi, Peskin, and Wolff 1979; Gelobter 1988; Wernette and Nieves 1992); 2) contaminated fish consumption (West, Fly, and Marans 1990); 3) the location of municipal landfills and incinerators (Bullard 1983, 1987, 1990, 1991a); 4) the location of abandoned toxic waste dumps (United Church of Christ Commission for Racial Justice 1987); and 5) lead poisoning in children (Agency for Toxic Substances and Disease Registry 1988).

Lead poisoning is a classic case in which race, not just class, determines exposure. It affects between three and four million children in the United States—most of whom are African Americans and Latinos living in urban areas. Among children five years old and younger, the percentage of African Americans who have excessive levels of lead in their blood far exceeds the percentage of whites at all income levels (Agency for Toxic Substances and Disease Registry 1988, p. I-12).

The federal Agency for Toxic Substances and Disease Registry found that for families earning less than $6,000 annually an estimated 68 percent of African-American children had lead poisoning, compared with 36 percent for white children. For families with incomes exceeding $15,000, more than 38 percent of African-American children have been poisoned, compared with 12 percent of white children. African-American children are two to three times more likely than their white counterparts to suffer from lead poisoning independent of class factors.

One reason for this is that African Americans and whites do not have the same opportunities to "vote with their feet" by leaving unhealthy physical environments. The ability of an individual to escape a health-threatening environment is usually correlated with income. However, racial barriers make it even harder for millions of African Americans, Latinos, Asians, Pacific Islanders, and Native Americans to relocate. Housing discrimination, redlining, and other market forces make it difficult for millions of households to buy their way out of polluted environments. For example, an affluent African-American family (with an income of $50,000 or more) is as segregated as an African-American family with an annual income of $5,000 (Denton and Massey

1988; Jaynes and Williams 1989). Thus, lead poisoning of African-American children is not just a "poverty thing."

White racism helped create our current separate and unequal communities. It defines the boundaries of the urban ghetto, *barrio,* and reservation, and influences the provision of environmental protection and other public services. Apartheid-type housing and development policies reduce neighborhood options, limit mobility, diminish job opportunities, and decrease environmental choices for millions of Americans. It is unlikely that this nation will ever achieve lasting solutions to its environmental problems unless it also addresses the system of racial injustice that helps sustain the existance of powerless communities forced to bear disproportionate environmental costs.

The Limits of Mainstream Environmentalism

Historically, the mainstream environmental movement in the United States has developed agendas that focus on such goals as wilderness and wildlife preservation, wise resource management, pollution abatement, and population control. It has been primarily supported by middle- and upper-middle-class whites. Although concern for the environment cuts across class and racial lines, ecology activists have traditionally been individuals with above-average education, greater access to economic resources, and a greater sense of personal power (Buttel and Flinn 1978; Morrison 1980, 1986; Dunlap 1987; Bullard, 1990; Bullard and Wright 1987; Bachrach and Zautra 1985; Mohai, 1985, 1990).

Not surprisingly, mainstream groups were slow in broadening their base to include poor and working-class whites, let alone African Americans and other people of color. Moreover, they were ill-equipped to deal with the environmental, economic, and social concerns of these communities. During the 1960s and 1970s, while the "Big Ten" environmental groups focused on wilderness preservation and conservation through litigation, political lobbying, and technical evaluation, activists of color were engaged in mass direct action mobilizations for basic civil rights in the areas of employment, housing, education, and health care. Thus, two parallel and sometimes conflicting movements emerged, and it has taken nearly two decades for any significant convergence to occur between these two efforts. In fact, conflicts still remain over how the two groups should balance economic development, social justice, and environmental protection.

In their desperate attempt to improve the economic conditions of their constituents, many African-American civil rights and political leaders have directed their energies toward bringing jobs to their communities. In many instances, this has been achieved at great risk to the health of workers and the surrounding communities. The promise of jobs (even low-paying and hazardous ones) and of a broadened tax base has enticed several economically impoverished, politically powerless communities of color both in the United States and around the world (Center for Investigative Reporting and Bill Moyers 1990; Bullard 1990; Bryant and Mohai 1992). Environmental job blackmail is a fact of life. You can get a job, but only if you are willing to do work that will harm you, your families, and your neighbors.

Workers of color are especially vulnerable to job blackmail because of the greater threat of unemployment they face compared to whites and because of their concentration in low-paying, unskilled, nonunionized occupations. For example, they make up a large share of the nonunion contract workers in the oil, chemical, and nuclear industries. Similarly, over 95 percent of migrant farmworkers in the United States are Latino, African-American, Afro-Caribbean, or Asian, and African Americans are overrepresented in high-risk, blue-collar, and service occupations for which a large pool of replacement labor exists. Thus, they are twice as likely to be unemployed as their white counterparts. Fear of unemployment acts as a potent incentive for many African-American workers to accept and keep jobs they know are health threatening. Workers will tell you that "unemployment and poverty are also hazardous to one's health." An inherent conflict exists between the interests of capital and that of labor. Employers have the power to move jobs (and industrial hazards) from the Northeast and Midwest to the South and Sunbelt, or they may move the jobs offshore to Third World countries where labor is even cheaper and where there are even fewer health and safety regulations. Yet, unless an environmental movement emerges that is capable of addressing these economic concerns, people of color and poor white workers are likely to end up siding with corporate managers in key conflicts concerning the environment.

Indeed, many labor unions already moderate their demands for improved work-safety and pollution control whenever the economy is depressed. They are afraid of layoffs, plant closings, and the relocation of industries. These fears and anxieties of labor are usually built on the false but understandable assumption that environmental regulations inevitably lead to job loss (Brown 1980, 1987).

The crux of the problem is that the mainstream environmental movement has not sufficiently addressed the fact that social inequality and imbalances of social power are at the heart of environmental degradation, resource depletion, pollution, and even overpopulation. The environmental crisis can simply not be solved effectively without social justice. As one academic human ecologist notes, "Whenever [an] in-group directly and exclusively benefits from its own overuse of a shared resource but the costs of that overuse are 'shared' by out-groups, then in-group motivation toward a policy of resource conservation (or sustained yields of harvesting) is undermined" (Catton 1982).

The Movement for Environmental Justice

As this book testifies, activists of color have begun to challenge both the industrial polluters and the often indifferent mainstream environmental movement by actively fighting environmental threats in their communities and raising the call for environmental justice. This groundswell of environmental activism in African-American, Latino, Asian, Pacific Islander, and Native-American communities is emerging all across the country. While rarely listed in the standard environmental and conservation directories, grassroots environmental justice groups have sprung up from Maine to Louisiana and Alaska (see map below).

These grassroots groups have organized themselves around waste-facility siting, lead contamination, pesticides, water and air pollution, Native self-government, nuclear testing, and workplace safety (Alston 1990; Bullard 1990, 1992; Bryant and Mohai 1992). People of color have invented and, in other cases, adapted existing organizations to meet the disproportionate environmental challenges they face. A growing number of grassroots groups and their leaders have adopted confrontational direct action strategies similar to those used in earlier civil rights conflicts. Moreover, the increasing documentation of environmental racism has strengthened the demand for a safe and healthy environment as a basic right of all individuals and communities (Commission for Racial Justice 1991; Bullard and Wright 1987, 1990; Bryant and Mohai forthcoming).

Drawing together the insights of *both* the civil rights and the environmental movements, these grassroots groups are fighting hard to improve the quality of life for their residents. As a result of their efforts, the environmental justice movement is increasingly influencing and winning support from more conventional environmental and civil rights organizations. For example, the National Urban League's *1992 State of Black America* included—for the first time in the seventeen years the report has been published—a chapter on the environmental threats to the African-American community (Bullard 1992b). In addition, the NAACP, ACLU, and NRDC led the fight to have poor children tested for lead poisoning under Medicaid provisions in California. The class-action lawsuit *Matthews v. Coye,* settled in 1991, called for the state of California to screen an estimated 500,000 poor children for lead

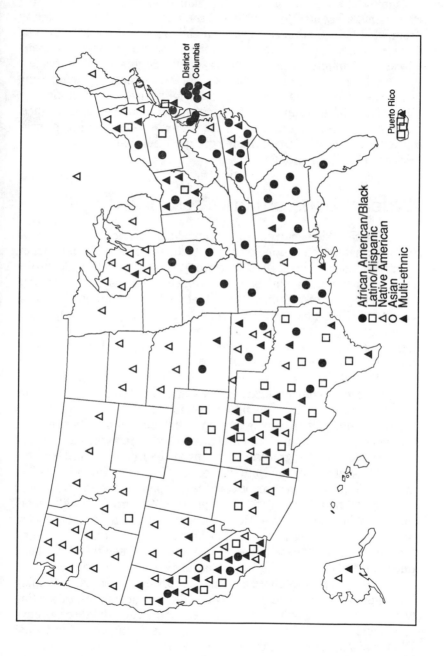

poisoning at a cost of $15 to $20 million (Lee 1992). The screening represents a big step forward in efforts to identify children suffering from what federal authorities admit is the number one environmental health problem of children in the United States. For their part, mainstream environmental organizations are also beginning to understand the need for environmental justice and are increasingly supporting grassroots groups in the form of technical advice, expert testimony, direct financial assistance, fundraising, research, and legal assistance. Even the Los Angeles chapter of the wilderness-focused Earth First! movement worked with community groups to help block the incinerator project in South Central Los Angeles.

Case Studies from the Grassroots

For all of their current and potential significance, however, little research has yet been done on these African-American, Latino, Asian, Pacific Islander, and Native American organizations which make up the grassroots environmental justice movement. The research discussed here focuses on environmentally threatened communities of color in Houston (TX), Dallas (TX), Los Angeles (CA), Richmond (CA), Kettleman City (CA), Alsen (LA), and Rosebud (SD). Each of these communities is embroiled in a wide range of environmental disputes against both government and private industry.

We had three major objectives in looking at these nine communities: 1) to examine the organizations and the dispute mechanisms people of color use in resolving environmental conflicts, 2) to explore the conditions and circumstances under which communities of color mobilize against an environmental threat, and 3) to assess the level of external support that grassroots groups of color receive from environmental, social justice, and other groups. To gather this information, in-depth interviews were conducted with opinion leaders, who were identified through a "reputational" approach. We started out with a small number of local informants. The informants were asked to "identify the *most* influential person or persons who had played a role in resolving the local dispute." These influential leaders were later asked the same question, and this second group of leaders was also interviewed.

The interviews focused on a number of key issue areas, including the nature of the dispute, leadership and external support, opposition tactics, and dispute outcomes. The questions included: Were the environmental problems caused by the government and/or corporations? Did the dispute involve a proposed or existing facility? Was the community group started as an environmental group? Do its leaders and members see themselves as environmentalists? Were equity and social justice concerns dominant organizing themes? Who led the local citizen opposition in the disputes? What kind of support did the local groups receive from environmental and other organizations? What tactics did the groups use? Which were most effective? How was the dispute resolved?

A summary of the various communities, grassroots groups, and types of environmental disputes included in this study are presented in Table 1. Here is a more detailed overview of each community's situation.

Houston: In the 1970s, Houston was dubbed the "golden buckle" of the Sunbelt (Bullard 1987, 1990). In 1982, it became the nation's fourth largest city with 1.7 million inhabitants. Its black community of some 450,000 is the largest in the South. For decades, Houston boasted that it was the only major city without zoning. During the "boom" years of the 1970s, this no-zoning policy contributed to haphazard and irrational land-use planning and infrastructure chaos (Bullard 1983). A mostly African-American suburban neighborhood was selected as the site for a municipal landfill. The Northeast Community Action Group (NECAG) formed to block the construction of the landfill.

Dallas: Dallas is the seventh largest city in the nation with a population of just under one million. The 265,594 African Americans who live in Dallas represent 29.4 percent of the city's population. West Dallas is one of many segregated black enclaves in the city. It has a population of 13,161, of which 85 percent is black. The neighborhood has lived with a polluting lead smelter for five decades (Nauss 1983; Bullard 1990). Early on, West Dallas residents formed the Neighborhood Coalition on Lead Pollution to get the smelter closed and the area cleaned up. Another group, West Dallas Coalition for Environmental Justice, continued the fight after the Neighborhood Coalition for Lead Pollution was disbanded.

Alsen (LA): Alsen is an unincorporated community on the Mississippi River several miles north of Baton Rouge, Louisiana's state capital. It had a population of 1,104 individuals in 1980, of which 98.9 percent were African Americans. Alsen lies at the beginning of "Cancer Alley," the 85-mile stretch of land from Baton Rouge to New Orleans, an area that accounts for one-fourth of the nation's petrochemical production (See Maraniss and Weisskopf 1987; Anderson, Dunn, and Alabarado 1985; Bullard 1990; Bullard and Wright 1990). Much of Louisiana's hazardous waste is disposed of in the Rollins Environmental Services incinerators located near Alsen. The resi-

Table 1
Summary of Community Disputes

Group (Year Founded), Location	Type of Dispute	Facility
Northeast Community Action Group (1979), Houston, TX	Solid waste landfill	Existing
Neighborhood Committee on Lead Pollution (1981), Dallas, TX	Lead smelter	Existing
West Dallas Coalition for Environmental and Economic Justice (1989), Dallas, TX	Lead smelter	Existing
Coalition for Community Action (1979), Alsen, LA	Hazardous waste incinerator	Existing
Concerned Citizens of South Central Los Angeles (1985), Los Angeles, CA	Solid waste incinerator	Proposed
Mothers of East Los Angeles (1985), Los Angeles, CA	Hazardous waste incinerator	Proposed
People for Clean Air and Water (1990), Kettleman City, CA	Hazardous waste incinerator	Proposed
West County Toxics Coalition (1989), Richmond, CA	Petrochemical refinery	Existing
Good Road Coalition (1991), Rosebud, SD	Solid waste landfill	Proposed

dents formed Coalition for Community Action to challenge the Rollins hazardous waste incinerator operation.

Los Angeles: Los Angeles is the nation's second largest city with a population of 3.5 million. It is one of the nation's most culturally and ethnically diverse big cities. People of color (Latinos, Asians, Pacific Islanders, African Americans, and Native Americans) now constitute 63 percent of the city's population. Residents of South Central Los Angeles, a neighborhood that is over 52 percent African-American and about 44 percent Latino, was slated to host the city's first state-of-the-art municipal solid waste incinerator. Local residents organized Concerned Citizens of South Central Los Angeles to fight the incinerator (Sanchez 1988; Russell 1989; Blumberg and Gottlieb 1989; Hamilton 1990).

Just as Los Angeles's largest African-American community was selected as a site for a city-sponsored municipal incinerator, East Los Angeles, the city's largest Latino community, was chosen as a site for a hazardous waste incinerator (Russell 1989). Officially, the incinerator was planned for Vernon, an industrial suburb that has only 96 people. But, several East Los Angeles neighborhoods (made up of mostly Latino residents) are located only a mile away and downwind from the proposed site. The group Mothers of East Los Angeles (MELA) took the lead in fighting the proposed hazardous waste site (Pardo 1991).

Richmond (CA): Richmond has a population of 80,000. Over half are African Americans and about 10 percent are Latinos. Most of the African-American population live next to the city's petrochemical corridor—a cluster of 350 facilities that handle hazardous waste (Citizens for a Better Environment 1989). The five largest industrial polluters in the city are the Chevron oil refinery, Chevron Ortho pesticide plant, Witco Chemical, Airco Industrial Gases, and an ICI pesticide plant (formerly Stauffer Chemical). Chevron Ortho generates over 40 percent of the hazardous waste in Richmond. The bulk of it is incinerated on the plant's grounds. Local citizens founded the West County Toxics Coalition to address the problem of toxic emissions.

Kettleman City (CA): Kettleman City is a small farmworker community of approximately 1,200. Over 95 percent of the residents are Latino. It is home to a hazardous waste landfill operated by the world's largest waste-disposal company, Chemical Waste Management (see Corwin 1991; Siler 1991). The company proposed that a new incinerator be built in Kettleman City. Residents organized an opposition group called El Pueblo para el Aire y Agua Limpio (People for Clean Air and Water).

Rosebud Reservation (SD): As state environmental regulations have become more stringent in recent years, Native-American reservations have become prime targets of waste disposal firms (Beasley 1990b; Tomsho 1990; Kay 1991b). Many waste-disposal companies have attempted to skirt state regulations (which are often tougher than the federal regulations) by targeting Native lands (Angel 1992). Because of their quasi-independent status, Native-American reservations are not covered by state environmental regulations. The threat to Native lands exists for the Mohawk Indians in New York to the Mission Indians (i.e., Campo, La Posta, Los Coyotes, Morongo, Pala, and Soboda) in southern California to the Gwichin people in Alaska (Kay 1991b). The problem is typified in the case of the Rosebud Reservation in South Dakota. RSW, a Connecticut-based company, proposed in 1991 to build a 6,000-acre municipal landfill on Sioux lands (Daschle 1991). Local residents founded the Good Road Coalition to block the landfill.

What We Learned

Eight of the nine community opposition groups were started as environmental groups. Mothers of East Los Angeles was the only exception. It grew out of a six-year dispute involving a proposed 1,450-bed state prison in East Los Angeles (Pardo 1991). MELA also fought a proposed underground pipeline through their neighborhood. Its fight against the incinerator is an extension of this earlier battle.

All of the groups have multi-issue agendas and incorporate social justice and equity as their major organizing themes. The leaders see their communities as "victims" and are quick to make the connection between other forms of discrimination, the quality of their physical environment, and the current dispute. Some of the leaders have worked in other organizations that fought discrimination in housing, employment, and education.

It is clear that the local grassroots activists in the impacted communities provided the essential leadership in dealing with the disputes. The typical grassroots leader was a woman. For example, women led the fight in seven of the nine cases examined. Only the West Dallas Coalition for Environmental Justice and Richmond's West County Toxics Coalition were headed by men.

Women activists were quick to express their concern about the threat to their family, home, and community. The typical organizer found leadership thrust upon her by immediate circumstances with little warning or prior training for the job. Lack of experience, however, did not prove an insurmountable barrier to successful organizing.

The manner in which the local issue was framed appears to have influenced the type of leadership that emerged. Local activists immediately turned their energies to what they defined as environmental discrimination, for discrimination is a fact of life in all of these communities. Most people of color face it daily.

The quest for environmental justice thus extends the quest for basic civil rights. Actions taken by grassroots activists to reduce environmental inequities are consistent with the struggle to end the other forms of social injustice found throughout our society—in housing, education, employment, health care, criminal justice, and politics.

The mainstream environmental groups do not have a long history of working with African-American, Latino, Asian, Pacific Islander, and Native-American groups. For the most part, they have failed to adequately address environmental problems that disproportionately impact people of color. Despite some exceptions, the national groups have failed to sufficiently make the connection between key environmental and social justice issues.

The experience of the organizations discussed here suggests that the situation is beginning to change for the better. While still too little, the mainstream environmental movement's support of environmental justice struggles has visibly increased between the first Earth Day in 1970 and Earth Day 1990. Certainly, the early environmental struggles by communities of color were less likely than more recent ones to attract significant support from the mainstream groups.

Because of the redefinition of "environmentalism" spurred on by grassroots challenges to the elitism and environmental racism of the mainstream groups, more mainstream groups now acknowledge and try to address the widespread inequities throughout our society. Many of these groups are beginning to understand and embrace the cause of social justice activists mobilizing to protect their neighborhoods from garbage dumps or lead smelters. These first steps have been a long time in coming, however. For many conservationists, the struggle for social justice is still seen as separate from environmental activism. Because of this, environmental activists of color have usually had better luck winning support for their cause by appealing to more justice-oriented groups. For example, Houston's Northeast Community Action Group (NECAG) was able to enlist support from a number of local social justice activists in their dispute with Browning-Ferris Industries. The anti-discrimination theme was a major tool in enlisting the Houston Black United Front (an African-American self-help group), the Harris County Council of Organizations (an African-American voter education and political group), and a Houston chapter of ACORN (Association of Community Organizations for Reform Now).

The situation in Dallas somewhat resembled that found in Houston. Leaders of West Dallas's Neighborhood Committee on Lead Pollution received no assistance from any outside environmental group in resolving their dispute. Instead, they relied exclusively on a grassroots self-help group, the Common Ground Community Economic Development Corporation, to get their grievances publicly aired. Common Ground not surprisingly has a long history of working on equity issues in the city's African-American community.

The Neighborhood Committee on Lead Pollution disbanded after the lead-smelter dispute was resolved. In 1989, the West Dallas Coalition for Environmental Justice, a multiracial group, formed to fill the leadership vacuum. It pressed for cleanup of the RSR site in West Dallas, closure of the Dixie Metals lead smelter in Dallas's East Oak Cliff neighborhood, and pollution prevention measures for the remaining industries in the neighborhood. The multiracial coalition has about 700 members and 20 volunteers. It has worked closely with Common Ground and Texas United, a grassroots environmental group affiliated with the Boston-based National Toxics Campaign. The local Sierra Club also wrote several letters endorsing the actions taken by the West Dallas group to get their neighborhood cleaned up.

Leaders in Alsen, on the other hand, did receive support (although late in their struggle) from several environmental groups. Rollins' proposal to burn PCBs in the Alsen incinerator had gotten the attention of several national environmental groups, including Greenpeace, Citizens' Clearinghouse for Hazardous Waste, and the National Toxics Campaign.

Alsen residents also enlisted the support of the Louisiana Environmental Action Network (a mostly white group) and Gulf Coast Tenants Organization (a mostly African-American group). Gulf Coast has, for example, led Earth Day "toxics marches" from New Orleans to Baton Rouge.

The four California community groups examined in this study all had great success in getting support from and forming alliances with both grassroots and national environmental groups. Again, the level of outside support was greatest for the groups fighting new facilities proposals.

The African-American leaders of Concerned Citizens of South Central Los Angeles found allies and built strong working relationships with a diverse set of international, national, and grassroots environmental groups. Greenpeace was the first national group to join Concerned Citizens in their fight to kill LANCER 1 (Russell 1989; Blumberg and Gottlieb 1989). Others joined later, including Citizens for a Better Environment (CBE), National Health Law Program, and the Center for Law in the Public Interest. Concerned Citizens also forged alliances with two white Westside "slow-growth" groups: Not Yet New York (a coalition of environmental and homeowner groups) and the anti-incineration group California Alliance in Defense of Residential Environments (CADRE).

Mothers of East Los Angeles lined up the support of groups such as Greenpeace, the Natural Resources Defense Council, the Environmental Policy Institute, the Citizens' Clearinghouse on Hazardous Waste, the National Toxics Campaign, and the Western Center on Law and Poverty. These allies provided valuable technical advice, expert testimony, lobbying, research, and legal assistance.

The Kettleman City dispute attracted widespread attention and became a topic on prime-time newscasts. The local group, El Pueblo para el Aire y Agua Limpio (People for Clean Air and Water), got a lot of support from both national and grassroots environmental and social justice groups. The dispute brought together environmental leaders of color from inside and outside California. The decision to site a hazardous waste incinerator in Kettleman City also acted as a rallying point for many environmental justice groups ranging from Greenpeace to the Albuquerque-based Southwest Network for Environmental and Economic Justice (a coalition of environmental activists of color from eight states in the Southwest).

The Richmond-based West County Toxics Coalition was founded with assistance from the National Toxics Campaign. It then got the Sierra Club (headquartered just across the Bay in San Francisco) involved in their struggle. The San Francisco-based Citizens for a Better Environment (CBE) furnished the group with technical assistance and documentation of the local environmental problem (see the 1989 report *Richmond at Risk*). The report offers graphic evidence of the threat posed by polluting industries in the city's African-American and Latino communities.

Disputes involving Native lands present special problems to conventional environmental movements. Given the long history of exploitation and genocide directed at Native Americans by whites, environmental disputes take on larger historical and cultural meanings. However, the Good Road Coalition was able to enlist the support of Greenpeace activists and two Native-American groups (the Indigenous Environmental Network and the Natural Resource Coalition).

Organizing Tactics

The grassroots environmental groups and their allies have used a wide range of tactics to fend off what they see as a threat to family, home, and community. The leaders have borrowed many of their tactics from the earlier civil rights movement. All of the groups have used public protest, demonstrations, petitions, lobbying, reports and fact-finding, and hearings to educate the community and intensify public debate on the dispute. In addition, leaders organized community workshops and neighborhood forums to keep local residents informed on the disputes and new developments.

All of the grassroots groups targeted local, state, and federal governments for their direct or indirect influence in siting and enforcement decisions. For example, the leaders of Houston's Northeast Community Action Group directed their actions toward both the local and state government bodies responsible for permitting the facility.

A number of tangible results emerged from the Houston dispute. First, the Houston City Council, acting under intense political pressure from local residents, passed a resolution in 1980 that prohibited city-owned garbage trucks from dumping at the controversial landfill in the Northwood Manor subdivision. Second, the council also passed an ordinance restricting the construction of solid-waste sites near public facilities such as school and parks. (This action was nothing less than a form of protective zoning.) And, third, the Texas Department of Health updated its requirements for landfill permit applicants. Applications now must include detailed land-use, economic impact, and sociodemographic data on areas where proposed municipal solid waste landfills are to be sited.

The Neighborhood Committee on Lead Pollution challenged the Dallas Health Department for its lax enforcement of the city's lead ordinance and the repeated violations by the nearby smelter. Grassroots leaders in West Dallas extended their influence beyond the neighborhood by pressuring the Dallas mayor to appoint a government-sanctioned city-wide task force (the Dallas Alliance Environmental Task Force) to address lead contamination. The impetus for the task force came from the local West Dallas group.

The two Los Angeles neighborhood groups also sought to have the city intervene in their dispute. The LANCER dispute was injected into local city politics and became a contributing factor in both the defeat of the pro-LANCER City Council President Pat Russell and the election of environmental advocate Ruth Galanter. Concerned Citizens of South Central Los Angeles and its allies proved that local citizens can fight city hall and win. Opponents of the city-initiated incinerator project applied pressure on key elected officials, including Mayor Tom Bradley. Bradley reversed his position and asked the city council to kill the project, which had been in the planning stage since 1969 and included a commitment to contribute $12 million (Russell 1989).

Mothers of East Los Angeles, in its struggle, targeted the South Coast Air Quality Management District (AQMD), the California Department of Health Services (DHS), and the U.S. Environmental Protection Agency (EPA)—the agencies responsible for awarding a permit for the Vernon hazardous waste incinerator project. The facility was to be California's first "state-of-the-art" toxic-waste incinerator.

To block the project, Mothers of East Los Angeles and its allies arranged for more than 500 residents to attend a 1987 DHS hearing on it. They pressed their demands in other public forums as well. The alliance questioned DHS's 1988 decision that allowed California Thermal Treatment Services (CTTS) to move the project forward without preparing an environmental impact report (EIR). The City of Los Angeles, MELA, and others joined in a lawsuit to review the decision. The federal EPA, however, approved the permit without an EIR.

This prompted California Assemblywoman Lucille Roybal-Allard to lead a successful fight to change the California law and require EIRs for all toxic waste incinerators. In December 1988, as CTTS was about to start construction, the AQMD decided that the company should do the environmental studies and redesign its original standards to meet the new, more stringent clean air regulations. CTTS legally challenged the AQMD's decision all the way up to the State Supreme Court and lost.

The Coalition for Community Action (Alsen, LA) focused its attack on the Louisiana Department of Environmental Quality and its less-than-enthusiastic enforcement of air quality standards in North Baton Rouge and the African-American communities affected by emissions from the nearby polluting industries. The group also worked on getting the federal EPA more actively involved in pollution prevention efforts in "Cancer Alley."

Richmond's West County Toxics Coalition worked to get both state and federal government agencies involved in reducing emissions from the nearby polluting industries. On the other hand, Kettleman City's People for Clean Air and Water focused its attention on the Kings County Board of Supervisors, the California Department of Health Services, and the federal EPA.

The Native Americans who founded the Good Road Coalition appealed to their Tribal Council (the government of the sovereign Sioux Nation on the Rosebud Reservation) to rescind the contract signed with RSW to build the 6,000-acre landfill on the reservation. Tribal Chairman Ralph Moran had supported the construction. It is interesting that six of the nine grassroots groups used litigation as a tactic. The three groups that did not were the West Dallas Coalition for Environmental Justice (its predecessor had already filed a lawsuit), Richmond's West County Toxics Coalition, and Rosebud's Good Road Coalition. All of the groups that filed lawsuits used their own lawyers. Three of them (Concerned Citizens of South Central Los Angeles, Mothers of East Los Angeles, and People for Clean Air and Water) applied to public interest law centers to file their lawsuits.

The West Dallas and East Los Angeles groups were joined in their lawsuits by the local government: both the city of Dallas and the Texas Attorney General joined the West Dallas plaintiffs, while the city of Los Angeles joined MELA.

Three of the neighborhood groups (the two in West Dallas and the one in Richmond) used negotiations as a dispute resolution tactic. The West Dallas groups were able to negotiate two different cleanup plans—the first in 1984, the second in 1992.

Richmond's West County Toxics Campaign brought in the Reverend Jesse Jackson of the National Rainbow Coalition to negotiate with Chevron, the major polluter in the community. Richmond's Mayor George Livingston helped arrange the May 7, 1990 meeting with Chevron that included representatives from the West County Toxics Coalition, the National Rainbow Coalition, and the Sierra Club. Jackson described the negotiations as a "test case, a test example, both with dangers and possibilities." He and the West County Toxics Coalition presented Chevron with a six-point plan (Reed 1990, p. A1):

- Annually set aside 1 percent of the cost of Chevron's proposed $1 billion modernization for a cleanup fund. The fund should employ Richmond's unemployed to help clean up the environment, and should also be used to finance health care and new pollution-reduction technology;
- Establish a 24-hour, fully funded clinic to provide medical attention to those harmed by the dozens of polluting industries in Richmond;
- Reduce the tons of toxic waste destroyed in Chevron's Ortho Chemical plant incinerator. (Chevron, which currently burns about 75,000 tons annually in the furnace, is seeking state permits to double the incinerator's capacity);
- Bring together representatives of other polluting industries and pressure them to reduce their companies' toxic emissions;
- Divest from South Africa; and
- Negotiate a timetable for accomplishing the above goals.

Nobody knows what these negotiations will yield or how long it will take to get tangible results. Nevertheless, both sides appear willing to talk. Of course, talking about emission reduction is different from actual emission reduction. But the Coalition and its allies did get Chevron to agree not to bring in outside waste to burn at the Richmond site.

The other concrete result of the negotiations was an agreement to meet again to negotiate specifics. Nevertheless, the meeting itself represented a major community victory in that the West County Toxics Coalition finally won the right to bargain with Chevron, something local leaders had unsuccessfully attempted to do since 1987.

Resolutions and Outcomes

These case studies demonstrate that African Americans, Latino Americans, and Native Americans are actively pursuing strategies to improve the overall quality of life in their neighborhoods. The grassroots leaders have not waited for "outsiders" or "elites" to rush to their rescue; they have taken the initiative themselves.

As expected, the groups had more success in blocking proposed facilities than closing those already operating. The West Dallas residents were successful in shutting down the lead smelter and in winning an out-of-court settlement worth over $45 million—one of the largest awards ever in a lead pollution case in the country. It was made on behalf of 370 children—almost all of whom were poor, black residents of the West Dallas public housing project—and 40 property owners.

The lawsuit was finally settled in June 1983 when RSR agreed to a soil cleanup program in West Dallas, a blood-testing program for the children and pregnant women, and the installation of new antipollution equipment. The equipment, however, was never installed. In May 1984 the Dallas Board of Adjustments, a city agency responsible for monitoring land-use violations, requested that the city attorney order the smelter permanently closed for violating the zoning code. It had operated in the neighborhood for some 50 years without the necessary use permits.

The 1984 lead cleanup proved inadequate. A more comprehensive cleanup of West Dallas was begun in December 1991—20 years after the first government study of lead smelters. Some 30,000 to 40,000 cubic yards (roughly 1,800 truckloads) of lead-tainted soil are to be removed from several West Dallas sites, including schoolyards and about 140 private homes (Loftis 1992). The project will cost between $3 to $4 million. The contaminated soil was originally planned to be shipped to a landfill in Monroe, Louisiana—a city that is 60 percent African-American.

The municipal landfill in Houston, the hazardous waste incinerator in Alsen, and the petrochemical plant (and on-site hazardous waste incinerator) in Richmond are still operating. Although the three groups and their allies fell short of completely eliminating the threat by bringing about actual plant closures, they were able to extract concessions from the polluting industries in the form of capacity reduction and emission controls. In Alsen, after more than six years, a 1987 out-of-court settlement was reached between Rollins and the residents. It was reported to be worth an average of $3,000 per resident. The company was also required to reduce emissions from its facilities.

Construction of four proposed facilities were prevented: the two waste facilities in Los Angeles (South Central and East Los Angeles), the one on Rosebud Reservation in South Dakota, and the one in Kettleman City. The two lawsuits filed on behalf of South Central and East Los Angeles residents never reached the trial or settlement stage, for the two construction proposals were withdrawn. The city-sponsored LANCER project was killed by the mayor and city council. In May 1991, CTTS decided to "throw in the towel" because the lawsuits threatened to drive up costs beyond the $4 million the company had already spent on the project (Dolan 1991). The Vernon hazardous waste incinerator became a dead issue.

On the other hand, the Good Road Coalition blocked plans to build the 6,000-acre landfill on the Rosebud Reservation through the electoral process. A majority of the residents voted the proposal down. In 1991, former tribal chairman Ralph Moran, who had favored the landfill proposal, was defeated in the tribal primary election and residents convinced the tribal council to cancel the agreement to build the facility. The proposal was resurrected in 1992 in yet another offer to the tribal council by RSW. Again, the plan was rejected by the council.

Although part of the lawsuit involving the Kettleman City incinerator dispute is still pending, People for Clean Air and Water won a major victory in delaying construction. A superior court judge in January 1992 overturned the Kings County Board of Supervisors' approval of the Kettleman City incinerator, citing its detrimental impact on air quality in the agriculture-rich Central Valley of California.

The judge ruled that Kings County's environmental impact report was inadequate and that county leaders had failed to involve the local residents in the decision by not providing Spanish translations of material about the project. This court ruling represents a victory since the waste-disposal company must now begin the permit process all over again if it is still interested in siting the facility.

Conclusion

The mainstream environmental movement has proven that it can help enhance the quality of life in this country. The national membership organizations that make up the mainstream movement have clearly played an important role in shaping the nation's environmental policy. Yet, few of these groups have actively involved themselves in environmental conflicts involving communities of color. Because of this, it's unlikely that we will see a mass influx of people of color into the national environmental groups any time soon. A continuing growth in their own grassroots organizations is more likely. Indeed, the fastest growing segment of the environmental movement is made up by the grassroots groups in communities of color which are increasingly linking up with one another and with other community-based groups. As long as U.S. society remains divided into separate and unequal communities, such groups will continue to serve a positive function.

It is not surprising that indigenous leaders are organizing the most effective resistance within communities of color. They have the advantage of being close to the population immediately affected by the disputes they are attempting to resolve. They are also completely wedded to social and economic justice agendas and familiar with the tactics of the civil rights movement. This makes effective community organizing possible. People of color have a long track record in challenging government and corporations that discriminate. Groups that emphasize civil rights and social justice can be found in almost every major city in the country.

Cooperation between the two major wings of the environmental movement is both possible and beneficial, however. Many environmental activists of color are now getting support from mainstream organizations in the form of technical advice, expert testimony, direct financial assistance, fundraising, research, and legal assistance. In return, increasing numbers of people of color are assisting mainstream organizations to redefine their limited environmental agendas and expand their outreach by serving on boards, staffs, and advisory councils. Grassroots activists have thus been the most influential activists in placing equity and social justice issues onto the larger environmental agenda and democratizing and diversifying the movement as a whole. Such changes are necessary if the environmental movement is to successfully help spearhead a truly global movement for a just, sustainable, and healthy society and effectively resolve pressing environmental disputes. Environmentalists and civil rights activists of all stripes should welcome the growing movement of African Americans, Latinos, Asians, Pacific Islanders, and Native Americans who are taking up the struggle for environmental justice.

CHAPTER 2

Beyond Toxic Wastes and Race

Charles Lee

> Racism is racial prejudice plus power. Racism is the intentional or unintentional use of power to isolate, separate and exploit others. This use of power is based on a belief in superior racial origin, identity or supposed racial characteristics. Racism confers certain privileges on and defends the dominant group, which in turn sustains and perpetuates racism. Both consciously and unconsciously, racism is enforced and maintained by the legal, cultural, religious, educational, economic, political, environmental and military institutions of societies. Racism is more than just a personal attitude; it is the institutionalized form of that attitude (Commission for Racial Justice 1987, p. x).
>
> —Rev. Benjamin Chavis, Jr.
> *Toxic Wastes and Race*

The federal government has traditionally been assumed to have the major responsibility for protecting the health and well-being of the nation. During the 1980s, however, an alarming trend emerged. The "New Federalism," ushered in by the Reagan administration, signaled a reduction of domestic programs to monitor the environment and protect public health.

The Reagan era and its policies have resulted in a number of negative actions by federal agencies, the most startling perhaps being a 1985 U.S. Labor Department ruling that farm owners were not required by federal law or regulations to provide water and field sanitation facilities for farmworkers. In his decision, Labor Secretary William Brock stated that while there was clear evidence of "unacceptable risks" from the lack of such facilities, he felt "action by states would be preferable, and more effective." In striking down this ruling, a three-judge panel in Washington, D.C., labeled it part of a "disgraceful chapter of legal neglect" (Noble 1987, p. A1).

During these same years, the U.S. Environmental Protection Agency (EPA) pursued a policy of delegating more and more responsibility for hazardous waste management to state agencies. This policy has serious implications. The Congressional Office of Technology Assessment cautions that this program may present "an unacceptable combination of shifting increasing responsibilities to the States without corresponding increases in necessary resources" (Office of Technology Assessment 1983). In 1984, 25 states reported a 63.5 percent shortfall in funds for hazardous waste enforcement (U.S. General Accounting Office 1983). Thus the federal policy has resulted in an abdication of, rather than a shifting of, the EPA's responsibilities (Vig and Draft 1984).

The reduced efforts to protect public health are especially disturbing in light of the many citizens who unknowingly may be exposed to substances emanating from hazardous waste sites. The U.S. General Accounting Office (GAO) reported in December 1986 that potentially large numbers of hazardous waste sites have remained unidentified. According to the GAO, the EPA division director responsible for hazardous waste identification stated that "the EPA does not know if it has identified 90 percent of the potentially hazardous wastes or only 10 percent" (U.S. General Accounting Office 1986).

Unfortunately, African Americans, Latinos, Asians, Pacific Islanders, and Native Americans in the United States are the citizens most likely to be victimized by this emerging trend. Indeed, racial and ethnic communities suffer from the most severe environmental pollution (Bullard and Wright 1986). For example, air pollution levels in the Washington, D.C., metropolitan area were found to be higher in poorer areas of the city and where the African-American population lives. A similar situation exists in New York, Chicago, Denver, Los Angeles, and San Francisco (McCaull 1976; Gelobter 1988). Nationally, higher percentages of African Americans and Latinos live in areas with poor air quality than do whites (Wernette and Nieves 1992, p. 16). According to panelists at the Fourth National Policy Institute—a conference co-sponsored by a wide range of organizations including the Joint Center for Political Studies, the Congressional Black Caucus and the National Conference of Black Mayors—African Americans are disproportionately burdened by environmental problems because they are more likely to hold industrial jobs in plants where chemical processing or manufacturing poses health risks. This problem is exacerbated by the residential concentration of blacks in urban areas, often in proximity to hazardous waste dumps or polluting factories (Joint Center for Political Studies 1984).

In recent years, a conflict has arisen over whether or not racial and ethnic communities will be placed in greater jeopardy by the location of new hazardous waste management facilities.

During 1982, the United Church of Christ's Commission for Racial Justice, under its former executive director, Dr. Charles E. Cobb, joined ranks with residents of rural Warren County, North Carolina, in opposing the establishment of a polychlorinated biphenyl (PCB) disposal landfill. North Carolina's plan to site this hazardous waste facility in a predominantly black and poor county sparked heated local opposition, which culminated in a massive nonviolent civil disobedience campaign. This brought in national media attention and led to more than 500 arrests. Among the demonstrators arrested were Walter E. Fauntroy, congressperson from the District of Columbia; Dr. Joseph Lowery, president of the Southern Christian Leadership Conference; Dr. Benjamin F. Chavis, Jr., the current executive director of the UCC Commission for Racial Justice; and the Rev. Leon White, director of the Southern Regional Office of the Commission for Racial Justice in Raleigh.

The protests in Warren County raised the question of how many other racial and ethnic communities were similarly harmed by hazardous wastes. Evidence was soon documented. The U.S. General Accounting Office (GAO) conducted a study in 1983 at the request of congressperson Fauntroy. It examined the racial and socio-economic makeup of communities surrounding four hazardous waste landfills in the southeastern United States. A key finding was that blacks comprised the majority of the population in three of the four communities studied (U.S. General Accounting Office 1983). The GAO study, however, was limited in importance by its regional scope. It was not designed to examine the relationship between the location of hazardous waste facilities throughout the United States and the racial and socio-economic characteristics of persons residing near them.

One of the earliest independent efforts to document and challenge the reality of environmental racism was the 1987 study *Toxic Wastes and Race,* commissioned by the United Church of Christ Commission for Racial Justice. The involvement of the Commission in this type of research marked a clear departure from its traditional protest and direct action activities. However, the Commission's staff reasoned, if oppressed people are to advance the cause of social justice in the future, they must have timely and reliable information about the crisis of survival that confronts them.

The success of a democracy depends on the full participation of its citizenry. The hazardous waste issue is admittedly a complex one. Decisions related to it require an informed public, particularly in directly impacted communities. Blacks, Hispanics, Asians, Pacific Islanders,

Native-Americans and other racial and ethnic groups need to adopt a more proactive posture with respect to this critical issue; they need to be able to clearly define their own interests within the context of the various social ills confronting them.

The availability of proper information is thus critical to determining how communities respond to environmental problems. As a whole, community activists have found the acquisition of needed information to be a difficult task. A recent survey of 110 community groups found that "nearly nine out of every ten groups (88 percent) perceived obstacles to obtaining information. Almost half (45 percent) claimed that government agencies blocked their learning process" (Freudenberg 1984, pp. 444-448). Institutional resistance to providing information is likely to be even greater when agencies are confronted by groups, such as those among racial and ethnic communities and the poor, who are perceived to wield less political clout.

The information in the report is also particularly necessary to help communities avoid being taken in by economic blackmail. Hazardous waste issues have become very much linked to the state of the economy in our communities. Many racial and ethnic communities have highly depressed economies and alarming unemployment rates; they are thus particularly vulnerable to those who advocate the siting of a hazardous waste facility as an avenue for employment and economic development.

In recent years, a school of thought has emerged which raises the idea of compensating communities which agree to host hazardous waste facilities (O'Hare et al. 1983; Kunreuther 1985). This theory argues that economic incentives can be offered to local residents so that the perceived benefits outweigh the perceived risks (Portney 1985). To advance such a theory in the absence of the consideration of the racial and socio-economic characteristics of host communities and existing forms of institutionalized racism leaves considerable room for potential discrimination and racist exploitation.

The Commission's influential study was the first effort to present a comprehensive national analysis of the relationship between hazardous wastes and racism. Its findings offer a good starting point for grassroots organizations, public health professionals and policymakers, communities of color, and organizations concerned with environmental justice.

The Basic Toxics Problem

Before exploring the study's findings on environmental racism, however, it is important to understand the general danger of hazardous wastes. According to the EPA, the term "hazardous wastes" means the byproducts of industrial production that present particularly troublesome health and environmental problems. Such wastes are toxic, ignitable, corrosive, or dangerously reactive. Many common materials may ultimately become hazardous; for example, varnish and detergents, used dry-cleaning solvents, and mercury from used batteries all become hazardous wastes.

Until the late 1970s, most hazardous wastes were discarded without considering the dangers they posed. Moreover, proper care was discouraged when waste management regulations created a permissive atmosphere for discarding wastes in the cheapest possible ways. Throughout the 1970s, as the EPA itself admits, up to 80 to 90 percent of hazardous wastes were disposed of without adequate safeguards for human health and the environment (Greenberg and Anderson 1984).

The EPA uses the term "uncontrolled hazardous waste sites" for a wide range of closed and abandoned sites that pose a present or potential threat to human health and the environment. They may be indiscriminately placed dumps, abandoned or closed disposal facilities, accidental spills, illegal discharges, or closed factories and warehouses where hazardous materials have been produced, used, or stored. In 1984, the EPA reported that "uncontrolled hazardous waste sites may present some of the most serious environmental and public health problems the nation has ever faced" (U.S. Environmental Protection Agency 1984).

Environmental damage from contamination by hazardous wastes is among the most difficult and costly conditions to ameliorate. The ultimate cost of cleaning up these sites could easily exceed $100 billion (Office of Technology Assessment 1985). More importantly, Landrigan and Gross assert that "there are already in our environment sufficient quantities of hazardous wastes to provide a legacy of disease and death to our descendants for generations yet to come" (Landrigan and Gross 1981).

The problems caused by human exposure to uncontrolled hazardous wastes are national in scope. By 1985, the EPA had inventoried approximately 20,000 uncontrolled sites across the country (U.S. Environmental Protection Agency 1986). The potential health problems associated with their existence are highlighted by the fact that between 40 and 50 percent of Americans depend primarily on groundwater for their drinking water. Approximately 75 percent of U.S. cities derive their water, in total or in part, from groundwater (Pye, Patrick, and Quarles 1983).

Few Americans were aware of these problems a decade ago. Within a remarkably short period of time, the issue became a top concern for U.S. citizens. Indeed, seldom have so many citizens expressed such unanimity of opinion in conveying their desire to see these problems solved (Epstein, Brown, and Pope 1982).

Laws to Address the Problem

To address this growing national problem, Congress enacted two major laws in the 1980s and 1990s: the Resource, Conservation, and Recovery Act (RCRA) and the Comprehensive Environmental Response, Compensation, and Liability Act (CERCLA). Both stipulated that newly generated hazardous wastes must be managed in an approved facility. The EPA defines a "facility" as any land and structures thereon which are used for treating, storing, or disposing of hazardous wastes (a TSD facility). Such facilities include landfills, surface impoundments, and incinerators (40 Code of Federal Regulations, Part 260.10). TSD facilities are regulated by the EPA under the authority granted to it by Congress.

The RCRA established a "cradle-to-grave" approach to regulating the generation, storage, transportation, treatment, and disposal of newly generated hazardous wastes. Under RCRA, states and the federal government share responsibility for this task. The EPA has promulgated regulations applicable to generators, as well as transporters, of hazardous wastes. It has also issued design and operational standards for TSD facilities. In addition, RCRA requires operators of TSD facilities to obtain permits which contain requirements for operation of such facilities. These requirements are generally site-specific.

Among the provisions of RCRA is one delegating responsibility to the states for "siting," approving the location of a new TSD facility, subject to federally defined technical criteria. The public is granted certain rights under RCRA. Under its penalty provisions, citizens may sue any company, or in some instances the EPA, for violations of applicable regulations. In addition, any person may petition the EPA to promulgate, amend, or repeal any regulation issued under the law. The act directs the EPA and the states to provide for, encourage, and assist public participation in the "development, revision, implementation and enforcement of any regulation, guideline, information or program" under it. Finally, it permits a state to assume primary responsibility for managing hazardous wastes within its borders following the EPA's approval of a plan submitted by the state.

By the time RCRA was enacted, the nation's hazardous waste problem was widespread. The act's provisions did not provide for the cleanup of areas such as Love Canal, New York, where in 1977 chemicals had bubbled into the homes of the town's residents. So, in 1980, Congress enacted CERCLA, commonly known as the "Superfund" act. It authorizes the federal government to finance the cleanup of hazardous waste sites from a trust fund established with revenues from taxes levied on certain products (petrochemicals, inorganic raw materials, domestic crude oil, and imported petroleum products). It also permits the federal government to require parties responsible for causing the release, or creating the uncontrolled hazardous waste site, to finance cleanup. CERCLA requires states to participate in any cleanup action within their borders; they may either cooperate with the EPA or take the lead themselves.

Existing uncontrolled hazardous waste sites are identified by the EPA in the Comprehensive Environmental Response, Compensation and Liability Act Information System (CERCLIS). Those requiring long-term "remedial action" are listed on the National Priorities List (NPL), which the agency has established. Only those listed on the NPL are eligible for federal cleanup funds under the Superfund bill.

The 1986 amendments to the bill require that health assessments be performed for each family affected by the sites listed on the NPL. They also require public notification of, and participation in, the plans for remedial action initiated under this law. By mid-1987, all states were to establish emergency response commissions, which were then to appoint local emergency planning committees to implement the new community right-to-know provisions.

The EPA maintains the toll-free RCRA/Superfund Hotline and ten regional offices around the country where citizens may seek information and assistance on hazardous waste problems. The EPA also employs a hazardous waste ombudsman in Washington, D.C., who responds to citizen grievances and suggestions, as well as provides them information. Citizens also may seek assistance from agencies in their states responsible for managing hazardous wastes.

Waste and Communities of Color

Notwithstanding the enactment of legislation and other efforts to address hazardous wastes and the environment, communities of color have, until recently, only been marginally involved with these issues. Thus, it is critical that the issues surrounding hazardous wastes and people of color be properly highlighted and understood. Today most African Americans and other people of color are beset by rising unemployment, increasing poverty, worsening housing, and declining educational and health status. It would be very difficult to properly address issues of environmental quality outside the broader context of these equity concerns. In short, communities of color cannot afford the luxury of only being concerned about the quality of their environment when confronted by a plethora of other pressing problems related to their day-to-day survival.

This does not mean, however, that people of color do not care about the quality of their environment and its effect on their lives. Research has suggested that residents of visibly polluted communities, regardless of race or socio-economic status, are becoming more conscious of this problem (Cutter 1981). Throughout the course of the Commission for Racial Justice's involvement with issues of hazardous wastes and environmental pollution, it has found numerous communities of color actively seeking to deal with this problem in their communities. Indeed, the League of Conservation Voters credits the Congressional Black Caucus as having one of the best voting records on environmental issues (Taylor 1982, pp. 51-52).

According to *Toxic Wastes and Race,* people of color have far more reason than other people to become active against hazardous waste— their communities are disproportionately targeted as sites for these hazards. The report presents findings from two cross-sectional studies on demographic patterns associated with 1) commercial hazardous waste facilities and 2) uncontrolled hazardous waste sites. The first study revealed a striking relationship between the location of commercial hazardous waste facilities and race. The second was descriptive and documented the widespread presence of uncontrolled toxic waste sites in minority communities throughout the United States.

Among the many findings that emerged from these studies, the following are most important:

- Race proved to be the most significant among the variables tested in association with the location of commercial hazardous waste facilities. This represented a consistent national pattern.
- Communities with the greatest number of commercial hazardous waste facilities had the highest composition of minority residents. In communities with two or more facilities or one of the nation's five largest landfills, the average minority percentage was more than three times that of communities without facilities (38 percent vs. 12 percent).
- In communities with one commercial hazardous waste facility, the average minority percentage of the population was twice the average minority percentage of the population in communities without such facilities (24 percent vs. 12 percent).
- Although socio-economic status appeared to play an important role in the location of commercial hazardous waste facilities, race

still proved to be most significant. This remained true after the study controlled for urbanization and regional differences. Incomes and property values were substantially lower when communities with commercial facilities were compared to communities in the surrounding counties without facilities.

- Three out of the five largest commercial hazardous waste landfills in the United States were located in predominantly black or Hispanic communities. These three landfills accounted for 40 percent of the total estimated commercial landfill capacity in the nation.

As the number of people of color in a community increases, the probability that some form of hazardous waste activity will occur also increases. This skewed concentration of commercial hazardous waste facilities and uncontrolled toxic waste sites is well illustrated by the 41 U.S. communities where the highest level of commercial hazardous waste activity is taking place.

Thirty-three such communities have populations exceeding 10,000. While collectively they have an inordinately high number of uncontrolled toxic waste sites (378), sixteen communities have ten or more. Findings on the location of these sites can be summarized as follows:

- Three out of every five African Americans and Hispanic Americans lived in communities with uncontrolled toxic waste sites.
- More than 15 million African Americans lived in communities with one or more site.
- More than 8 million Hispanics lived in communities with one or more site.
- African Americans were heavily overrepresented in the populations of metropolitan areas with the largest number of uncontrolled toxic waste sites. These areas include: Memphis, TN (173 sites); Cleveland, OH (106 sites); St. Louis, MO (160 sites); Chicago, IL (103 sites); Houston, TX (152 sites); and Atlanta, GA (94 sites).
- Los Angeles, CA, has more Hispanics living in communities with uncontrolled toxic waste sites than any other metropolitan area in the United States.
- Approximately half of all Asians, Pacific Islanders, and Native-Americans lived in communities with uncontrolled toxic waste sites.

Other examples of this concentration of hazardous wastes are the following counties: Los Angeles County, California; Cook County, Illinois; Wayne County, Michigan; the three northern New Jersey counties of Essex, Hudson, and Union; and Cuyahoga County, Ohio. The major cities in these areas are Los Angeles, California; Chicago, Illinois; Detroit, Michigan; Newark, New Jersey; and Cleveland, Ohio.

Among the 50 metropolitan areas with the greatest numbers of African Americans living in a community with a hazardous waste site, 73.5 percent are near uncontrolled sites. In addition, in ten metropolitan areas, 200,000 or more African Americans reside in a community with an uncontrolled site.

In seven of the ten metropolitan areas with the greatest number of uncontrolled sites, African Americans constitute more than 20 percent of the population. In ten metropolitan areas, more than 90 percent of the African-American population live near uncontrolled sites. The most prominent of these is Memphis, Tennessee. An estimated 99.8 percent of its African-American population resides in areas with uncontrolled sites. It ranks as the metropolitan area with the greatest number of such sites in the nation. A comparable pattern can be found for the Latino population in the United States: at least six metropolitan areas have more than 100,000 Hispanics living in communities with uncontrolled toxic waste sites.

The findings in *Toxic Wastes and Race* suggest that uncontrolled sites in African-American and Hispanic communities represent a substantially greater threat to their quality of life than previously suspected. Since these communities already suffer serious health and environmental problems, the contribution of these sites to the lower health status of minority populations needs to be examined immediately.

The findings of *Toxic Wastes and Race* expose a serious void in present government programs addressing minority concerns in this area. The study firmly concludes that eliminating hazardous wastes in African-American, Hispanic, and other minority communities should be made a policy priority at all levels of government. Yet, this issue is not currently at the forefront of the nation's attention. Therefore, concerned citizens and policymakers who are cognizant of this growing national problem must make it a priority issue.

Bringing a Movement Together

The general public widely believes that people of color have not expressed concern about environmental issues. This is a gross misconception rooted in the narrow definition of environmental issues advanced by traditional environmentalists, conservationists, and the media. People of color have taken on environmental issues as part of their struggle around community, labor, and human rights issues.

Their involvement in the environmental justice movement has spawned a transformation in the thinking and action of those serving these communities in the United States and around the world. A growing body of research subsequent to *Toxic Wastes and Race* points to the beginning of a convergence of the environmental and social justice movements. With a long tradition of connection to the land, concern for the natural world, and struggle for social justice, people of color are beginning to restructure and redefine our understanding of environmentalism (see Bullard 1990; United Church of Christ Commission for Racial Justice 1992; Bryant and Mohai 1992).

Grassroots activists of color are demanding that this nation address many of the critical issues of our time, including housing, employment, energy, defense policy, resource exploitation, public health, and self-determination. At present, environmental policies in the United States have failed to truly engage all Americans. Specifically, African Americans, Latino-Americans, Asian Americans, and Native Americans have yet to play a substantive role in the environmental policy debate. Moreover, the nation's environmental agenda, as reflected in the work of both governmental and nongovernmental organizations (NGOs), has not taken into account the environmental injustices people of color suffer in their daily lives.

The need for greater involvement by people of color in shaping national environmental policies is clear. An essential first step toward meeting it is the development of a national agenda of action. Such an agenda will need to involve the broadest possible representation of U.S. communities, so that it enfranchises all Americans in environmental policymaking. It will need to be planned and executed by people of color in key leadership roles.

This was the objective in convening the First National People of Color Environmental Leadership Summit. The Summit was held in October 1991 in Washington, D.C., and was attended by over 650 delegates, participants, and observers. The participants included environmental activists, civil rights advocates, trade unionists, farmworkers, scientists, environmental lawyers, and representatives from the philanthropic community. Delegates from communities of color represented all 50 states, Puerto Rico, Chile, Mexico, and the Marshall Islands. The Summit achieved both a high level of multiracial representation and gender balance; of the 301 delegates, 55 were Native-American, 158 were African-American, 64 were Latino-American, and 24 were Asian-American or Pacific-American. Equal numbers of men and women attended.

The four-day event provided a forum in which leaders from communities of color could participate with other leaders in shaping an "inclusive" environmental agenda. The Summit served to strengthen and empower grassroots leaders and build a broader multiracial environmental and social justice network. It addressed three fundamental areas: 1) the environmental/social crisis in general, 2) the particularly problematic forms of environmental pollution impacting communities of color, such as hazardous and solid waste, air pollution, radioactive waste, pesticide exposure, and lead poisoning; and 3) the historical experience and cultural perspectives of communities of color in the United States regarding the environment.

The hard work that went into convening the Summit is already paying off. Regional and national grassroots networks have formed, or old networks have been strengthened. Communication lines have been opened for a serious dialogue with mainstream environmental groups. Activists of color have been further mobilized, energized, and galvanized by the call for environmental justice for all communities.

CHAPTER 3

Environmentalism and the Politics of Inclusion

Dorceta E. Taylor

Since at least the 1830s, European-American individuals and groups have championed the cause of the environment. In the early years, two concerns dominated this movement: natural resource conservation, and wilderness and wildlife preservation (Nash 1982; Paehlke 1989, pp. 4-22; Fox 1985; Devall and Sessions 1985; Pepper 1986; Bramwell 1990). While these two dominant perspectives often conflicted with each other, they also overlapped in their primary concern with the management of large, sparsely populated, public wildlands.

From the 1950s and 1960s onward, a third concern began to increasingly be seen as an essential aspect of modern environmentalism: human welfare ecology. As Robyn Eckersley notes, "The accumulation of toxic chemicals or 'intractable wastes'; the intensification of ground, air, and water pollution generally; the growth in new 'diseases of affluence' (e.g., heart disease, cancer); the growth in urban and coastal high rise development; the dangers of nuclear plants and nuclear wastes; the growth in the nuclear arsenal; and the problem of global warming and the thinning of the ozone layer have posed increasing threats to human survival, safety, and well-being" (Eckersley 1992, p. 36). It was on the basis of these concerns that the environmental movement finally emerged as a significant mass movement by the 1970s. Like its predecessors, however, this new wing of the modern environmental movement tended to operate without significant minority participation (Buttel and Flinn 1974; Lowe *et al.* 1980; Paehlke 1989; Fox 1985; Mohai 1990; Taylor 1989).

The Rise of an Inclusive Environmental Movement

This pattern changed dramatically with the emergence of the multiracial environmental justice movement in the late 1980s. In recent years African Americans and other ethnic groups have organized around environmental issues at an unprecedented rate. New groups are constantly being formed, and older ones are continually expanding their agenda. Thousands of people of color have joined environmental groups, coalitions, and alliances in the United States (Bullard 1992a). Hundreds have served as founders, leaders, organizers, researchers, academics, policymakers, board members, campaign managers, and environmental educators. The Citizens Clearinghouse for Hazardous Wastes estimates it works with over 7,000 community and grassroots groups nationwide. Just two years ago, CCHW's estimate was about 2,200 (Citizens' Clearinghouse for Hazardous Waste 1991; Suro 1989, p. 18; Collette 1987, pp. 44-45; Montague 1990; Ruffins 1990).

Like many people attracted to the modern environmental movement, activists of color were shocked when they learned of the dangers to their communities caused by acute and chronic exposures to toxins and other environmental hazards. As more and more communities woke up to find themselves suffering from chronic exposures to toxins, they started making connections between previously mysterious illnesses and environmental hazards. The environmental disasters at Love Canal (New York), Triana (Alabama), Institute (West Virginia), Warren County (North Carolina), and Emelle (Alabama)—along with research linking race and poverty to the siting of hazardous facilities—spawned a whole new breed of environmental activists.

These people looked directly at the relationships among class, race, political power, and the exposure to environmental hazards. They thus rejected conventional NIMBYism (Not In My Backyard campaigns). They refused to say "not in my backyard" without questioning or caring about whose backyard the problem ended up in. In addition to asking "why in my backyard?" they insisted that such hazards should not be located in anyone's backyard.

Herein lies a key distinction between the environmental justice movement and much of the white-dominated, well-to-do, community environmental organizations which have sought to protect their own neighborhoods from pollutants and hazardous wastes. Activists of color were more experientially equipped to perceive the injustice in the distribution of environmental hazards and envision a world where these burdens would be eliminated, reduced, or, where unavoidable, distributed equitably in the future.

As noted, research played a vital role in the growth of the environmental justice movement. In recent years, minority researchers have thoroughly documented the link between environmental hazards and race and poverty. They have also developed concepts such as "environmental blackmail," "environmental racism," and "environmental equity" to challenge and clarify the rest of the environmental movement's thinking.

As the research and discussion papers multiplied, conferences and roundtables were also convened to discuss and debate these issues. Notable among these conferences were the Urban Environmental Health Conference (1985), the Race and the Incidence of Environmental Hazards Conference (1990), and the first National People of Color Environmental Leadership Summit (1991). The Urban Environment Health Conference was particularly important. It was the first forum to raise the issue of toxic exposures on the job as well as in the community and pointed out how poor people and people of color were being forced to choose between their sources of income and their health and safety.

During these same years, several journals, magazines, and newsletters sprang up to cover environmental justice issues. Foremost among them are *Race, Poverty, and the Environment* (Earth Island Institute), *Toxic Times* (National Toxics Campaign), *Everyone's Backyard* (Citizens' Clearinghouse for Hazardous Waste), *RACHEL's Hazardous Waste News* (Environmental Research Foundation), *Panna Outlook* (Pesticide Action Network), *Voces Unidas* (Southwest Organizing Project), *The Workbook* (Southwest Research and Information Center), and *The Egg: A Journal of Ecojustice* (Network Center for Religion, Ethics and Social Policy). In addition, other environmental magazines such as *Environmental Action* and *Green Letter* have carried substantial sympathetic coverage of environmental justice issues.

The most vital element in the rise of the environmental justice movement, however, was the emergence of grassroots activists willing to lay everything they have on the line. People with little previous knowledge of environmental issues or experience with political activism have been compelled to take radical action. For example, as we have seen in Warren County, North Carolina, African-American women, men, and children militantly stood and lay in front of trucks to prevent them from taking PCB-laced soil to the dump (Geiser and Waneck 1983; LaBalme 1988). Scenes like these have been repeated all over the country with people of various racial and ethnic groups participating. Increasingly distant are the days when communities of color would remain silent or refuse to question the nature of the new jobs promised them when companies manufacturing dangerous products moved into town, or when landfills, incinerators, or other toxic dumps were placed in their neighborhoods. While the more established sectors of the environmental movement were content to fight professional battles in quiet courtrooms and the lobbies of Congress, the participants of the grassroots environmental justice movement took much greater risks and made larger personal sacrifices.

This new movement has become well rooted throughout the country. According to Bullard (1991a, pp. 6-10), 11 percent of the current multiracial environmental justice groups were formed prior to 1970, 24 percent between 1970 to 1980, and the rest during the 1980s and 1990s. For example, groups like Citizens for a Better America in Virginia and the Franklin Park Coalition in Boston (Roxbury) have been established for about 17 years. Citizens for a Better America is a multi-issue environmental group, and the Franklin Park Coalition is a park restoration and conservation group. Other groups like the Gulf Coast Tenants Organization (Baton Rouge, Louisiana), Southwest Organizing Project (New Mexico) have also been established for more than a decade.

While the issue has been highlighted in recent years, it would be a mistake to think that all minority environmental groups focus on community anti-toxins campaigns as do such grassroots groups such as Toxic Avengers, West Harlem Environmental Action, Mothers of East Los Angeles, Concerned Citizens of South Central Los Angeles, and Native Americans for a Clean Environment. Nor are the concerns of the environmental justice movement bounded by expanding the anti-toxins concern to include toxins on the job, as represented by such groups as the Labor/Community Strategy Center, the Michigan Association of Minority Environmental Services and Technologies, the Oil Chemical and Atomic Workers, and various local committees for occupational safety and health.

This diverse new movement actually includes professional networks (African American Environmental Association and the American Association of Blacks in Energy in Washington, D.C.); community gardens and farm cooperatives (Cambodian Gardens in Houston, Inner City Coop Farm in New Haven); business-environmental forums (Forum for Community Transformation in Portland, Oregon); Greens (African-American Black and Green Tendency in California); water and energy conservationists (Center for Environment, Commerce, and Energy in Washington, D.C.); wilderness activists (Flora, Folk and Fauna in Washington, D.C.); research, advocacy, and training organizations (Southwest Organizing Project, Gulf Coast Tenants Association, Center for Third World Organizing); environmental educators seeking access to the outdoors for inner city youths (Natural Guard in Connecticut); and groups combining an understanding of African-American history with an understanding of natural history (Underground Railroad in Kansas and Minnesota). Typically, environmental justice groups start off working on a single issue but quickly move on to multi-issue agendas and a diversity of strategies and tactics.

As this local activism has increased and national conferences and movement media have brought people together, a more coordinated, multi-issue national movement has emerged. Most early environmental justice groups engaged in solitary struggles. However, as the 1980s drew to a close and national clearinghouses, public information services, and regional networks (for information dissemination, training, testing, and organizing) were established, many of these groups started gathering together under one umbrella. Their approach also more and more distinguished itself from the other sectors of the environmental movement.

One key distinction, of course, is the racial diversity of the movement. Environmental justice groups range from those that are all, or primarily, African-American, Native-American, Puerto Rican, Latino, and Asian to multiracial coalitions, some including European Americans as members. For instance, the Labor/Community Strategy Center in Los Angeles is a multiracial coalition, while Mothers of East Los Angeles is all Latina, and Concerned Citizens of East Los Angeles is made up primarily of African Americans. Toxic Avengers is a Puerto Rican group in Brooklyn, while the People United for a Better Oakland (PUEBLO) is a multiracial group. A national conference of the environmental justice movement thus looks quite different from the national conferences of the Sierra Club or Friends of the Earth.

Women's leadership is also very strong in the environmental justice movement. In many instances women are founders or are the heads of these organizations. Native Americans for a Clean Environment, Mothers of East Los Angeles, and Concerned Citizens of South Central Los Angeles were all founded and headed by women and maintain primarily female memberships. In other instances, groups like Citizens for a Better America and West Harlem Environmental Action were co-founded by women along with men and their membership is more mixed. Women's participation in these organizations is still vital and valued, however.

The environmental justice movement is also more ideologically inclusive than more traditional ecology groups. It integrates both social and ecological concerns much more readily and pays particular attention to questions of distributive justice, community empowerment, and democratic accountability. It does not treat the problem of oppression and social exploitation as separable from the rape and exploitation of the natural world. Instead, it argues that human societies and the natural environment are intricately linked and that the health of one depends on the health of the other. It understands that if the human environment is poisoned, if there are no opportunities for economic survival or nutritional sustenance, or if there are no possibilities to be sheltered, then we have an inadequate environmental program. The environmental justice movement thus represents a revolution within the history of U.S. environmentalism.

Impact on the Traditional Movement

The environmental justice movement blasts apart the widely held myth within the traditional environmental movement that poor people and people of color are unconcerned with environmental issues. The fact that so many environmental groups of color have emerged and operate within the ideological framework of environmental justice demonstrates to the "mainstream" movement that people of color have always been interested in environmental issues. They simply remained outside the existing movement because of the ways in which environmental issues were framed, the kinds of issues which were focused on, and the ways those issues were strategically addressed.

Some white environmentalists dismiss this new sector of the environmental movement as radical social justice extremists and stubbornly ignore the potential insights to be gained by exploring their experience. For them, it is still business as usual. Others have sought to make just enough changes within their organizations to avoid charges of racism and negative press coverage. Still others have responded to this new sector of the movement by beginning to imagine more powerful and inclusive ways of furthering the environmental cause. The current impact of the environmental justice movement on the other sectors of the environmental movement is thus still inconclusive. But the seeds of change can be seen nearly everywhere. Directly or indirectly, the environmental justice movement has widened various debates, changed many of the terms of discussion, and altered the ways several issues are conceptualized and campaigns organized.

One example of this dynamic is the internal organizational policy changes that are underway. Several prominent environmental organizations, even some of those with the most conservative agendas, have felt compelled to racially diversify their staff, boards, and coalition partners. It has become increasingly hard to claim that there are not qualified people of color to sit on their boards, do research in their organizations, make policy, or teach environmental education. The environmental justice movement has begun to attract a growing number of people of color who are professors, researchers, policymakers, health and safety specialists, and environmental activists. People of color have become the members and volunteers that fuel the rapidly expanding environmental justice movement.

In light of this, several funding organizations are tying some of their funding to conventional environmental organizations to successful racial diversification efforts. We are increasingly seeing new opportunities for people of color to work and study within the environmental field. Today there are numerous minority internship programs, most notably those run by the Center for Environmental Intern Programs (CEIP). Other have launched collaborative efforts with minority environmental groups aimed at increasing the presence of people of color in the field. Greenpeace, for example, works closely with the Center for Environment, Commerce, and Energy to place interns.

While helpful, these efforts alone can not go very far beyond cosmetic tokenism. Hiring a few people of color can satisfy funders, the press, and liberal members, but it does not necessarily address the deeper questions raised by the environmental justice movement or help the wider movement grow and win significant victories. Alliance-building and logistical support are needed, not tokenism and cooptation.

One of the strengths of the multiracial environmental justice movement is that it provides the opportunity for people of color to lead instead of being led, to initiate and produce research instead of relying on someone else's, and to define the issues that are most pressing to them instead of having their issues defined by others. While traditional environmental organizations should continue to racially diversify, they should also support the new multiracial grassroots environmental organizations. For if recent trends hold, people of color will continue flocking to the grassroots environmental justice movement where they are immediately welcomed as contributing members. The chance for a majoritarian movement for social and ecological renewal will be lost if the traditional environmental movement does not develop respectful alliances with these new constituencies and sources of political energy. This, of course, requires activists in the traditional movement to move beyond their often unconscious stance of white superiority.

The relationship between white and minority environmental groups has traditionally been one of distrust, distance, discomfort, and misunderstanding. With a large number of groups of color emerging with a radical politic, the relationship between minority and nonminority environmental groups could easily get worse. However, both sides are now expending considerable effort to achieve mutual understanding and find common ground. They are working to identify the issues that keep them apart as well as the radical changes needed to bridge the distance.

Prospects and Prognosis

Participation of people of color in the environmental justice movement will probably continue to increase, but to reach the largest number of people possible will require intense work by today's activists. First and foremost, they must meet the crying need of their constituents for environmental education. This should begin early in people's lives. Children in school need to be exposed to these issues so as to ensure that new generations of environmental activists and specialists can be nurtured. Not only should they be taught the basic facts and principles of the field, but they should also learn how traditional fields such as medicine, law, education, or public health can be applied to environmental work. Some Native Americans have already formed their own environmental law firms to handle their communities' legal battles.

Secondly, alliances need to be built between the environmentalists and labor activists. Environmentalists and labor activists have often been at odds historically, a happy state of affairs for big business. However, they can be a good allies for one another. Many unions are fighting for worker health and safety. If environmentalists of color collaborate with them and help create environmentally sound jobs and train people for them, the animosity between the two movements will probably subside.

In addition, the environmental justice movement needs to continue to emphasize community organizing. Militant environmental campaigns must be waged for access to green space, toxic cleanup, inclusion of environmental issues in school curricula, pesticide reduction, clean air and water, healthier lifestyles among people of color, and a reduction and redistribution of environmental risks. More active organizations of color are needed.

People of color have to be especially vigilant to prevent continued exposure of their communities to hazardous materials. It is estimated that the Defense Department alone will spend $22 billion over the next fifteen years on cleanup projects. In addition, between $25 and $50 billion will be spent to comply with the Clean Air Act through the installation of scrubbers and other smokestack devices. The Department of Energy estimates it will spend about $200 billion over the next 30 years to clean up 3,700 Superfund sites where nuclear materials are stored. In 1992 alone, more than $159 billion will be spent on all aspects of hazardous waste cleanups in the United States. This figure is expected to grow by about 10 percent a year as more sites are discovered. Yet, which sites will be targeted for cleanup? Where does the cleaned-up material go? Will the path of least resistance to dumping continue to lead polluters to minority communities?

Environmental justice groups also have to build alliances with other sectors of the social justice and environmental movements. The resources of these movements need to be combined to design and execute large-scale collaborative research projects, to create databanks on environmental health issues, and to build funding bases for future undertakings. Similarly, efforts to mount joint campaigns should be increased. More regional networks like the Southwest Network for Environmental and Economic Justice and the Southern Organizing Committee for Economic and Social Justice will enhance joint activities.

On another front, people of color should pressure the Congressional Black Caucus (CBC) and such formations to provide more high-profile leadership in these struggles. The CBC has already compiled one of the most outstanding and consistent environmental voting records in Congress. Yet, more needs to be done. The Caucus should let environmentalists know that it provides them their strongest congressional support and help further break down the myth that people of color have little interest in their relationship to the environment. Caucus members also need to make clear their support for these issues to their local communities. Caucus members should make environmental issues an even more prominent focus of their campaigns. Such legislative support will complement the efforts of grassroots groups.

People of color will also have to hold elected officials (regardless of their race) accountable for local environmental hazards. Those winning our support should champion the cause of environmental justice since their constituents have a better-than-average chance of being adversely affected by pollution. Those already elected should be held accountable for the factories, incinerators, landfills, etc., that they invite into communities to provide jobs. Activists should pursue elective office themselves to ensure that they have an actual say in the environmental health of their communities.

While the chances are good that many more groups of color will join the growing ranks of the environmental justice movement, these activists of color have an enormous task ahead of them. They have to continue the struggle for environmental justice, but also educate and organize their communities generally. In addition, they have to work closely with one another to increase funding for their projects and organizations, expand job-training and job-creation opportunities, enhance the political influence of their members, and ensure political accountability from elected officials. Finally, they must also find a way to link their local struggles with the larger ones in the national and international arenas.

CHAPTER 4

Coping with Industrial Exploitation

Cynthia Hamilton

The consequences of industrialization have forced an increasing number of African Americans to become environmentalists. This is particularly the case for those who live in central cities where they are overburdened with the residue, debris, and decay of industrial production. Social scientists have been fascinated with the relationship between race, development, and the environmental crisis. They have found that the costs and benefits of industrial expansion are not equally distributed in our society: some communities pay more of the costs, others receive more than their fair share of benefits.

This chapter examines the urban industrial problems faced by people of color. Environmental problems in these communities can best be understood in terms of the much-discussed "crisis of growth and development." People of color are the first to feel the irony of living in a country that represents 6 percent of the world's population and consumes 45 percent of its resources, including 60 percent of its energy resources.

The Price of Growth

Growth and development are sources both of wealth and destruction. Growth also reproduces inequality. Is it possible to limit growth and distribute goods more equitably? Hazel Henderson (1981, p. 7) contends that it is never a matter of growth vs. no growth. What is crucial is what is growing, what is declining, and what must be maintained. Uneven development and trade have shaped power relations between nations and individuals over the past three centuries. These relationships have been named in several ways: colonialism, imperialism, underdevelopment, internal colonialism, and institutional racism.

The most advanced stage of industrial development has been the most toxic, thanks particularly to the petroleum, electronics, and aerospace industries. Such industries have left a trail of horrors in communities of color. Children of farmworkers have suffered birth defects as a consequence of their mothers' pesticide exposure at work during pregnancy. In and around farmworker communities, child cancer rates are unusually high. Children whose mothers work in low-wage, hazardous jobs in high-tech industries, where the use of dangerous chemicals is common, have high rates of birth defects. And children living around military installations have high rates of cancer and other illnesses.

Ecological disasters similar to those we find in Haiti (massive soil erosion, devastated forests, dead rivers, and extinct species of animals, plants, and even butterflies—to say nothing of the poor quality of life of the people) are usually dismissed as rare and explained as aberrations. But today these conditions are commonplace. What nation has *not* experienced at least some of them? Industrial development has not only produced its opposite, underdevelopment, but is itself self-destructive. Unrestrained, it has had disastrous effects on society, including the slow destruction of the ozone, the increase of acid rain, and chemical contamination of water, food, and air.

So-called socialist and capitalist economies alike have long operated on a fallacy that the earth's resources and capacity to absorb pollution are inexhaustible. There is growing official recognition, however, that unchecked growth, based on excessive resource consumption and use of nonrenewable resources, can no longer be sustained. Even the authors of the cornucopian theory of unlimited industrial growth and development have begun to modify their positions. Walt W. Rostow wrote in *Getting from Here to There* (1987) that by the year 2000 we must develope new renewable energy sources, recycle them, and control pollution. This is the conviction of a strong proponent of unlimited growth.

One of the byproducts of unlimited growth along the petrochemical route is the toxic waste crisis. The United States produces between 250 and 400 million metric tons of toxic waste per year or about one ton per person per year. To date, no viable solution has been found to deal with this mounting waste problem. There are more than 6,000 industrial plants in the United States producing dangerous chemicals. Many, if not most, are found in working-class districts with high percentages of people of color. The waste products of this production are also frequently stored in such communities or sent to the Third World (Center for Investigative Reporting and Bill Moyers 1990; Alston 1990). This waste export pattern has aptly been tagged "toxic imperialism."

Africa has become a prime dumping ground for toxic industrial and pharmaceutical residues and even deadly radioactive material (see Greenpeace 1990). Shipments arrive there from Norway, France, Italy, Belgium, Luxembourg, the Netherlands, West Germany, Canada, and the United States. South America and Central America, as well as the Caribbean islands, face the same problem, largely from U.S. exports. As organized local resistance raises consciousness, governments simply move the problem elsewhere. At the same time, banks are eager to acquire equity in Third World debtor countries and have thus initiated "debt for nature swaps" where debts are reduced in exchange for unspoiled land. Communities of color in the United States, like their counterparts in the Third World, are offered economic incentives in exchange for accepting the toxic consequences of hazardous waste storage.

To date, our legal and political system has protected those who are destroying our future. In the name of private property and free enterprise, corporations are allowed to pollute the air, water, and soil we all share. In the name of progress and development, industries consume vital resources and transform harmless elements into hazardous by-products. This depletion of resources and industrial destruction of the environment are now constants, not occasional externalities. Herbert Marcuse echoed this view when he stated:

> Concentration camps, mass exterminations, world wars, and atom bombs are no "relapse into barbarism," but the unre-pressed implementation of the achievements of modern science, technology and domination (1961, p. 4).

We must now weigh our philosophical and policy alternatives with this knowledge as our backdrop. We need a reconceptualization of evolution that would include a decentralization of power and allow for new forms of political participation to emerge before totalitarian measures are imposed to control the crisis of resource scarcity and environmental degradation.

Conventional Perspectives and the Need for Alternatives

Both Western liberalism's and conservatism's notions of individualism, private property, and the free market provide the philosophical basis of industrial "democracy" that dominates modern thought and society. The industrial revolution also gave rise to Marxism, of course. Yet, ironically, though Marxism rested on a chronicle of the inequities and irrationalities of capitalism, it accepted industrial development and the technological domination of nature by human society as a precondition for a liberated, communist society. Indeed, applied Marxism stands alongside liberalism and conservatism in its defense of industrial growth and development. Even liberal policies that emphasize fairness, opportunity for all, and state regulation of production are predicated on the promise of growth. The greatest defense, then, of those corporations most active in the destruction of the environment is the common left-liberal-conservative commitment to industrial development.

Our legal, cultural, and economic systems have promoted the "good" of the few over the "good" of the majority. The corporations' achievement of legal "personhood" has allowed them to place narrow profit above the broader concerns of real people and their communities. We now need to break with the school of thought that excludes community, nature, and justice from our consideration.

To halt this self-destructive march of industrial growth and development, citizen action is necessary. It must be guided by a critical approach to community development and industrial production and transcend isolated, individual crises so as to confront the national and transnational consequences of corporate, industrial behavior. So far, environmental activists and theorists have been slow to develop a theory of political action or community development because of their focus on instrumentalities: rules, bureaucracy, and administration (in the tradition of liberal and conservative thought). What's needed instead is the creation of an "economic democracy" that institutionalizes decentralized, local, and regional approaches to development, production for use, and the greening of urban environments as well as preservation of the wild.

It is very important that we rebuild our cities, for they have become centers of social injustice as a result of our current development models. According to the World Commission on Environment and Development (WCED), "the future will be predominantly urban, and the most immediate environmental concerns of most people will be urban ones" (WCED 1987, p. 255). This connection between the urban and environmental crises was further developed at WCED hearings in 1986:

> Large cities by definition are centralized, manmade environments that depend mainly on food, water, energy, and other goods from outside. Smaller cities, by contrast, can be the heart of community-based development and provide services to the surrounding countryside.
>
> Given the importance of cities, special efforts and safeguards are needed to ensure that the resources they demand are produced sustainably and that urban dwellers participate in decisions affecting their lives. Residential areas are likely to be more habitable if they are governed by individual neighborhoods with direct local participation. To the extent that energy and other needs can be met on a local basis, both

the city and surrounding areas will be better off (WCED 1987, p. 243).

New planning must be undertaken, with the assistance of people from multiple disciplines, to achieve this goal of neighborhood empowerment. In the area of technological alternatives, we must focus on renewable resources and conservation (e.g., solar energy and recycling) to replace our dependence on nuclear energy and fossil fuels.

Our new call for an ecological democracy must also recognize the class interests in both Western and developing societies. We must highlight the political intentions and consequences of existing growth and development strategies, which often mean the destruction of working-class communities in central cities. We must now reject a view of development as simply a neutral technological advancement.

A new social contract between citizens and their governments must be made. Our communities must resist transnational corporations that use their economic power to influence political officials and render them unresponsive to citizens and their communities. Accountability requires new leadership and new forms of citizen participation in governance. Multiple decisionmaking units (like neighborhood councils) should regulate development and ensure citizen input on economic and environmental decisions. Centralized political decisionmaking, as well as centralized planning, must be replaced by decentralized methods. This is the essence of what Henderson calls "thinking globally and acting locally" (Henderson 1981, p. 355).

To develop a more complete definition of social justice and democracy, we must transcend the limitations of private property, recognize environmental rights as human rights, and embrace community activism in pursuit of the common good. Liberal and conservative political philosophies have only served to justify industrial development and sanctify unlimited individual rights. As a consequence, we are a long way from achieving environmental or "earth" rights.

The Politics of Reconceptualization

Given these problems and needs, it is reassuring to know that the basis for alternative policies and institutions is being developed through grassroots struggles in communities of color around the country. The contradictions resulting from U.S. development strategies have put African-American and other communities of color (primarily Latinos and Native Americans because they too have been victims of de facto segregation) on the cutting edge of the 21st century. Indeed, the effects of those strategies on communities of color in the United States have made most grassroots organizations wary of development models emphasizing capital intensive projects such as building highways, office towers, shopping malls, and condominiums.

It is no accident that the crisis of industrialization would manifest itself most dramatically within communities of color, for they have experienced the most severe economic underdevelopment and the most contamination from industrialization. The health consequences already have been catastrophic. Many others will not manifest themselves for years. Even now we know that Navajo teenagers have a rate of organ cancer seventeen times the national average; that 50 percent of the nation's children suffering from lead paint poisoning (resulting in low attention spans, limited vocabulary, behavior problems, etc.) are African-American. These are the *real* implications of U.S. institutional racism and development strategies that ignore human and social costs as well as environmental costs. All of this has badly eroded the quality of life in the urban United States.

Many of these problems emanate from discriminatory land-use decisions, which ensure that poor people and people of color live in close proximity to polluting industries. Noise and pollution from factories, warehouses, and stockyards have become the trademark of African-American communities, further ensuring de facto segregation. As whites left the inner city to escape its deafening noise, congestion, foul air, water, and land, African Americans were allowed to move into the houses left behind. The boundaries of African-American communities are often formed by rivers or lakes on whose banks we find factories, warehouses, stockyards, and other nonresidential structures.

The central business district of cities in the early 20th century was where people of lower socio-economic status generally lived. In many cities, African Americans replaced the European, working-class people completely in these areas by the end of World War II. In many instances, housing had been built on marshes and landfills. Frequently, in the Northeast and Midwest, elevated trains traversed the length of the African-American neighborhoods as business continued as usual beneath them. The geographic concentration of industries and households increases the likelihood that a huge volume of waste will be transformed into dangerous pollution.

After the major drive to organize unions in the 1930s, industries often relocated to the urban periphery. To escape their workers' increasing demands, industries began to move even further away from the urban core into the suburbs. Later, during the 1970s, industries again sought new locations, this time in the Sunbelt in order to take advantage of this region's cheap land and labor (Perry & Watkins 1977; Feagin 1988; Bullard, 1987, 1989). The government helped by providing subsidies for production and new building by industries engaged in the military-industrial complex and by financing public housing and highway construction to facilitate the transit of workers and commodities. This desertion of the inner city left a decaying core. Indeed, this is an international condition. As noted by the WCED:

> [Industrial] cities account for a high share of the world's resource use, energy consumption, and environmental pollution...Many [industrial cities] face problems of deteriorating infrastructure, environmental degradation, inner-city decay, and neighborhood collapse. The unemployed, the elderly, and racial and ethnic minorities can remain trapped in a downward spiral of degradation and poverty as job opportunities and the younger and better-educated individuals leave declining neighborhoods. City or municipal governments often face a legacy of poorly designed and maintained public housing estates, mounting costs, and declining tax bases (1987, p. 24).

The WCED report also notes that because the resources exist to solve the urban environmental crisis in industrial countries, "the issue for most industrial countries is ultimately one of political and social choice" (WCED 1987). In most instances, the choice has been to build a new urban core, displace the poor, and create a new corporate city to fulfill a new set of functions. Cities are now no longer needed for the centralization of production but rather for the housing of administrative and financial headquarters.

As the role of finance capital has expanded, centers to facilitate transactions have become more elaborate. They now contain housing banks, stock exchanges, insurance companies, brokerage firms, etc. The old industrial city has now taken a new "corporate" form—not only a new appearance, but new inhabitants, as the poor and working class are displaced. Corporate decentralization and urban sprawl have replaced clear, functional, central cities. Lost too are the institutions of urban policies that provided some measure of social justice for poor people and communities of color. Now, left to their own devices, communities of color have organized themselves to fill gaps in services provided by local governments. This has been true even when many people of color have been elected to key governmental leadership positions in these restructured cities.

Land-use decisions have always reflected class and racial bias (Logan and Molotch 1987; Bullard 1984, 1987; Bullard & Feagin 1991; Feagin 1988). Because they reflect the distribution of power in society, they cannot be expected to produce an equitable distribution of goods and services or a balanced sharing of social responsibilities. This is true in inner-city ghettos, middle-class suburban neighborhoods, and even affluent subdivisions inhabited largely by African Americans. African-American communities are systematically redlined by banks, savings and loan associations, and insurance companies (Bullard & Feagin 1991). Yet, now citizens in these communities are expected to assist in the bailout of the failed savings and loans institutions, many of which engaged in illegal redlining practices for years.

These same communities also host an unfair share of prisons, highways, sewerage treatment facilities, bus garages, salvage yards, hazardous waste treatment centers, storage and disposal facilities, and other polluting industries. As in the Third World, rising poverty, unemployment, unpayable debt, aid with strings attached, trade barriers, and export-driven economics are at the root of many environmental problems in the United States. Ironically, the art of justifying or "selling" communities on development projects that are *not* in their best interest has become a new business specialty for consultants.

The mainstream environmental movement has not yet taken leadership in resisting these projects. Resistance has fallen to the movement for environmental justice led by the residents of poor neighborhoods and communities of color most affected by virtue of their proximity to the major sources of pollution. As long as land can be acquired cheaply and easily in communities of color, and as long as zoning and other regulations can be minimized, these communities will continue to be prime targets, particularly for waste disposal waste-to-energy incinerators. This will likely intensify as landfill space decreases.

Avoiding Western Chauvinism

Participation by mainstream environmentalists in the decisions to move poison from one community to another more vulnerable community does not move us any closer to viable alternatives. Communities of color begin their organizing with a recognition of limited options and allies. These communities start with a clear view of the link between the exploitation of the environment and their own exploitation. They recognize industrial and environmental inequities precisely because their communities have been so neglected.

We must understand that the way we conceptualize economic development can produce very different cultural attitudes and behavior. For example, Native Americans have always insisted that their culture (as embodied in their religion) is the source of their economic system and values. These values emphasize harmony with Mother Earth and the Creator. On the other hand, Western thought emphasizes humanity's control of nature. Nature and "wildlands" are thus seen as needing to be controlled, tamed, and dominated. It is not by chance that the symbols and mythical heroes (like Prometheus) of Western culture are the embodiment of domination and production. The anti-heroes, (Orpheus, Narcissus, Dionysus) are the antagonists of domination, and considered weak and disruptive. However, it is through these anti-heroes that the symbolic opposition between "man" and nature, subject and object, can be overcome (Marcuse 1961, p. 151). For Marcuse, they represent a much different reality:

> [T]heirs is the image of joy and fulfillment; the voice which does not command but sings; the gesture which offers and receives; the deed which is peace and ends the labor of conquest; the liberation from time which unites man with god, man with nature (1961, p. 147).

It is not surprising that the characteristics of these anti-heroes were attributed by Hegel to "Africa...the land of childhood, lying beyond the day of self-conscious history...," or dismissed by other Western philosophers as effeminate.

Not surprisingly, Western scholars are quick to characterize Africa's proximity to nature as a source of weakness. Feelings, emotions, and sensations—not reason—are said to characterize the "Sons of Ham." This idea was stood on its head by African and West Indian writers and activists from French colonies in the 1930s as they launched the Negritude movement. The technological achievements of the West were presented as symbols of colonialism and oppression, of a "civilization of machine and cannon." The African Renaissance movement offered "humanism" as a tool to tame technology and subjugate it to human needs. These writers extolled those qualities denigrated by the West. As Leopold Senghor wrote in "Prayer to the Masks":

> For who would teach rhythm to a dead world of cannons and machines? Who would give the shout of joy at dawn to wake the dead and orphaned? Tell me, who would restore the memory of life to men whose hopes are disemboweled? (Kennedy 1975, pp. 132-133)

But, these were not voices rejecting technology as such. Rather, they sought to point out the misuse of technology and the need to infuse it with the spirit of people. They, therefore, point to alternatives. Here is but one example of their poetic critique of industrialization and technology:

[Blessings] for those who never invented anything,
Who never explored anything,
Who never conquered anything,
But who abandon themselves to the essence of all things,
Ignorant of surfaces, caught by the motion of all things,
Indifferent to conquering but playing the game of the world...

Listen to the white world,
Horribly weary from its enormous effort,
Its rebellious joints crack beneath the hard stars,
Its rigid, blue steel penetrates the mystic flesh;
Hear its traitorous victories trumpet its defeats;
Hear the grandiose alibis for its sorry stumbling,
Pity for our conquerors, omniscient and naive!
(Kennedy 1975, p. 76)

Ironically, those in the West who have been responsible for industrial development have been least likely to explore its consequences. Quite possibly the reason is their alienation from the land and nature. Some poets have suggested that the alienation of most immigrant Americans comes from their lack of contact with the mythic beginnings of the land. They contrast this with the experience of Native Americans, who trace their own development alongside that of the land.

The early Negritude critics shed light on the persisting criticism by non-Westerners of environmental destruction and domination and articulate clearly the direction the designers of new paradigms must explore. Those who present an alternative analysis of development must continue where this critique ends. Development, as it has been made manifest in the world, is more than increased industrial production.

Women and Alternative Models

Some feminists scholars suggest that the domination of nature provides a context for viewing the domination of women (Merchant 1981; Shiva 1990; Hamilton 1990; Adair 1990). They suggest that the status of women actually declines with modernization and industrial development. Their integration into low-wage jobs and their access to a multitude of household appliances has not enhanced women's equality. Not all sectors of the women's movement would agree, of course. Many accept the claim that women can be beneficially integrated into existing development models.

Yet, focusing on women also helps to put the critique of development in perspective. Historically the domination of women was linked to their isolation in the private sphere, away from formal economic work and community politics. A "women's place" was limited to "the home." At one time community life was an extension of home, but with the transformation of neighborhoods and the industrial destruction of settled communities, women lost a very important arena for political action that placed them at the center of community-based politics, working on schools, churches, youth activities, and voluntary organizations.

The isolation of suburban living and that of new urban housing projects not only has decreased the public space for women's voices, but also has increased their physical vulnerability. It thus may not be mere coincidence that urban women are now fighting back and at the forefront of movements to preserve community and oppose unhealthy development and destructive environmental exposure (Hamilton 1990; Pardo 1990).

This is particularly true of women of color in urban settings. For them, urban environmental issues are a "natural." Because the urban crisis threatens personal health, family, and the neighborhood community, women of color have frequently found themselves in leadership roles (Hamilton 1990). Some analysts have suggested that women of color have inherited the language of participation and political confrontation from the civil rights struggles of the 1960s:

> The 1960s revolt of central-city minority neighborhoods invented a political vocabulary which has been embraced not only by service professionals choosing to reside in the central city, but by the suburban dwellers as well. This has induced government agencies and local political leaders to become much more neighborhood-oriented and participation-oriented at least in their rhetorical style (Mollenkopf 1981, p. 331).

The organized environmental efforts by women of color have great potential and are already seen as a threat by corporate elites. For example, the Trilateral Commission identified, over a decade ago, the challenge to corporate interests presented by such social movements. In its 1975 report *The Crisis of Democracy,* the Commission expressed its fear of true democracy, citizen participation, and civic notions of the "common good":

The vulnerability of democratic government in the United States [thus] comes not primarily from external threats, though such threats are real, nor from internal subversion from the left or the right, although both possibilities could exist, but rather from the internal dynamics of democracy itself in a highly educated, mobilized, and participant society...Previously passive or unorganized groups in the population—Blacks, Indians, Chicanos, white ethnic groups, students, and women—[have] now embarked on concerted efforts to establish their claims to opportunities, positions, rewards, and privileges, to which they had not considered themselves entitled before (Sklar 1980, pp. 3 and 37).

Clearly, when groups previously left out of formal parliamentary and electoral processes of participation began to demand institutional access or to develop new methods of civic involvement, capitalism and elite politics were threatened. The grassroots environmental struggles of women of color reflect just such a struggle for noncorporate alternatives. Nonhierarchical, decentralized structures are frequently advanced by these women. In their struggles, they encourage individual initiative while emphasizing respect for interdependence and cooperation, thus breaking with both the individualistic and bureaucratic extremes of modern life. Their life experience leads them to start questioning the private ownership of common resources and the elite domination of modern "democratic" politics. It encourages them to ask: What are our rights regarding quality of life? What are the rights of those already victimized by environmental abuse?

Conclusion

After years of struggle for civil rights, communities of color see their victories threatened by unjust environmental decisions. Many land-use and siting decisions place municipal landfills, toxic waste dumps, incinerators, and polluting industries in their communities. Persistent problems of lead poisoning in urban areas and pesticide poisoning in rural areas are also key concerns. Addressing these problems requires new perspectives, new leaders, new organizations, and new actions.

Changing government policy is simply no longer enough. The problems of development and unlimited economic growth have emerged from the economic/corporate arena where government is only a junior partner. Current organizing efforts to defend the families, homes, and communities of people of color from environmental degradation need to address this reality directly. They need to not only demand greater accountability from elected officials who are all too often beholden financially to the corporate elite through Political Action Committee money and corporate donations, but they also need to demand greater democratic control of economic ownership, production, and investment. The environmental justice movement cannot allow questions of land use, land rights, and land ownership to remain the province of corporate decisionmakers. It needs instead to create a democratic alternative.

This is beginning to happen. While the public is trained to look for leadership among those considered exceptional in our society, the environmental justice movement is turning this idea on its head. Ordinary women and men have been at the forefront of fighting toxics and other environmental problems in low-income, working-class communities of color. According to Lois Gibbs of the Citizens Clearinghouse for Hazardous Wastes, our society has begun to witness "ordinary people doing extraordinary things" (Gibbs 1982). New grassroots leadership is developing to challenge both business executives and political officials who place corporate interests over those of "ordinary" citizens (Gottlieb and Ingram 1988; Bullard 1992a). This struggle is even beginning to transform the agenda of the mostly white, mainstream environmental movement.

The long-term promise of the environmental justice movement also depends on its transcending the limited views of progress, growth, and environmental ethics so deeply embedded in the modern Western worldview, and even common among many of its critics. It must become understood that human progress in the Western world has largely been seen as synonymous with the alienation of human beings from each other and the natural world. Domination and the rise of corporate capitalism can be explained, in part, as a consequence of this alienation. Individuals and societies can no longer stand apart from nature and other people. Overcoming the divisions within society and between society and the natural world must be the goal of the environmental justice movement. Only this struggle against alienation's perversion of humanistic and ecological values can bring us closer to an alternative way of life predicated on a healthy, just, and sustainable relationship to the natural world and each other. This must become our ultimate task.

CHAPTER 5

Getting the Lead Out of the Community

Janet Phoenix

Lead poisoning, while completely preventable, is one of the most common environmental health diseases in the United States (Agency for Toxic Substances and Disease Registry 1988). Some of the symptoms of lead toxicity are fatigue, pallor, malaise, loss of appetite, irritability, sleep disturbance, sudden behavioral change, and developmental regression. The more serious symptoms include clumsiness, muscular irregularities, weakness, abdominal pain, persistent vomiting, constipation, and changes in consciousness. Lead exposure is particularly harmful to children. It damages their developing brains and nervous systems. Indeed, even low-level lead exposure can lead to attention disorders, learning disabilities, and emotional disturbances that can affect a child for the rest of his or her life. While once controversial, the effects of lead poisoning have now been carefully analyzed by several investigators and have gained wide acceptance within the public health field (Needleman *et al.* 1992; Dietrich *et al.* 1987; Baghurst *et al.* 1987; Environmental Defense Fund 1990; Alliance to End Childhood Lead Poisoning 1991).

One key source of lead poisoning has been dramatically reduced over the last two decades. A reduction in the mean blood lead level in the U.S. population occurred between 1976 and 1980 when the sale of leaded gasoline declined in this country. Yet, the problem of lead poisoning is still widespread. It has been estimated that between four to five million U.S. children are routinely exposed to lead in sufficient amounts to be considered dangerous to their health. As pointed out by the Centers for Disease Control:

> Childhood lead poisoning is one of the most common pediatric health problems in the United States today, and it is entirely preventable. Enough is now known about the sources and pathways of lead exposure and about ways of preventing this exposure to begin the efforts to eradicate permanently this disease. The persistence of lead poisoning

in the United States, in light of all that is known, presents a singular and direct challenge to public health authorities, clinicians, regulatory agencies, and society (Centers for Disease Control 1991).

In 1988, the Agency for Toxic Substances and Disease Registry (ATSDR), a division of the Public Health Service within the U.S. Department of Health and Human Services, issued a report to Congress on the nature and extent of lead poisoning in children. It contained estimates of the extent of childhood lead poisoning in Standard Metropolitan Statistical Areas (SMSA) and provided breakdowns by race, income, and urban status (Agency for Toxic Substances and Disease Registry 1988). The estimates of affected children are largely based on the numbers of children in these areas who live in pre-1950 housing, where lead paint is most common, though data generated by childhood lead poisoning screening programs was also incorporated for the cities where such programs exist. Given the fact that the study focused on lead paint and largely ignored other common sources of lead exposure, it is possible that this study actually underestimates the extent of the problem. The sources of continuing exposure include lead-based paint and paint dust, but also include contamination at work and neighborhood pollution by nearby industries and waste treatment facilities.

Whatever the limitations of this study, it does clearly show that lead exposure is not randomly distributed across population groups. Its distribution is directly related to both class and race. A disproportionate impact, for example, is felt in African-American communities, as are so many environmental health problems (Agency for Toxic Substances and Disease Registry 1988). Indeed, African Americans, at all class levels, have a significantly greater chance of being lead poisoned than do whites.

Given the de facto residential and occupational segregation that still affects African Americans and other minorities, such a finding should probably not come as a surprise. Yet, the figures are astounding. According to ATSDR's report to Congress, 49 percent of African-American inner-city children are exposed to dangerous levels of lead, compared to 16 percent of white inner-city children. Outside the nation's large urban areas, 36 percent of African-American children are exposed to dangerous levels, compared to 9 percent of white children. This disparity has existed for decades (Agency for Toxic Substances and Disease Registry 1988; Schwartz and Levin 1992, pp. 42-44).

What makes these statistics even more alarming is the fact that the blood lead level deemed dangerous has gone down as a result of recent research. During the 1980s, the federal Centers for Disease

Control (CDC) mandated medical intervention for children with blood lead levels of 25 ug/dl or higher. In October 1991, the CDC issued a statement, *Preventing Lead Poisoning in Young Children,* lowering the acceptable blood lead level from 25 ug/dl to 10 ug/dl. Today, the average level for all children in the United States is under 6 ug/dl (Schwartz and Levin 1992, p. 43). However, the Second National Health and Nutrition Examination Survey II (NHANES II), conducted between 1976 and 1980, found that the average blood lead level for African-American children was 21 ug/dl, and for poor African-American children in the inner city, 23 ug/dl. This average has gone down along with the decline of lead gasoline. Yet, the average blood lead level in African-American children is still well above 6 ug/dl. Indeed, many African-American children have blood levels well above the 10 ug/dl limit.

Lead poisoning has been termed the *silent epidemic,* for it most often leaves no outward sign of its arrival. Years after lead levels return to normal it becomes apparent in the difficulty a child has in school, in frank mental retardation, or in the onset of kidney disease in a previously healthy adult. Yet, health policy in the United States largely leaves prevention, screening, and treatment to individuals rather than taking a proactive, public health approach that does not penalize poor people without sufficient means to pay for screening and treatment or moving out of dangerous housing, jobs, and neighborhoods. Nor has a proactive policy been developed to break through the de facto segregation that keeps people of color trapped in contaminated houses, jobs, and communities. Activists of color thus need to ask: Where does lead come from? How does it damage the health of those who come into contact with it? What can we do to mitigate the damage? What can be done to prevent it?

Lead Paint and Dust in the Home

In 1989-1990, the U.S. Department of Housing and Urban Development conducted a national survey of lead-based paint in housing. The results were published in its *A Comprehensive and Workable Plan for the Abatement of Lead-Based Paint in Privately Owned Housing* (1990). It details the prevalence of lead-based paint in housing stock, as well as the average lead-dust levels in the researched housing units. The HUD researchers discovered that 57 million of the 100 million housing units in the United States contain lead-based paint on interior or exterior surfaces. Some seventeen million of them are in a deteriorated condition and pose an immediate hazard. Three to four million of these homes are occupied by children under six, those at greatest risk of being poisoned.

Most of the homes in the worst condition are in our inner cities, and a disproportionate number of the inhabitants are people of color. Part of the danger comes from children eating peeling lead-based paint chips, yet paint dust is perhaps an even more significant problem since dust covers a larger surface area and is more readily absorbed into the bloodstream from a child's stomach. Those who inhale the dust absorb it through their lungs, and from there it enters their bloodstream. Such exposure can cause lead poisoning even though it may take place over only a short period of time. Lead dust is also harder to clean up. Children come into contact with it because it clings to toys, collects on flat surfaces (especially around windows), and then sticks to children's hands. So when they put their hands in their mouths, they swallow lead dust. Over time, enough can accumulate to poison a child. Studies done in Cincinnati "support the hypothesis the peeling paint is eventually ground into dust which then contaminates hands, toys, and food" (Bornschein et al., 1986). Large amounts of lead dust are frequently generated during home renovation projects. This dust can remain airborne for up to 24 hours after work has ceased, during which time it can be inhaled, posing a hazard to workers as well as the families living in the homes. Adults as well as children are poisoned this way. The dust settling out of the air coats household surfaces (including children's toys) and can travel a long distance from where the work is being done. Because work done on the outside of a building can contaminate rooms on the inside, a thorough cleanup is necessary. Pregnant women and children should not enter a renovated home for 24 hours after the work has been completed and a thorough cleanup has been done.

One study subclassified the type, age, and condition of housing that poses the greatest paint chip and dust dangers to children. The four housing classifications included:

- Public and private housing built after World War II, having relatively low levels of paint and dust lead.
- Rehabilitated housing, originally built before World War II, having low levels of paint lead but moderate levels of exterior dust lead.
- Pre-World War II housing of satisfactory appearance, but having relatively high paint lead and moderate dust lead.
- Deteriorating or dilapidated pre-World War II housing, having relatively high paint and dust lead.

When the threshold for childhood lead poisoning was 25 ug/dl, only Group 4 housing posed a hazard. But with the new standard of 10 ug/dl all four groups do. These findings correlate well with estimates of leaded housing stock which appear in the HUD report cited earlier.

A good case study of lead problems in the home is provided by Jeremy, a two-year-old living in a well-maintained, older apartment building in a large urban center in the eastern United States. His family always had trouble with the apartment's old wooden windows. The maintenance people had to come in at least twice a year to scrape and repaint them. Because it seemed to Jeremy's dad that as soon as they left the paint would start to peel again, he was constantly complaining.

The workers never thoroughly scraped off all the old paint, and so the new layer began to blister and peel almost immediately after they left. Also, when they worked on the outside of the apartment building, they never covered the ground. Chips would fall into the yard, and lead dust blew into the urban garden plots next door, where Jeremy's family had gardened for three years.

While Jeremy's parents had not yet noticed any behavioral changes, his mother regularly took him to the neighborhood health clinic for routine checkups. She was very upset when his lead test came back positive. The clinic outreach workers who visited the house talked about cleaning up paint chips, but Jeremy's mother was always careful to sweep up the chips after the renovation workers left. Moreover, she tried to make sure that Jeremy never ate paint chips in the yard. At first everyone was puzzled by how such a high level of lead contamination could happen.

Paint chips would have been the obvious answer had Jeremy's mother not been so conscientious. The paint chip samples taken from the windows tested positive as lead-based paint. The city lead inspector had brought in an XRF (a hand-held device which aims X-rays at painted surfaces and measures how much is reflected) and used this to determine how much lead was in the paint on their walls and windows.

The main problem was the dust, however. A lot of dust was released when the workers came in to scrape and repaint the windows twice a year. Regardless of his mother's thorough cleaning, Jeremy should have stayed elsewhere until the cleanups had been completed, preferably using a high phosphate dishwasher powder which has proved useful for cleaning up lead dust.

Furthermore, before the situation was researched, no one suspected that lead dust from the maintenance work on the nearby apartment building had settled in the adjacent garden plots. Yet, soil lead levels in the garden were well above 1,000 parts per million (ppm). The U.S. Environmental Protection Agency has determined that 500-1,000 ppm and greater are toxic levels of lead in soil. Growing vegetables can concentrate this lead in vegetables thus endangering everyone who eats vegetables grown in the contaminated soil. This was a very likely source of contamination for Jeremy. His parents were active gardeners and very proud of the vegetables they grew to supplement their diet. As active gardners, they also brought lead dust into the home on their hands and work clothes.

Jeremy's blood lead level was 16 ug/dl, high enough to do damage but not high enough to cause obvious symptoms. Other children are not so lucky. A fifteen-month-old named Vincent seemed to be progressing well; he had learned to say a few words. He liked to rise early and play vigorously. Yet, it was not long before his parents noticed a marked change in his behavior: he seemed to forget how to talk and stopped wanting to play. Instead, he would take his blanket into a corner and lie quietly. Food no longer interested him. His lead level was 45 ug/dl.

Unlike Vincent, Jeremy did not need to be hospitalized for the expensive procedure of chelation therapy which cleans the blood of lead contamination. His parents were simply told to eradicate the sources of contamination in his environment and have him tested every three months until his level fell below 10 ug/dl. Eradicating the source of contamination is a difficult proposition for poor families, however. Jeremy's family, for example, cannot afford to move out of the apartment, nor are they allowed to remove the paint themselves. They can stop growing and eating food from their garden, but this only makes their food costs more expensive. To help cover their medical and home improvement costs, Jeremy's parents hired an attorney to file a lawsuit against their landlord for not properly maintaining the building and contributing to Jeremy's poisoning. No settlement has yet been reached, however.

In spite of their financial limitations, Jeremy's family has done a good job in lowering his lead level. They covered the window sills and walls with contact paper, washed Jeremy's hands more frequently, and supplemented his diet with iron and calcium. (Such nutritional supplements have been found to help limit lead contamination.) His mother also used trisodium phosphate (TSP, a powdered detergent, usually found in hardware stores, which is good at cleaning up lead dust) to wash the floors and the toys. After a few months, Jeremy's lead level came down.

No one knows whether Jeremy will suffer any permanent damage from his early exposure to lead, or if he will suffer mental retardation. Little can be done at his age to diagnose the long-term effects of his lead exposure. His parents have been told that when his language skills are more fully developed, he can undergo developmental testing, provided they can afford it. These tests can pinpoint learning disabilities. Yet, even if problems are discovered, it would be difficult, if not impossible, to "prove" they were caused by the lead exposure. Many lead-poisoned children live in a harsh environment that lacks those elements children need to compensate for learning disabilities and realize their potential.

It is not easy to separate the general effects of poverty and racism from the specific effects of lead. Yet, we do know that lead causes attention deficit disorder and other behavioral problems which interfere with school performance. Lead-poisoned children have trouble learning to speak and write. They may not have the same problem-solving ability as other children. Jeremy's mother worries that he may have trouble in school in the future, although he seems bright and alert right now.

For any individual child it is difficult to predict the effects of lead exposure. We do know that children whose lead levels rise above 50 ug/dl are much more likely to suffer profound damage, such as mental retardation. At levels of 50 ug/dl, or even below, hearing can be affected as well as Vitamin D metabolism and synthesis of the oxygen-carrying components of the blood. Also, as the blood lead level rises above 50 ug/dl, disorders such as colic (a complex of symptoms ranging from abdominal pain or cramps to constipation) may result. Effects of lower levels of exposure are much less predictable but no less real.

Contamination
on the Job and in the Community

Perhaps the most common source of contamination for adults is at their workplace. Hazardous industries with well-known lead exposure problems include battery manufacturing plants, lead smelters, brass foundries, firing ranges, radiator repair shops, and construction sites. Large industries are required to inform their employees of these hazards and to test their blood lead levels regularly. Some states mandate that levels above 25 ug/dl be reported to a state occupational registry maintained by occupational health departments that monitor hazardous work sites. Also, when employees are removed from a work site because of elevated blood lead levels, the state's occupational health department is supposed to monitor their progress. (State requirements normally reflect federal regulations.) Furthermore, retesting has to take place before the employee can return to work. Unfortunately, such state efforts are often underfunded and the actual regulation is often completely inadequate. Furthermore, small businesses often escape from taking precautions because they don't employ enough people for federal or state regulations to apply. This leaves many workers unprotected.

A good case study of these problems is provided by Randall, a former worker in a battery manufacturing plant who worked with lead every day. Written warnings about lead had been handed out when he was first hired; but Randall could not read well and so hadn't understood the warnings. Also, he was afraid to question his employer closely about the dangers because he desperately needed the job.

After several months, Randall started to have stomach cramps and headaches, but they were not bad enough to stop him from working. They merely robbed him of the joy of his leisure time by making him not feel good. A colleague complained one day that although lead tests were supposed to be given periodically to workers at the plant, none had been given since the physical exams they had received when hired. Blood had been taken then, but the results had not been shared with the workers.

This comment sparked Randall's couriosity and he asked the co-worker to explain the dangers of lead to him. What he learned concerned Randall enough that he sought out a clinic in his neighborhood and asked to be tested. Because his lead level was 92 ug/dl, the clinic doctor recommended that he be hospitalized immediately for therapy. When his employer learned of the hospitalization, Randall was laid off. He thus had to be hospitalized in a charity hospital because he was no longer covered by health insurance.

Randall was treated with chelation therapy to remove the lead from his blood. Although his lead level was high enough to kill a child, as an adult he was in no danger of dying. His physicians were concerned, however, about his developing hypertension and kidney damage. As noted, lead can affect the kidneys, the reproductive system, the gastrointestinal system, and the nervous system.

Fortunately, Randall recovered almost completely and was released from the hospital. He was told, however, that he could not return to his trade or other similar work because of the risk of re-exposure, which in even small amounts could send his lead level soaring again because a significant amount of lead was now stored in his bones which would render a new round of chelation therapy much less effective.

Randall and his wife were also concerned that their children may have been exposed to the lead dust he brought home on his clothing. While people who work in lead-related industries are often unaware of the hazards they pose to their families, secondary exposure of children whose parents work with lead is quite common. If those who work with lead handle their children before removing their work clothing, they can contaminate them. If their work clothing is washed with the rest of the family's laundry, further contamination can take place. Over time, lots of lead dust can accumulate in the home through such exposure and cause the blood lead levels of family members to rise. Clothes, upholstered furniture, automobile upholstery, and carpets are common accumulation sites for lead dust.

Randall's wife took the children to the clinic, where they too were tested and found to have high blood lead levels. The local children's hospital offered outpatient treatment for the children, but the family had to scramble to find the money to pay for it. With Randall no longer employed, his wife's income was the only source of support for the family. Randall felt he should have received some consideration and benefits from his employers, but the company denied all responsibility. Randall has since applied for unemployment compensation and workmen's compensation but his case has not yet been acted on.

A small community in an eastern state provides a good case study of primary lead poisoning of poor communities through industrial pollution. This community sits in the midst of a solid waste incinerator, an oil company, and a water pollution control plant. The plant has been operating over capacity for years and spills hazardous wastes into the adjacent river. The oil company has spilled approximately 17 million gallons of petroleum into underground areas, thus contaminating the aquifer of the community. The incinerator receives solid wastes above 25 ug/dl from neighboring communities. Although scrubbers are in place in its smokestacks, these scrubbers do not yet efficiently remove heavy metal particles from the smoke. Hazardous metals such as lead, cadmium, and mercury are regularly emitted which adversely affect human health.

These heavy metals have settled into the air, soil, and water of this community and adjacent ones. Their residents, mostly people of color, are being assaulted on a number of fronts. The workers in these plants—and their families—are not only at risk from these facilities; the entire community is poisoned and becomes contaminated simply by living near these facilities. It has been estimated that three-fourths of the children in this community have elevated blood lead levels.

Waste incineration may soon rival lead-based gasoline and lead smelting as major sources of lead in the air. Researchers project that millions of pounds of lead per year will be emitted from the nation's waste incinerator facilities in the next few years. All of it is being released into the environment, despite what we know about its hazardous effects. Little has been done to improve the capacity of these facilities to clean the air they release.

Communities Fight Back

Changes need to be made to prevent this very preventable disease. Some of these changes involve educating individuals on how they can better protect themselves and their children. However, other needed changes are deeply political and require greater social and economic justice, a more responsive democracy, and a socially responsible economic system that does not make profit the sole or highest guide to economic decisionmaking. Such changes will certainly require the growth and strengthening of a grassroots social movement for environmental justice that can educate local communities and hold governments and corporations accountable to the needs and desires of oppressed communities.

Happily, this is already beginning to happen. A report on the hazardous conditions facing communities of color and low-income communities in one state was recently prepared and presented to the state legislature. The following goals were recommended in the report:

- establishment of a Task Force on Environmental Equity;
- research on the health and safety impacts of environmental conditions in at-risk communities;
- greater public notice of hazards through publications that target communities of color and their organizations;
- research and documentation of fish consumption patterns and resulting health concerns in the rivers and lakes of the state;
- training and certification of lead inspectors, abatement contractors, and others who engage in the inspection, removal, covering, or replacement of paint, plaster, or other material containing a lead hazard;
- state-funded lead poisoning prevention, inspection, education and abatement programs;
- mandatory lead screening for children at the age of six months, one year, and annually thereafter until age six;
- a "safe house" program that provides free temporary housing during the abatement and cleanup of contaminated homes; and
- research and documentation of the sources and prevalence of occupational disease and the need for occupational health services for residents in low-income communities and communities of color.

Other communities have gone even farther. Recently a state government opted to study three counties to determine if lead poisoning existed in their state and, if so, to what extent. The state had not regularly screened its citizens since the early 1980s, when federal funds earmarked for lead poisoning prevention had been cut. At that time, the funding was shifted into the Maternal and Child Health Block Grant program, which left it up to individual states to decide whether, and to what extent, to fund lead poisoning prevention. During the study, children, as well as soil and paint samples, were tested for lead. The data from the three counties were then used to make estimates for the state as a whole.

In one county, families whose children had been screened became concerned about the results, but the state refused to release the data until the final drafting of the report could take place. The data was politically explosive. It indicated that more than 20 percent of the children in the county were lead poisoned. It also showed that 67 percent of the African-American, Latino, and Asian children were found to have lead levels greater than 10 ug/dl. Many of the minority families tested came together and formed a new community organization.

In 1989, this grassroots organization undertook its own health survey, covering 1,012 households in which eight different languages were spoken (Calpotura 1991). The survey revealed that:

- 33 percent of the households had no health insurance;
- 98 percent had no lead screening for household members;
- 31 percent had received no immunizations for children in the household;
- outpatient clinics which they frequented had little or no bilingual or multilingual capacity; and
- 96 percent of people eligible for the existing free testing program were unaware of it.

The community also continued to hold public meetings, focusing on:

- the results of its own health survey and the need to obtain results of the lead screening done by the state;
- the need for lead testing of playgrounds and schools;
- the need to gain access to free testing programs; and
- the need for fully funded lead abatement programs.

The organization's initial successes included:

- obtaining the results of the state survey;
- expansion of free testing services; and
- an agreement by the city to test selected school and playground sites for lead contamination.

Later the organization campaigned for a Comprehensive Screening and Abatement Program and got the town council to pass it. The county residents and the organization they formed will continue to work for implementation of their plan. Revenue from the property tax on older housing will go into a fund to be used for the lead abatement of low-income dwellings, as well as educational programs for the county residents. Training low-income people to do lead abatement work is also an integral part of the plan.

The community organization has mobilized the county's citizens to devise and implement a successful strategy to address lead poisoning on a community-wide basis. It has thus served as an example for other communities in the country. Similar efforts have been made in other parts of the country. In 1991, for example, a coalition of civil rights, environmental, and public health advocates in Alameda County (NAACP Legal Defense and Educational Fund, ACLU, Natural Resources Defense Council, National Health Law Program, and the Legal Aid Society of Alameda County) obtained an agreement from the state of California to screen an estimated 500,000 poor children for lead poisoning at a cost of $15-20 million (Lee 1992). The agreement is part of an out-of-court settlement in a class-action lawsuit, *Matthews v. Coye*. The plaintiffs charged California with failure to routinely conduct blood lead testing of some 557,000 Medicaid-eligible children below the age of five—a violation of the federal Medicaid Act and its implementation guidelines.

Needed Public Health Policies

At present a great need exists for free or affordable blood lead screening. The resulting data can be used not only to help the screened children but also to indentify lead hazards in the community and determine the nature and extent of lead poisoning in a given community. Without such data, many corporate and government officials will continue to claim there is not a serious problem. Unfortunately, Massachusetts is the only state so far to mandate universal screening of children. Since this practice began quite recently, only preliminary data have been reported thus far. Yet, the initial data confirm that the problem is much more widespread then previously believed and involves children from all communities and socio-economic levels.

Some excellent first steps besides the Massachussetts effort are already being taken, however. The Centers for Disease Control lead poisoning surveillance effort, for example, is currently underway in five states and should be expanded to include all 50 states. It is a laboratory-based reporting system in which all laboratories that do blood lead analysis convey their findings to the CDC, using a standard software package designed for the purpose. This data is then compiled by the CDC so that statewide incidence and prevalence can be calculated.

This system is a vast improvement over previous data collection efforts. Most states have not had the capacity to distinguish between a reported blood lead level for a child being screened for the first time from a repeat test result. This has meant that incidence could not be reliably determined at all, and prevalence estimates had to be corrected to account for existing cases in which children were being retested for medical management purposes. Until all states are participating in this program, however, no national incidence and prevalence data can be generated. Correlation and followup in adult blood lead surveillance systems is also needed.

The quarterly *Morbidity and Mortality Weekly Report* publishes information on prevalence of childhood lead poisoning. This information is being generated as part of the five-state agreement on screening and reporting. The first report gave data from the New York City program. The other states have not yet generated sufficient data for inclusion in a report, but are expected to do so soon. This reporting effort is being coordinated by the Lead Poisoning Prevention Branch, Division of Environmental Hazards and Health Effects, of the Center for Environmental Health and Injury Control.

Besides universal screening efforts, universal use of a risk questionnaire for childhood lead poisoning should be filled out with the help of parents starting when a child is six months of age. This should be done whenever a child under six has a regularly scheduled health visit. Research has shown that the most rapid rates of increase in blood lead levels occur in children between six and twelve months of age. Parents should be questioned about:

- the age of their housing;
- the presence of chipping or peeling paint;
- whether a child's siblings or playmates have had elevated blood lead levels;
- occupational exposure for those living in the child's household; and
- recent, ongoing, or planned renovation of their housing.

We also need to assess the communities in which families live. Access to an environmental health assessment is a fundamental right of any community. This is especially true of those with known hazards such as older housing stock, industrial pollution, municipal incinerators, and a history of using lead gasoline.

Currently, many states do not have adequate laboratory capacity to expand their screening and reporting programs. Less than 25 states have enough private or public laboratory capacity to provide universal blood lead tests. This is an enormous problem. Because lead poisoned people are often asymptomatic, diagnosis and treatment rely almost entirely on accurate measurement of blood lead (B-Pb) and/or erythrocyte protoporphyrin (EP).

The problem is even worse with regard to laboratory analysis of environmental samples of soil, water, dust, and paint chips. While some state laboratories do provide these services, they will often do so only after someone has already obviously been lead poisoned. Environmental assessment is simply not available in many parts of the country, and those private facilities that can do the work vary in quality and cost. Hence, access to lead-testing services does not exist for many residents of minority and low-income communities.

Also, once lead-exposed children and communities are identified, we must ensure equitable, comprehensive, and compassionate medical treatment. A first step, of course, is to make sure that third-party private and public insurers cover all citizens and fully reimburse families and businesses associated with screening for or treatment of lead poisoning. Too many families are faced with very high costs in pursuing medical treatment for lead poisoning. Some health maintenance organizations and insurance companies have even refused to pay for screening their enrollees. This forces families to go without care or to cover the costs of hospitalization, chelation therapy, and followup testing out their own pockets.

We also need changes in service delivery. Incorporating educational and preventive efforts into medical management is vitally important. One necessary innovation is serving affected families through the use of multidisciplinary teams of professionals, ideally consisting of:

- a physician or health care provider to provide medical assessment and make decisions on the need for nutritional supplementation and/or medication;
- a nurse or clinical specialist who provides nursing assessment, education about common sources of lead, and referrals to other agencies; and
- a social worker who assists in obtaining financial assistance for indigent families, finding alternative housing, determining a family's legal rights, locating community resources, and educating families how to minimize exposure to lead hazards.

One of the most important public policy questions is developing methods of financing lead abatement programs for low-income homeowners and landlords. The earlier-mentioned HUD report was the first to provide estimates of the cost of abatement (the process of removing the source of exposure to the environmental hazard). For most of the homes, abatement is estimated to cost $2,500 or less. Of course, a large home with many leaded surfaces may cost much more than this to abate.

The most difficult situations arise when low- to moderate-income homeowners discover a lead problem in their own home, but obtain financing for deleading. They may attempt to do the work themselves by sanding, scraping, or burning off the old lead paint, but this generates tremendous amounts of lead dust which can further poison family members and neighbors. Such scenarios should not be viewed as problems for individuals to solve. The existence of immediate lead hazards in over 17 million individual homes in the United States is not a just a problem for those 17 million individual homeowners. It is a widespread public health problem which necessitates the allocation of public resources in order to address it.

Low-interest loan programs, use of community development block grants to delead properties, tax credits for abatement, and property tax increases to cover deleading have all worked in parts of the country. The high concentration of lead-contaminated buildings in certain communities demands a very systematic approach. Comprehensive planning by city housing officials should incorporate planning for lead removal from the housing stock.

Communities should now begin by deleading blocks of homes at a time instead of waiting until a child is poisoned on the premises. Many lawsuits have been filed by tenants with poisoned children in an attempt to force landlords to delead properties and/or compensate them for the injuries to their children. For these children, however, the damage has already been done and is probably irreversible, even if the property is abated. We need to begin to prevent these catastrophes before they occur.

This is as true at work as it is at home. No individual should work at a site where he or she is exposed to dangerous levels of lead. Certainly no workers should be without access to warning information about the health risks of their job or regular screening, treatment, and continuous counseling in their native languages about potentially adverse health effects of the exposure. In general, communities must begin to devise preventive strategies to remove lead and other toxins from their environments.

Conclusion

Lead poisoning is unquestionably a national health problem of monumental proportions. It can no longer be dismissed as a rare problem that affects only the children of inattentive parents in old homes who do not monitor their children's activities or keep a clean house free of peeling paint chips. The studies clearly show harm is being done to a sizable segment of the population, though minority children in central cities are disproportionately affected. The studies also show that lead contamination comes from a variety of sources at home, at work, and in the community.

Basic justice demands that every individual and every community should have access to services for screening, environmental investigation of lead hazards, and counseling and followup services for adults and children. Psychometric evaluation must also be made available and affordable for children who have already been identified as lead poisoned. Yet, these are just first steps. Ultimately, every individual and community will need to win the right to a clean and healthy environment. Relying on government officials and corporate officers will not help us reach this goal. People must organize themselves into a powerful grassroots movement for environmental justice if these long-range goals are ever to be achieved.

CHAPTER 6

Race and Waste
in Two Virginia Communities

Robert W. Collin and William Harris, Sr.

We begin our chapter by defining, justifying, and providing a brief history of environmental planning in the Unites States. Then we describe some of its traditional concerns about socio-economic equity. Next we examine the case studies of two counties in Virginia—Halifax and King and Queen County.

The Planner's Code of Ethics contains one of the strongest affirmations of the need for economic redistribution ever made by any profession. The housing and community development area of professional planning has focused on these issues of equity, while traditional environmental planning has not, however. In the case studies, we will discuss the reasons for this. Most importantly, we will examine the forces that are bringing about a merger of environmental and socio-economic equity concerns in U.S. planning. As the profession adapts to changes in society, environmental planning at the grassroots, neighborhood level will become increasingly important in the struggle for environmental justice, a struggle that has tremendous implications for people of color. We will conclude the chapter with a discussion of planning as it relates to environmental equity.

The Role of Environmental Planning

Planning encompasses both theory and practice. While planning as a human practice is perhaps as old as human experience, it was not formalized as a profession until the turn of this century. Intellectually, it is a relative newcomer, essentially becoming a recognized academic enterprise only after World War I. Planning today comprises three primary orientations. It is futurist in perspective, logical (or process-oriented) in approach, and strategy-building in methodology. Nearly all definitions of planning include these orientations. Edward Alexander presents a summary of these three different social postures reflected in planning definitions. He concludes that planning is never viewed as a trial-and-error process, but always as a calculated effort to influence the future. It is

> the deliberate social or organizational activity of developing an optimal strategy of future action to achieve a desired set of goals, for solving novel problems in complex contexts, and attended by the power and intention to commit resources and to act as necessary to implement the chosen strategy (Alexander 1986, p. 43).

This definition is important because it denies planners any excuse for inaction. They are not free to transfer their power and resources to others, particularly decisionmakers. They must be both researchers and advocates for the implementation of their plans.

In the U.S. context, planning is justified as an appropriate means to achieve purposeful social change. As all governments seek first their own stability and preservation, planning becomes their instrument for rationalizing activities designed to ensure their continued stability and improving the quality of life for their citizens. However, the history of social change in the United States has been characterized by volatile, aggressive behavior by those citizens who believed they had been denied some part of the American Dream (Harding 1980, p. 150). Spurred by the story of the 18th-century American revolutionaries, disenfranchised groups have sought to attain social, economic, and political equity.

The ongoing struggle of African Americans against oppression has been their most important contribution to our nation (King 1984, pp. 52-53). In this struggle for equality of opportunity and development, planning has played a varied role. When public policy has been constructed to limit the opportunities and development of African Americans and other people of color, the planning community, unfortunately, supplied the rationale, supportive data, and plans of action.

The case studies in the other chapters of this book testify to this. As a consequence, the black community has grown to distrust planning and its professional practitioners. On the other hand, when African Americans have experienced the benefits of positive public policy, it usually has been the result of their own successful challenges to the Establishment through self-advocacy and risk-taking. Planners are not usually seen as friends of the black community. Few have worked on behalf of the poor or the African Americans as a whole.

Because positive planning requires an appropriate exercise of power, it is important to the social and physical health of the nation. It should be used by public and private officials to test for consensus on issues among the population. Planning can also prove productive when it allows an orderly process to evolve that takes advantage of the ideally pluralist nature of U.S. decisionmaking. Finally, planning should provide the decisionmaker, consumer, and producer an opportunity to assess the degree to which stated social objectives have been achieved.

It is important, too, to appreciate the potential value of planning in a complex human-ecological environment. Given the many levels of decisionmaking, the complex organizational arrangements, and the many vested interests, planning can help over time to increase efficiency. It is this conflict between environmental complexity, the need for efficiency, and the varied competing interests that underscores the need for ethical principles in the planning profession.

The Case of King and Queen County

The events that form the basis of an important lawsuit in this county began in 1969. The community first began organizing around the issue of environmental racism when it created RISE (Residents Involved in Saving the Environment). This biracial, nonprofit community organization opposed development of a regional landfill in a predominantly African-American neighborhood. Its membership is composed primarily of property owners in the area surrounding the proposed landfill.

King and Queen County, Virginia, is 50 percent white and 50 percent African-American. In 1988, the federal government ordered a redistricting, which resulted in an increase in the number of county supervisors from three to five. The two new supervisors were African-American. In Virginia, each county's board of supervisors makes most of the land-use decisions. To facilitate that process, it appoints a planning commission, which makes nonbinding recommendations. Typical decisions concern permit and variance requests. However, in Virginia, localities can only make decisions about those matters that the state has expressly delegated to them.

In 1987, Virginia promulgated new regulations for solid waste disposal in landfills. As in many counties, these regulations increased the expense of waste disposal in King and Queen County. Up until this period waste disposal had been almost entirely unregulated. It was estimated that closing the three existing landfills in the county, all of which violated the new regulations, would cost $1.7 million. During the trial, the court held that "the County could not afford to close the existing landfills and develop a new landfill that would comply with the new regulations" (*RISE v. Kay* 1991).

To solve its waste problems, the county began negotiating with the Chesapeake Corporation about a joint-venture landfill. This project would have entailed 1) Chesapeake's building the landfill and using it for its own waste disposal, and 2) the county's operating it in exchange for free use. The two sides identified a 420-acre site, known as the Piedmont tract, and tested it to determine its suitability as a landfill. In the summer of 1988, Chesapeake Corporation abandoned the negotiations.

In January 1989, two members of the board of supervisors tried to purchase the Piedmont tract from the corporation. On December 11, 1989, the board executed a purchase-option agreement with Chesapeake for the land. Two board members abstained from voting to approve the purchase because they were employees of the corporation. Since the board's public notices did not refer to the land as a potential landfill site or as a "regional landfill," residents never got the facts. However, the court presumed that they had, as the information "was well-publicized in local newspapers" (*RISE v. Kay* 1991).

Nonetheless, community opposition to the proposed landfill began to mount. On January 25, 1990, upset citizens met at the Second Mount Olive Baptist Church, very near the proposed site. They feared the landfill would increase noise, dust, and foul odor; reduce property values in the community; interfere with worship and social activities at the church; require expensive improvements on the access roads; and, in general, blight the venerable church and the community. The church, founded in 1869 by recently freed slaves, had subsidized an otherwise inadequately funded school for black children for many years. It remains the anchor of the county's black community.

On February 12, 1990, the supervisors held a public hearing, during which Browning-Ferris Industries (BFI) made a proposal on the operation of a landfill. Two-hundred-twenty-five citizens attended, fifteen of whom spoke in opposition to the landfill. The assembled citizens also presented a petition to the board signed by 947 people opposing the landfill. Nevertheless, the board approved the facility, and on August 13, 1990, passed a resolution leasing the Piedmont tract to BFI so it could operate the landfill.

Thirty-nine African Americans (64 percent) and 22 whites (36 percent) live within a half-mile radius of the site. Most of the landfill-bound traffic will move down a 3.2 mile stretch of road along which live 21 black families and five white families. Considered alone, this may seem only inadvertently racist. However, an analysis of the events surrounding construction of the four other landfills clearly shows a racist pattern of waste disposal siting. The race of those affected was the defining factor in each case.

The Mascot landfill was sited in 1969. The population living within a one-mile radius of the landfill was close to 100 percent African-American. Moreover, the landfill was only two miles from an African-American church, the Escobrook Baptist Church, which had been established many years earlier.

The Dahlgren landfill was sited two years later, in 1971. An estimated 95 percent of the population living in the immediate area were African-American. As of 1990, some 90 to 95 percent of the residents within a two-mile radius of the site were African-American.

The Owenton landfill, called Newtown by the nearby residents, was set up in 1977. The population living within a half-mile radius at the time was entirely African-American and is still predominantly so. The African-American First Mount Olive Baptist Church is located only one mile from the landfill. Given that no African Americans served on the County Board of Supervisors until 1988, it is not hard to see why the African-American community's needs were ignored during these years.

The white community was not completely unaffected by waste disposal sites. In 1986, King Land Corporation did set up and begin to operate a private landfill on a 120-acre site in a predominantly white area of King and Queen County. The white community was not only able to mount significant opposition to this site, but its concerns were soon seriously addressed by local political leaders. The county passed a zoning ordinance and obtained an injunction in the Circuit Court preventing King Land from continuing operation of its landfill under a state-issued permit. When the company sought permission to continue operation, the county zoning administrator turned them down. The company was turned down again after appealing the decision to the County Board of Zoning Appeals. The County Board of Supervisors later denied King Land's application for a variance, arguing that the landfill would result in a significant decline in the value of adjacent properties. The board also expressed concerns about King Land's poor record regarding the surrounding community's environment, health, safety, and public welfare. Thus, not only were four out of the five county landfills sited in predominantly black neighborhoods, but there was also a stark contrast between the *official responsiveness* accorded to white resistance to landfill development and the same concerns of black residents.

The Eastern District Court of Virginia did, finally, *as a conclusion of law,* rule that the placement of landfills in King and Queen County from 1969 to the present had disproportionately affected black residents. Yet, the court found no evidence of racial discrimination in these waste disposal decisions, arguing that the Board of Supervisors "appears to have balanced the economic, environmental, and cultural needs of the County in a responsible and conscientious manner." The court chose to ignore the racial bias demonstrated by the fact that in a county half black and half white, all four existing landfills were sited in black communities and the only landfill site shut down was located in a white community. They thus turned a blind eye to a clear case of institutional racism.

The case is now on appeal in the U.S. Court of Appeals for the Fourth Circuit. As it has unfolded, more and more direct evidence of racial bias has come forth. For instance, a white female RISE member gave an account of a racial slur made by the county administrator for King and Queen County. At a Board of Supervisors meeting, two black ministers expressed serious objections to siting the regional landfill so close to the major black church in the area. After the meeting, the RISE member reiterated these objections. The county administrator responded by declaring that the two black ministers should be given a one-way ticket back to Africa. A white male member of RISE, who attends the same church as one of the white supervisors, also gave damning testimony. He told the white female RISE member that "he had heard that the niggers in Second Mt. Olive Church had a petition to stop the landfill."

Through its suit, RISE hopes to expose this nation's pernicious new form of discrimination—environmental racism.

The Halifax County Case

Halifax County was the home of the first permanent English settlement in North America. A dozen years after the settling of Jamestown, a Dutch ship arrived there with 20 African indentured servants. This marked the introduction of slavery to North America. During the colonial period, Halifax County and the whole state of Virginia became a key center of the infamous African slave trade (Higginbotham, 1992), that "peculiar" institution of U.S. history. While most Africans who survived the Middle Passage were enslaved, some remained free. However, even they did not enjoy full rights as Virginia citizens.

A few of the "free" Africans in Halifax County were able to purchase land. Some intermarried with Native Americans, thus creating a greater unity between the two oppressed peoples. Even in the late 17th century, following Virginia's enactment of laws making every resident black a slave forever, some of these Africans acquired education and maintained a quasi-free status in the county. Since it continued to honor "free papers," a few more black families purchased land that some of their descendants have held onto ever since the colonial period. This history of relative black freedom and ownership of property gave rise to the struggle against environmental racism in Halifax County.

The county is located in the south-central part of Virginia. Primarily rural, the 1990 census reported a population of 11,393 African Americans and 17,504 whites. Even though African Americans have long been successful farmers in the county, black farm ownership has steadily declined over the past 45 years. In 1959, African Americans constituted 41 percent of the county's farm operators, as compared to only 15 percent in the rest of Virginia. By 1987, African-American farm operators in the county constituted only 25 percent of the total as compared to 4 percent in the whole state. Clearly, though, land remains important to blacks in Halifax County. In fact, its value is growing as African Americans lose more and more land.

In 1982, Congress passed a bill requiring that special protection be given to historical sites of significance to Native Americans and other minorities whenever federally funded waste facilities were to be constructed. Public Law 97-425, known as the Nuclear Waste Policy Act, was designed to prevent the development of hazardous waste sites in minority communities. Basing themselves on this law, Halifax County citizens sought to prevent the siting of a nuclear waste depository by the federal government.

In 1985 and 1986, Cora Tucker, a community organizer and life-long resident of the county, brought together African Americans and supportive whites to oppose the depository. She organized and became the president of the local chapter of Citizens for a Better America. The purpose of the organization is to improve the quality of life of all citizens, without regard to race, gender, or economic status. While the national organization offered some financial assistance and national publicity, it allowed Tucker to organize a grassroots effort that left control of the movement firmly in the hands of those African Americans whose properties were most at risk.

The U.S. Department of Energy had proposed that a particular section of Halifax County be designated a potential site for the storage of high-level nuclear wastes. Citizens for a Better America estimated that three-quarters of the population surrounding the site would be African Americans who owned land or rented property there.

The African-American community and its supporters based their opposition to the proposed site on two primary arguments. First, they believed the proposal to be racist in that it placed a disproportionate burden upon the lower-income, black community. Indeed, construction of the facility would result in further loss of black-owned farmland in the county. This trend was already well-documented by the U.S. Census

Bureau. Second, the group held that building the facility would run counter to the fundamental intent of Public Law 97-425, in that it would harm important historical sites in the county. A list of such sites was sent to the Department of Energy.

More than 1,400 residents of the county attended a public meeting in 1986 to express their opposition to the proposed nuclear waste site. Comments made at that meeting and reported in the *South Boston Gazette-Virginian* show clearly the wide range of people organized by Tucker and her supporters. Presentations were made by a U.S. senator, a state senator, a Pittsylvania County administrator, the Halifax town manager, a tobacco farmer, the vice-president of the Halifax County Farm Bureau, the director of the Southside Community Services Board, a representative from Community Hospital, the president from the local chamber of commerce, and community leaders from a wide variety of citizen organizations. Reverend Leon White, Director of the United Church of Christ Commission on Racial Justice, North Carolina-Virginia Field Office, summed up the crowds' mood:

> When I saw that one of the areas proposed for the site was in Halifax and Pittsylvania counties, I concluded that these were predominantly black counties and I discovered that to be true. The poor people and the black people are ready to fight (*South Boston Gazette-Virginian* 1986, pp. 10-14).

As is clear from the broad support garnered from both African-American and white community leaders, the organizing efforts of Citizens for a Better America were productive. In 1986, the Department of Energy decided to eliminate Halifax County from the list of potential nuclear waste sites. Two conclusions emerge from the record of the community's coming together to fight a policy that was clearly racist and environmentally unsound. First, African Americans are capable of generating broad support in their struggle to counter public policies that are detrimental to black citizens. This is especially so when their leadership is strong, persistent, and well informed. Second, benefits accrue to the African-American community when racist proposals affecting the environment are eliminated. The white community of Halifax County realized the advantages of not having a dangerous facility in the area, even if the site disproportionately threatened black neighborhoods. No part of a community is an island unto itself; all residents benefit or suffer when any of them do.

Equity Concerns in Planning

In perhaps oversimplified terms, an ethic is a guide to behavior based upon a perception of what is morally right. When imposed upon a professional group, an ethic is also designed to direct the group's practice toward fair ends. Within the planning profession, Peter Marcuse recognizes the difference between this lofty goal and the reality of professional practice:

> [P]rofessional ethics are likely simply to render more efficient the services provided by planners to those presently with the power to use them. Professional ethics are likely to be system maintaining rather than system challenging (1976, p. 274).

Since he issued his challenge to the profession to bring its practice into line with its ethical responsibility, the American Planning Association has formulated a Code of Professional Conduct to guide the professional behavior of its membership. Two of its ethical principles are fundamental to this discussion. The first is that the public interest should be served. The association makes this the highest moral obligation for all practicing planners. It requires each one to ensure, as far as possible, that the interests of the nation's citizens take precedence over any special interests, including, of course, those of the planner. The other essential principle promotes equitable redistribution: all planning should first serve those who have the most profound need. This is a powerful message in a racist, sexist, and class-dominated society such as the United States.

Unfortunately, due to the large gaps between principle and practice, the African-American community has been poorly served by planners in several areas, including housing, economic development, and environmental protection (Jaynes and Williams 1989; Bullard and Wright 1987; Bullard 1990). Consistent with the historic struggle by African Americans for justice and fairness in a society that has long been hostile to their development, the black community has reacted with understandable distrust to the denial of justice at the hands of professional social planners. The challenge then to the planning profession is to help bring oppressed citizens to some parity through a planned redistribution of resources and opportunities. To do so will bring planners into conflict with society's most powerful elites. It will also require planners to take greater risks and confront the very funding sources that maintain their profession. To fail to rise to this challenge is clearly unethical, as Marcuse warned more than fifteen years ago.

Against this background, planners must confront one of the most complex and difficult issues of the century: how to care for the environment while dealing with all of the social justice concerns of the affected communities. A wise approach to community development allows the nation to tackle the broad range of issues that determine the quality of life for all its citizens. The United Nations has defined community development as:

> the process by which the efforts of the people themselves are united with those of governmental authorities to improve the economic, social, and cultural conditions of communities, to integrate those communities into the life of the nation, and to enable them to contribute fully to national progress. This complex of processes is, therefore, made up of the people themselves in efforts to improve their level of living, with as much reliance as possible on their own initiative; and the provision of technical and other services in ways which encourage initiative, self-help and make them more effective. It is expressed in programmes designed to achieve a wide variety of specific improvements (United Nations 1963, p. 4).

While this model of development must be modified to accommodate the unique circumstance of the African-American community in the United States, its main thrust is entirely relevant: development demands strong internal (community) commitment and effort as well as external intervention and assistance from planners to solve complex problems (Harris 1976, pp. 26-27). Especially in environmental affairs, planners must commit themselves to their profession's code of ethics and acquire the high level of competence needed to successfully address the problems facing the African-American community.

To do this, the planner must be a social change agent, an advocate for disadvantaged and historically oppressed groups. In the United States, this role is made complicated by the need to combat racism, sexist, elitism, and other unhealthy social traditions. The challenge to planners working in the black community is particularly great because so few environmental planners are people of color. So far, few white planners have shown much serious interest in improving the quality of life for blacks through innovative environmental policymaking.

The nature and history of environmental policy in this country, as well as the educational background of the nation's current environmental planners, help explain the grave schism between the goals of environmental planning and requirements of liberating community development. Much environmental planning, as expected, has focused on the natural resource base: how to protect it and minimize its reduction. The goal is to ensure that development activities are sufficiently controlled or managed so they do not compromise important elements of the natural environment, such as wetlands and open space. Furthermore, the public at large must not be exposed to an unhealthy environment. Finally, planners usually emphasize conservation and preservation of resources, *not* the equity of social and economic arrangements. So when they and community developers do interact, it is usually as opponents.

Environmental planners are frequently in the position of advocating constraints on the use and development of natural resources—for example, setting limits on the filling of wetlands or the density of groundwater-recharge areas. Community development planners, on the other hand, often object to such proposals because of their impacts on the price of housing or because of the inequitable distribution these types of control entail.

The bias against considering social or economic equity in environmental planning also has clear roots in the decisionmaking methodologies traditionally applied to natural resources. Specifically, much environmental policy and legislation in recent years has reflected a blatantly utilitarian view of "correct use." The practice of selecting the policy or action that maximizes social benefits has become institutionalized to a significant extent through the heavy reliance on cost-benefit analysis. Executive Order 12291, for example, requires the Environmental Protection Agency (EPA) to conduct such an analysis for all proposed regulations, and, for approval, their benefits must be shown to exceed their costs (Smith 1986). Furthermore, many decisions on projects such as the construction of a water supply canal or a flood control dam are powerfully driven by cost-benefit analyses—indeed, they are often required by law.

Utilitarianism may well dominate work in bureaucracies like the EPA. From an ethical point of view, it can be argued that this is to some extent desirable in that it emphasizes the *collective* consequences of decisions and helps prevent those that serve only narrow private interests. On the other hand, utilitarianism and cost-benefit analysis are the quintessential *opposites,* ethically speaking, of concern for social and economic equity. If the collective benefits from a particular decision, say on the location of a hazardous waste facility, exceed its costs, the distribution of these benefits and costs is deemed largely irrelevant. That a minority community may incur a disproportionately large amount of risk is, in the context of a strict cost-benefit analysis, unimportant. Many such conclusions are made everyday in the regulatory and standard-setting practices of agencies like the EPA.

While the education of environmental planners increasingly incorporates discussions of environmental ethics, a tendency to underemphasize distributional equity still persists. Environmental ethics, and indeed the philosophy underlying the environmental movement, tends to stress certain particular notions of equity (though this word itself is rarely used), including those regarding our moral obligations to future generations and the intrinsic value of the natural world. While we do not wish to diminish the importance of these values, attention to the social and distributive implications of environmental policy and action is inadequate in both environmental planning practice and education, and must clearly be emphasized in the future.

Conclusion

More and more people from all sectors of society are working to protect the environment. This has finally reached the grassroots, neighborhood level. Community development, organization, and mobilization around environmental issues could eventually become a stronger force than traditional community development concerns. The environmental movement has recently made particularly strong efforts to form coalitions, though these coalition efforts now face their greatest challenge of inclusiveness.

Poor and minority communities that have suffered from environmentally degrading land uses are beginning to organize their own efforts for change. Unjust neighborhood boundaries caused by de facto segregation, lack of mobility, and a sense of victimization are conditions that strongly inspire community organization and mobilization. Environmental planning at the grassroots level confronts inequitable land-use and distribution equity head-on because the reality of benefits, burdens, and decisionmaking is more sharply revealed at this level.

Environmental planning is increasing at the grassroots level for several reasons. First, the solution to several key environmental problems, as so many other social problems, must ultimately be found at this level—where "the rubber meets the road." Unlike many other problems, however, environmental degradation is politically uncompromising. Everyone must participate in dealing with it. Hence fairness inevitably becomes an issue, for any broad human enterprise is only as strong as its weakest link.

It is well documented that decisions concerning toxic and hazardous wastes facility siting disproportionately threaten and burden minority communities. The facilities constructed contaminate airsheds and watersheds, not just nearby neighborhoods. Commonly, siting decisions are premised on varying expectations of encountering resistance and on assumptions that if the facilities are dangerous, their danger is limited only to those who live or work nearby. Although it is true that they are more dangerous the closer one is to them, they may very well threaten all of us. Because of the pervasive concerns about equity in community development and neighborhood planning, environmentalists are often faced with charges of elitism, paternalism, and racism as they attempt to deal with polluting facilities.

Overall, addressing the worst abuses of the environment has become a national, state, municipal, and neighborhood priority. This is reflected by changes in the law, media coverage, and the growth of environmental industries, and now also in neighborhood organizations and municipal land-use planning. Equity in siting decisions is thus becoming a higher priority in land-use decisions and community development.

One example comes from New York City, which recently adopted city charter siting guidelines that distribute the benefits and burdens of desirable and undesirable public facilities. They develop a general framework for describing the need for the facility and a process that assigns it to a particular neighborhood. If any neighborhood has more than its fair share of a certain type of facility, then the city must certify that the new project responds to a critical need, would operate for two years or less, or constitutes the only feasible alternative. This entire planning process is documented in the public record. New York City must publish a statement of needs, include a map showing the location of a proposed project, and specify plans for the facility's opening, closing, reduction, or expansion. The purpose of this public record is to encourage greater community involvement. These charter revisions are the first in the country to fully address inequitable land-use decisions. We endorse this approach in principle, but withhold final judgment until it has been implemented. Equity depends on both process and outcome.

Land-use planning is rapidly being incorporated into the implementation of recycling programs. The increase in this type of environmental planning is being spurred by recent state legislative initiatives that require a reduction in city and county solid-waste streams. As in King and Queen County, enforcement of new state regulations on waste disposal has uncovered a pattern of environmental racism.

Many of the zoning ordinances now under consideration should be based on more research on the type and magnitude of the particular waste stream envisioned. The cost of recycling is something many businesses, citizens, and planners need to know. Only research can provide this information. However, some municipalities have already implemented zoning ordinances designed to facilitate recycling. Many cities are setting on-site recycling-space standards for new construction or substantially remodelled structures. Los Angeles issues development permits on condition that a plan be submitted for facilitating recycling. The focus of these plans ranges from occupant-education programs to hauler-access designs. Most ordinances stop short of laying down specific space requirements because more information is generally needed, especially about building design. Issues such as retrofitting recycling designs into existing structures and getting a recycling program into private homes have yet to be resolved. Very few of these ordinances specifically address the problems of ethnic minorities, nor do they, therefore, decrease the growing environmental resistance to siting inequities. These ordinances do, however, reflect a growing awareness of the need for grassroots environmental planning.

Educational institutions that train planners have an ethical obligation to prepare them to make the difficult decisions regarding the environment. Many of the decisions will be unprecedented. As environmental planning reaches out to the grassroots, neighborhood level, more and more people are affected and so will demand greater accountability. Unlike most other social issues, environmental planning and management affects everyone and is uncompromising in its demands.

Environmental Politics in Alabama's Blackbelt

Conner Bailey, Charles E. Faupel, and James H. Gundlach

Both academics and activists have been attracted to the issue of environmental justice in recent years. Work by Bullard (1990), Bullard and Wright (1986, 1987), Mohai (1990), and others has greatly increased our understanding of social and environmental justice. Growing public awareness is also shown by the appearance in 1990 of the first issue of the *Race, Poverty and the Environment,* published by Earth Island Institute, and of a series of articles on the links between race and environmentalism in the newsletters of major environmental organizations (see Russell 1989; Truax 1990).

In 1990 a conference on this topic was held at the University of Michigan (Bryant and Mohai 1992). Scholars of color attending this conference pressured the Environmental Protection Agency (EPA) to form an Environmental Equity Workgroup to review evidence that racial minority and low-income communities bear disproportionately high environmental risk (U.S. Environmental Protection Agency 1992).

Yet, despite this heightened national awareness and activity, an effective alliance between the civil rights and environmental movements has not been successfully forged in Alabama. In this chapter we examine the dynamics of this situation through a case study of Sumter County, Alabama, the location of the nation's largest hazardous waste landfill. The population is overwhelmingly black and poor. Local opposition to the landfill for the most part has come only from a small group of white environmentalists. They have been largely unsuccessful in mobilizing the support of the local black community. Investigators attribute this failure to a combination of factors. Chief among them are the pervasive "mill town" atmosphere that favors the status quo and the failure of the white environmentalists to address the social, economic, and political concerns of the black population.

Evidence to support these views was obtained through field interviews conducted over a five-year period (1986-1991), archival research,
and two separate surveys. Hopefully, by understanding the inability of
white environmentalists and black civil rights activists to form a successful alliance, we can avoid such failures in the future. This is particularly
urgent given that our data show that there is little significant difference
in the negative attitudes and concerns about hazardous waste treatment
between white and black residents of the county. We will thus conclude
this chapter by recommending an approach that would strengthen the
link between the civil rights and environmental movements.

Sumter County, Alabama

Sumter County can best be described as predominantly black,
rural, and poor. Its 1990 population was just over 70 percent black
(Center for Demographic and Cultural Research [CDCR] 1991). Most
of the population is concentrated in the southern half of the county in
and around the towns of Livingston (pop. 3,500) and York (Pop. 3,100),
in which most of the whites live. The next largest community is in Cuba
(pop. 500), also in the southern half of the county. The hazardous waste
landfill near Emelle (pop. under 300) is located in the more sparsely
populated and predominantly black northern half the county.

The county has experienced a significant decline in population
over the past 50 years due to emigration to other areas. Between 1940
and 1990, the population declined by more than 40 percent, from 27,000
to fewer than 17,000 (Alabama Department of Economic and Community Affairs [ADECA] 1989; CDCR 1991). Just between 1960 and 1970,
more than 5,400 people left, more than a quarter of the 1960 population.
Between 1970 and 1980 the rate of emigration continued but at a slower
rate: over 1,400 residents moved away, about 9 percent of the 1970
population (ADECA 1984). Emigration also continued in the 1980s: the
net decline was over 1,800, almost 11 percent of the 1980 population
(CDCR 1991).

This pattern of emigration reflects the limited employment opportunities in the local economy. Agriculture, the historical base of the
economy, has suffered declining fortunes due in part to the soil depletion caused by almost continuous cotton production since the 19th
century. The demise of both sharecropping and the tenant farming
system, which began during the 1930s, led to a massive exodus of rural
blacks from Sumter County and the South generally (Hamburger
1978)). Farm mechanization further reduced agricultural employment
opportunities.

Strong prices for agricultural commodities (notably soybeans) during the 1970s gave way to declining prices in the 1980s. In recent years, local farmers have been unable to compete with those in the Midwest. Between 1978 and 1982, the number of local farms with over $20,000 in sales declined by 18.5 percent, while total acreage in production declined by 20 percent (ADECA 1984).

In 1982, cash receipts from agriculture totaled $18.2 million, slightly over half of which came from row crops (e.g., soybeans and cotton). Five years later, total cash receipts had declined to less than $14 million, with row crops accounting for most of this reduction, dropping from approximately $9 million in 1982 to less than $1.5 million in 1987 (ADECA 1989). By the end of the 1980s, cattle, and logging had largely replaced row-crop agriculture in the county.

Sumter County is rural but not isolated. It is served by Interstate Highway 59, which runs from Birmingham to New Orleans, an active railroad, and the Tennessee-Tombigbee Waterway. The combination of these transportation links and low wage rates made the county an attractive place for manufacturers relocating out of the Rustbelt in the northeast and midwest during the energy crisis of the 1970s. Several industries moved into the county during the early 1970s, but moved out a decade later—a pattern seen in many other small southern towns (Falk and Lyson 1987).

These economic vicissitudes have led to continued high unemployment and poverty rates. During most of the 1980s, the unemployment rate fluctuated between 12 percent and 22 percent. In 1990, Sumter County ranked a lowly 61, out of 67 counties in Alabama, in terms of per capita income ($9,803, compared to $13,669 for the state and $17,592 for the nation as a whole). Almost 30 percent of its residents received food stamps in 1990, compared to 11.2 percent for Alabama as a whole (CDCR 1991).

Black Political Empowerment

The majority black and the minority white populations of Sumter County live essentially separate social lives. They go to separate churches, bury their loved ones in separate cemeteries, and send their children to separate schools. The public school system remained officially segregated until 1969, when a federal court ordered it desegregated. Ten months later, the white community established the all-white, private Sumter Academy as a means of maintaining a segregated school system. Since 1970, the public schools have been almost exclusively black. Virtually all white residents send their children to the Academy.

Their interest in and support for the public schools is obviously limited. However, issues of funding and educational quality are central concerns of both black and white leaders and residents.

Race relations in the county are marked by the history of slavery and the continuing economic dominance of the minority white population, which controls most of the businesses in the area, from banks to retail establishments. In addition, most of the farm and timber land is owned either by local whites or absentee landlords. Here, as elsewhere, economic and political power go hand-in-hand. Unemployment and poverty are common experiences for blacks, thus creating black dependence on whites for jobs and other favors. These economic differences reflect both the history of racial discrimination and the contemporary reality of vastly different class positions.

For the county's black citizens, the 1970s and 1980s were decades of struggle with an entrenched, white political establishment (Sanders 1986). In the early 1970s, the Federation of Southern Cooperatives established its main training facility in Sumter County. Its stated purposes were to encourage the development of cooperatives, strengthen small black and white family farms by providing technical and managerial training, and offer those farmers the advantages of economies-of-scale in purchasing materials and marketing their produce. However, perhaps the Federation's most important impact on the county was in strengthening local black political organization. This helped hasten the disruption of white political hegemony.

In 1979, the white political establishment struck back at the Federation. In what has come to be known as the "Cotton Patch Conspiracy" (Bethell 1982), whites got political contacts in Washington, D.C., to initiate a federal grand-jury investigation of alleged Federation financial wrongdoing. This investigation had a chilling effect on Federation operations for two reasons. First, private foundations, which had provided an important financial base of support, adopted a wait-and-see attitude and suspended funding. Second, even though no evidence of wrongdoing was ever discovered, Federation leaders had to devote considerable energy to defending themselves and their organization during the two-year investigation. Local black leaders are convinced that the investigation was motivated by the white establishment's desire to undermine the Federation.

The political status quo in Sumter County first began to erode during the 1960s when blacks finally won the right to vote. With few exceptions, such as the attack against the Federation, the county's white establishment has been unsuccessful since then in maintaining control over local affairs. In 1982, the white monopoly of political power was finally broken when the first black was elected to public office as district judge. By 1986, black politicians represented the county in both the state senate and house of representatives and constituted a majority on both the board of county commissioners (responsible for budgetary and policy matters) and the county school board. Whites have, however, continued to hold the positions of mayor in Livingston and York.

In the 1984 and 1988 elections, the white probate judge fended off the challenges of a leading black politician by only the slimmest of margins and through very questionable means. In Alabama, a probate judge performs administrative rather than judicial functions, including the certification of candidates for elected office. In the 1988 election, the county's white judge refused to certify his black opponent, claiming a procedural irregularity. Shortly before the election, Alabama's attorney general forced him to back down; yet little time remained for campaigning at that point, and the black challenger lost by less than 50 votes.

During the past two decades, politics in the county have become largely a struggle between the white and black communities. Race has always been the key factor in determining political power, but it became an issue of contention only when blacks gained the right to vote and began to organize politically. It has taken two decades for them to consolidate their control over political life. This struggle for ascendancy absorbed most of the political energies of both groups, thus deflecting attention from other issues, including the environmental problem of hazardous waste disposal.

The "Cadillac" of Landfills

The initial move to establish the "Cadillac" of hazardous waste landfills in Sumter County was made by a small group of regional investors known as Resource Industries, Inc. In 1977, when they established the landfill, public hearings were not required. So the investors quietly established the necessary political connections through James Parsons, the son-in-law of then-governor George Wallace.

Parsons introduced these investors to Drayton Pruitt, who acted as their lawyer in negotiating the purchase of land near Emelle. It is widely believed that in 1977, Parsons also facilitated political contacts necessary to obtain an operating permit. In 1978, both the land and the permit were sold to Chemical Waste Management, Inc. (CWM). This company now owns about 2,700 acres in the county, only 350 of which are used for waste disposal. The remaining acres serve as a buffer and are managed as a wildlife reserve.

In a 1974 report to Congress, the EPA identified Sumter County as a potential site for a large-scale hazardous waste landfill, primarily because of its geological stability and the desirable physical characteristics of a rock formation known as the Selma Group. This formation is 700 feet thick and made up of relatively impermeable marine sedimentary materials (primarily calcium carbonate). The sparseness of the local population and the presence of an interstate highway also swayed the EPA.

CWM claims the Selma Group will protect against the movement of chemical contaminants into the underlying Eutaw aquifer for over 10,000 years (CWM 1989). However, independent researchers now believe the Selma Group may be less perfect as a final repository of hazardous wastes than originally thought (see, for example, Bittner, King, and Holston 1988; Donahoe and Groshong 1990). In addition to uncertainties regarding long-term risks, more immediate risks are associated with the CWM facility, including the possibility of tornado and other storm damage to above-ground facilities (e.g., large storage tanks for liquid waste). A more likely threat of contamination comes from the transportation of wastes to Emelle. During 1989, approximately 40,000 truckloads of wastes entered the county, whose emergency response capabilities remain limited (Faupel and Bailey 1989).

CWM is a major actor in the hazardous waste industry, owning four of the six largest landfills in the nation (EPA data, quoted in United Church of Christ Commission for Racial Justice 1987). These facilities account for over 50 percent of the nation's permitted hazardous waste landfill capacity. The Emelle facility alone accounts for nearly half of CWM's total. CWM also owns a variety of other facilities, including land-based incinerators and ships designed specifically for incineration of liquid hazardous wastes. It reported corporate profits of $176 million on revenues of $1.147 billion in 1990 (CWM 1991). The *Wall Street Journal* (October 27, 1989) reported that CWM revenues represent 40 percent of the entire industry total.

The company portrays itself as a good corporate neighbor that uses the best available technology to provide industry with a safe method for disposing of its hazardous waste. It organizes individual and group tours of the Emelle facility, pays for an "informational" supplement in a local newspaper, and supports numerous civic causes in the county. It regularly points out that its business is vital to the area's economic health.

Economic Impact of CWM

CWM is Sumter County's single largest employer, employing over 400 people: its 1987 payroll came to nearly $9 million (Todd 1988). In an area where underemployment and low wages are the norm, the company provides a large number of relatively well-paying jobs. In addition, it purchased local goods and services valued at $4 million in 1987 and pays a county user-fee on every ton of waste buried at Emelle. In 1989, approximately 790,000 tons of waste were brought to the facility, generating $3.8 million in revenues for the county. Todd (1988) estimated that CWM's total economic contribution (including a multiplier effect) to the county was $16.1 million in 1987, or approximately $950 per capita. This represented about 10 percent of total per capita income: $8,290 (ADECA 1989).

The importance of CWM to the local economy explains why most business and community leaders either publicly support or appear to accept the presence of the landfill in their midst. Since 1978, CWM has paid roughly $20 million to the county commission, which distributes funds to local agencies and organizations according to a formula established by the county's representatives in the state legislature. Among the recipients are the municipal governments of Livingston, York, and five smaller towns; ten government service agencies (e.g., library, rescue squad, and water authority); the local university; the county school board; and the county commission's general fund. The mayor of York, noting that 30 percent of that town's revenues come from the commission, has publicly expressed concern over local dependency on CWM. Other local critics of the commission claim the county has become a "hazardous waste junkie."

Mobilization of Opposition to CWM

The quiet manner in which the Emelle landfill was opened and operated in the late 1970s initially served to limit public opposition. "The thing was here in Sumter County before most people knew about it," remarked one local resident. Numerous rumors regarding the facility circulated at the time. Some people thought it was a brick factory; others, a cement kiln or fertilizer plant. A review of the weekly newspapers published in York and Livingston between 1978 and 1988 shows that the landfill attracted relatively little notice during its first ten years of operation (Faupel, Bailey, and Griffin 1991).

However, black leaders in the county played an early and important role in alerting the public to the presence and dangers of the Emelle landfill. In 1981, Wendell Paris led a loosely knit black organization called the Minority People's Council and organized a demonstration at the facility's main gate to protest unsafe working conditions at the plant. This generated unwanted media attention for CWM and evoked a two-fold response: an effort to improve working conditions and a high-visibility public relations campaign to portray CWM as a good corporate neighbor.

A very different approach was taken by the Sumter Countians Organized for the Protection of the Environment (SCOPE), organized shortly after the Emelle facility opened. SCOPE was a largely white, essentially moderate organization that sought rigorous monitoring of landfill operations, public access to reliable information on those operations, and direct accountability of the management to the public. A biologist on the faculty of Livingston University was the organization's most prominent member. SCOPE started out by organizing several public forums.

This moderate approach, however, did not satisfy all SCOPE members. A dissident faction formed a more radical activist group—Alabamians for a Clean Environment (ACE). It soon took the lead in organizing local opposition to CWM. Like its predecessor, ACE is a largely white organization with a membership of over 300 and a core leadership group of less than ten. Its claim of broad public support is hard to verify since few local citizens have attended its rallies and demonstrations. ACE leaders note that many local people are afraid to speak out because so many jobs and so much of the area's economy is linked to CWM.

ACE's primary goal is simple: to shut down the CWM facility. Because of this radical stance, local residents do not take ACE seriously, viewing them as, at best, a small band of highly idealistic, utopian environmentalists. One of our respondents described them as "a little local group... As far as their having any effect, it's about like a mouse trying to stomp an elephant."

ACE's importance as a political force has been greatly underestimated by local leaders, however. First, while it is outside the traditional power structure, it has tenaciously kept the issue of hazardous waste in the public eye. "[CWM has] often reacted to ACE like it was a pesky fly you keep swatting around," observed one of our respondents, adding that "anytime you can get someone to keep reacting to you, then you're powerful." Moreover, while ACE has typically been characterized as a small local group, its influence and recognition extends far beyond the county.

It is associated with other nationally based environmentalist groups, ranging from the Sierra Club and Greenpeace to the National Toxics Campaign and the Citizens' Clearinghouse for Hazardous Waste. In addition, in 1991, a prominent ACE leader formed Southern Women Against Toxics (SWAT). And two other ACE leaders serve on the steering committee of the state-wide Alabama Environmental Coalition. All these groups provide ACE more resources and a higher level of visibility, legitimacy, and technical expertise than it would have otherwise.

The group's leaders were prominently featured as speakers and organizers at a 1988 regional meeting of environmentalists (Southern Environmental Assembly '88) held in Atlanta. ACE also gained wide recognition when its past president was named 1988 Alabama Volunteer of the Year by Governor Guy Hunt. Just weeks later, she was among a dozen individuals from all over the country who were honored by President Reagan for voluntary service. She received an award in recognition of her environmental activism.

A Tentative Alliance

African-American leaders played a key role in the early opposition to CWM. They led the opposition against the all-white county government that was aiding and supporting the company's move into the community. However, because of racial divisions in the county, few white residents joined their struggle. It soon became apparent that CWM was not going to leave the county any time soon.

During much of the 1980s, the African-American community's attention was deflected from this environmental issue by the struggle for basic civil rights and political empowerment. African Americans were struggling to dismantle a cruel form of political apartheid, Alabama-style, in a predominantly African American county. The white-controlled government adamantly refused to share power. Most white residents were satisfied with the status quo, for their privileged position derived directly from white racism.

Because of this larger struggle, during the early and mid-1980s African-American leaders remained on the sidelines as CWM became entrenched. ACE, CWM's chief source of opposition, was then and remains essentially a white organization operating within an overwhelmingly African-American community. Attempts by ACE to attract African-American members and to involve them in the campaign against CWM proved largely unsuccessful until 1987.

In that year, ACE organized a rally in Montgomery, Alabama, followed by a caravan procession to the town of Livingston and then the gates of the CWM facility. ACE received assistance in this effort from Greenpeace and the Citizens Clearinghouse for Hazardous Wastes.

The rally theme, "Toxic Trail of Tears," was an explicit attempt to link hazardous wastes and minority populations. It referred to the forcible resettlement of Alabama's Creek Indians to Oklahoma during the 1830s. Sumter County had been an assembly point for the original "Trail of Tears." Native-American and African-American speakers protested the disproportionate number of hazardous waste sites in their communities. Civil rights songs and chants intermingled with those of the mainstream environmental movement. Wendell Paris, a key leader of the county's African-American residents, played a prominent role in the proceedings.

ACE's social and political position outside the traditional, white power structure makes the group much more amenable to forging a strong working relationship with the African-American community. "The only meaningful contacts with whites as equals comes from the people from ACE," claimed one of the county's African-American leaders. Since then, civil rights and environmental activists have begun to work together more closely, a pattern that is emerging elsewhere as well.

Nonetheless, an alliance between civil rights and environmental activists in Sumter County remains an unrealized goal. This is largely because ACE remains a single-issue organization, while African-American civil rights leaders are pursuing broader social justice goals as well. With the exception of Wendell Paris, most African-American leaders remain reluctant to speak out against CWM.

African Americans now control the public school system and the county government, both of which depend on CWM payments to finance a substantial portion of their operations. In addition, a large number of African-American residents of Sumter County work for CWM, which by local standards pays its employees extremely well. These workers, their families, and many of their kin are understandably reluctant to support actions directed at shutting CWM down. Indeed, the company's arrival is viewed by many residents as the only positive economic development to occur in the county in the last decade. Taking an anti-CWM position carries with it considerable political risks for African-American leaders. Few residents have spoken out against CWM, and among those who have, most have suffered social ostracism and public ridicule. Outside of ACE, opposition to CWM is almost always muted. Not a single politician, including Wendell Paris, has run an election campaign in which hazardous waste was presented as a significant issue.

Targets for Environmental Hazards

Many outside observers assume that poor people are concerned first and foremost with improving their immediate economic condition (see Cerrell Associates 1984). Poverty, the reasoning goes, makes poor people willing to accept certain risks that others would not. However, poor people did not bring CWM's hazardous waste landfill to Sumter County: a white-controlled county commission did. Just as Third World nations are pressured to accept loose environmental standards in order to attract foreign investment, many poor communities are presumed to be willing to trade an increased number of jobs for decreased environmental quality.

Community leaders in Sumter County often give voice to this sentiment in one form or another. They either deny or downplay the risks associated with CWM operations, while emphasizing the economic benefits the company has brought (Bailey et al. 1992). Yet, two surveys indicate that most residents—white and black—are seriously concerned about the hazardous waste landfill in their community. A mail survey was conducted in 1988 of a random sample of 200 residents, but the response rate among blacks was low (Bailey et al. 1989). To rectify this weakness, a set of questions from the survey was appended to a 1990 door-to-door survey of 366 households in which there were children receiving free or subsidized meals at the public schools. This sample was 99 percent black; it included only three whites. Table 1 presents selected characteristics of the two samples.

Table 2 shows that a majority of both groups of respondents agreed or strongly agreed that the CWM facility economically benefited the county. However, as Table 3 shows, most residents also supported strong environmental regulations, even at the expense of job creation. Two-thirds of the 1990 door-to-door survey respondents, who were predominantly poor and black, favored strict environmental laws even if that meant fewer new jobs. Seventy-eight percent of the respondents in the 1988 mail survey also strongly preferred strict environmental standards.

According to Table 4, a majority of both black and white residents view hazardous waste as a serious threat to their communities. Black respondents in the 1988 mail survey were even more likely than whites to view the CWM facility as a "very serious threat." Nearly 30 percent of the white respondents in 1988 felt the facility posed no threat or only a minimal threat, compared to 12.5 percent of the black respondents (Bailey et al. 1989, p. 78). Of the 1990 survey respondents, over half said that hazardous waste poses either a very serious or somewhat serious threat to their community.

Why then has the black population not supported ACE? Apparently, blacks feel they have other more pressing concerns than hazardous waste. According to Table 5, when asked to rank in order of importance the issues of education, race relations, hazardous waste, and unemployment, blacks decisively ranked education and unemployment ahead of hazardous waste.

Table 1
Demographic Characteristics of Respondents to Mail and Door-to-Door Surveys in Sumter County, in Percent*

Characteristic	1988 Mail (N=69)	1990 Door-to-Door (N=366)
Sex		
Male	67.6	7.4
Female	32.4	92.6
Race		
White	66.7	0.5
Black	29.0	99.2
Other	4.3	0.3
Household Income		
Less than $20,000	47.6	n.a.
$20,000 - $39,000	24.6	n.a.
$40,000 or more	27.7	n.a.
Education		
Less than high school	27.9	31.7
High school	30.9	54.1
More than high school	41.2	14.2
Age		
18-30	15.6	35.2
31-40	25.9	43.8
41-50	8.5	12.0
51-60	8.5	6.3
61-70	17.1	1.4
71+	23.1	1.1

* Percentages are based on the number of respondents who answered the question. Not all respondents answered all of these items.

The 1990 door-to-door survey found that ACE had failed not only to mobilize blacks in support of its agenda (as is true also of the largely white national environmental groups), but it had failed even to create an awareness of its existence. According to Table 6, when asked if there were any groups in the county that oppose CWM's operations, only 21 percent responded affirmatively; two-thirds said there was no such group. In followup questions, respondents were asked to name a group

Table 2
Percent Responses to Statement "The presence of the Chemical Waste Management facility is an economic benefit to Sumter County."

Response	1988 Mail (N=69)	1990 Door-to-Door (N=366)
Strongly agree	31.9	16.4
Agree	27.5	38.9
Undecided	11.6	25.5
Disagree	14.5	12.6
Strongly disagree	11.6	3.8
Don't know/refused to answer	2.9	2.8

Table 3
Percent Responses to Question "If you had to choose between making anti-pollution laws stricter to protect the public's health or relaxing those laws to create more jobs in Alabama, which would you choose?"

Response	1988 Mail (N=69)	1990 Door-to-Door (N=366)
Make laws stricter	78.3	67.8
Relax laws	10.1	28.4
Undecided/don't know	8.7	3.6

that opposed CWM's operations. Only 7 percent named ACE. As noted in Table 7, of these knowledgeable respondents, only half shared the views of ACE and not one claimed membership in the group.

Future Directions

Data from this and other studies clearly indicate that environmental concern is not a function of race or class. The poorest residents of Sumter County, one of the poorest counties in one of the nation's poorest states, strongly oppose weakening the environmental protection laws as

Table 4: Percent Responses to Statement "How serious a threat do you think hazardous wastes are to your community? Are they a..."

Response	1988 Mail (N=69)	1990 Door-to-Door (N=366)
Very serious threat	39.1	32.5
Somewhat serious threat	26.1	24.6
Minimal threat	11.6	13.1
Not a threat	7.2	23.0
Don't know/Refused	14.5	6.8

Table 5: Percent of Responses in the 1990 Door-to-Door Survey to Question "Please indicate how important you think each of the issues listed below is for Sumter County" (N=366)

Response	Education	Race Relations	Hazardous Wastes	Un-Employment
Extremely important	63.7	26.2	36.3	60.9
Very important	33.7	45.1	34.4	33.9
Somewhat important	1.6	15.6	12.8	2.2
A little important	0.3	5.7	7.4	1.1
Not important	0.0	6.3	6.3	0.5
Don't know/ Refused	1.1	1.1	2.8	1.4

a means of expanding economic opportunities. Likewise, poor African Americans in the county are strongly concerned about the dangers associated with having a hazardous waste landfill operating in their area.

Yet, on a daily basis, the people of Sumter County generally—black and white, rich and poor—face a complex set of problems stemming from their Deep South history and their economic and political marginality. Activists who focus on environmental issues without at-

Table 6: Percent of Responses in the 1990 Door-to-Door Survey to Question "Are there any groups in Sumter County that oppose Chemical Waste's operations?" (N=366)

Aware	Frequency	Percent
No	245	67.1
Yes	78	21.4
Don't know	43	11.5

Table 7: Percent of Respondents in the 1990 Door-to-Door Survey able to name any group the opposes CWM operations (N=366)

Group	Frequency	Percent*
Unable to mention any group	340	93.2
Alabamians for a Clean Environment (ACE)	24	6.6
Sumter Countians Organized for the Protection of the Environment (SCOPE)	3	0.8
Minority People's Council	7	1.9
Federation of Southern Cooperatives	24	6.6
Other groups	4	1.1

* Due to multiple responses by some able to identify groups, total responses add to more than 100 percent.

tending to the broader yet connected issues of economic and political justice are unlikely to succeed in fostering the natural alliances between those fighting for social justice and environmental quality.

While linkages have been established between civil rights and environmental activists in Sumter County, little progress has been made in bringing black and white residents together since the one day organized by ACE several years ago featuring multiracial rallies, songs, and speeches. To be sure, a long history of racial separation and a recent history of fear and bitter political struggle must yet be overcome. Such changes can be effected only by a conscious and concerted effort on the part of environmental activists to integrate their struggle as part of the multi-issue struggle waged by the local African-American majority.

As long as environmentalism is seen as a "white thing" under the direction of local white folks, it is unrealistic to expect African-American residents to devote their energies to a narrow environmental agenda. Only by working together with local African Americans to reduce the racial tensions and political divisions in Sumter County can white activists gain significant support from the African-American majority.

Cooperation depends on trust, a commodity in short supply in the county due to its sorry history of black-white race relations. White activists have made conscious efforts to reach out to progressive forces in the African-American community, but they need to play a more active part in helping improve the social, economic, and political conditions of the black majority. The cause of environmental justice has great potential as a force to break down the barriers erected under slavery and "Jim Crow" and maintained now for over 160 years. We have not yet reached that point, however—at least not in Sumter County, Alabama.

CHAPTER 8

Sustainable Development at Ganados del Valle

Laura Pulido

The environmental justice movement has not devoted enough attention to sustainable development—a proactive form of environmental organizing. Yet sustainable development is essential for all people of color. This is particularly so for Latinos who suffer not only from unwise environmental politics but also from growing poverty, cultural denigration, and a lack of political power.

Most environmental problems result from economic activity. Hence, it is necessary to confront the racist polices and environmentally damaging practices of U.S. and multinational corporations (Mann 1990, 1991). In addition, both our economic and environmental problems require stronger responses than increasing affirmative action or dealing with environmental problems on the consumer level.

This chapter presents a case study of Ganados del Valle, a community development group in northern New Mexico, which seeks to create environmentally sustainable alternatives to corporate economic practices by combining appropriate resource use, workplace democracy, and enhancement of the local culture. It exemplifies how culturally appropriate, sustainable development might occur in other disenfranchised communities.

Sustainable Development

Sustainable development has two aspects: ecological and social (Douglas 1984). Development is socially sustainable when it provides a livable wage and ensures that workers do not live under the threat of job loss. Likewise, it is neither racist nor sexist. It allows the development of each worker's skills and personality while building on diverse cultural backgrounds. Development is ecologically sustainable when it meets real human needs with only a minimal impact on the earth and its other life forms.

Many social justice issues are raised in formulating natural resource policy. Crucial questions must be asked and understood within the larger context of production. For example: What resources are being exploited? How are they being extracted from the earth? Who is being affected? What are the ecological implications? Will other components of the ecosystem be damaged? If so, who will that affect? Who is benefiting from resource exploitation? Are local residents getting jobs? Where are the raw materials transported? How will they be processed? Who will bear the burden of the resulting pollution? Are the products socially necessary, or only luxuries? Are they recyclable? Where does the waste from the manufacturing process go?

By asking these questions within a social justice framework, we can consider the implications of our actions in a more comprehensive way. Clearly, the problem of waste disposal is only the last consequence of a long process that creates numerous other problems. The essence of sustainable development was articulated well by Brundtland in the World Commission on Environment and Development report, *Our Common Future* (1990):

> [T]he "environment" is where we all live; and "development" is what we all do in attempting to improve our lot within that abode. The two are inseparable…
>
> Many critical survival issues are related to uneven development, poverty, and population growth. They all place unprecedented pressures on the planet's lands, waters, forests, and other natural resources, not least in the developing countries. The downward spiral of poverty and environmental degradation is a waste of opportunities and of resources. These links between poverty, inequality, and environmental degradation formed a major theme in our analysis and recommendations. What is needed now is a new era of economic growth—growth that is forceful and at the same time socially and environmentally sustainable (pp. xi-xii).

The concept of sustainable development is not new to U.S. environmentalists, though it is more commonly applied to the Third World (McNeely and Miller 1984; Guha 1989, 1990; Hecht and Cockburn 1989; Shiva 1988; Clay 1990; Rees 1990). A number of scholars have written about sustainable development in the so-called "core countries," but usually only in a fairly abstract context (Gorz 1980; Daly and Cobb 1989; Bookchin 1990; Young 1990; Chase 1991). The traditional approach to development in the United States has been to produce as much as possible with little thought to the social and environmental consequences. If productivity is high enough, it is assumed that enough wealth is generated to devote funds to the ecological cleanup after the fact. But as our world has rapidly changed, it has become glaringly apparent that this conventional path is no longer creating as much wealth, regardless of the social and environmental impacts.

In short, the environmental justice movement, having laid the groundwork for addressing social justice, now must take the next step. Unlike traditional trade unionism, it should both combat racism and discrimination and attend to the environmental impact of development. Unlike the mainstream environmental movement, it should both emphasize economic equity and community empowerment.

Environmental issues, whether related to toxins or natural resources, all revolve around the question of growth and development. Activists of color have always been aware of these links (Bullard 1990; Bullard and Wright 1987, 1991). It is time we insert ourselves into the debate in a new way, one that is proactive and constructive and does not depend on Anglo leadership.

The Case of Ganados del Valle

Ganados del Valle in northern New Mexico is an organization that has grappled with the complex intersection of community needs, development, and environmental quality. It was founded by locals in 1981 in response to the intense poverty in the region. To date, it has created a vertically integrated business that produces high-quality woven goods. To keep money in the area, members raise the sheep, wash the wool, spin and weave it, and sell their goods in Los Ojos. By promoting careful grazing practices and building on local culture, Ganados has gained acceptance by the community and given its members both a renewed sense of pride in their heritage and an alternative to emigrating out of the area or working at dead-end, low-wage tourist jobs. Ganados is based in the Chama Valley of Rio Arriba County, a sparsely populated region characterized by great scenic beauty (see Figure 1). The population is scattered among a series of small villages, which are enclosed by rolling hills, mesas, and mountains extending outward in all directions. The high country contains three preserves known as Wildlife Management Areas (WMAs), which were created by the state of New Mexico to protect the elk population of the area.

The Chama area, like most of northern New Mexico, has a long history of human settlement (deBuys 1989). Under both Spanish and Mexican governments, it was settled under a system of community land

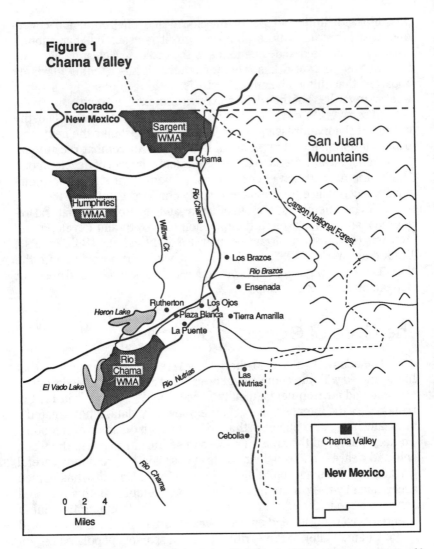

**Figure 1
Chama Valley**

grants intended to populate the area (Swadesh 1974). Chama was itself once part of the Tierra Amarilla land grant (Ebright 1985). Because of the aridity of the region and the short growing season in the north, ranching became the primary economic activity (Weigle 1975). For the most part, "Hispanos," as the settlers were known, lived in a fair degree of isolation, thus allowing them to develop their own unique traditions, which blended elements of Spanish, Mexican, and Plains Indian culture.

In the 1800s, several events radically altered the Hispano way of life: the coming of the railroad, U.S. acquisition of Mexico, and an influx of Anglo settlers. These changes engendered overgrazing, deforestation, and a corrosive market economy—something the Hispanos did not readily adapt to (Peña 1991a). Most important, however, was the loss of millions of acres of communal and private land through fraud, swindling (by both Anglos and Hispanos), lawyers' fees, and outright selling of the land (Carlson 1990; Knowlton 1973; Westphall 1983; Ebright 1985, 1987, 1989).

The loss of their land base, coupled with the area's adoption of a market economy, dealt a serious blow to the Hispanos, who had to cope with a changing set of social relations without an adequate resource base. Many emigrated but later returned to their villages with the deepening of the Great Depression (Deutsch 1987). Tragically, they found that with an increased population but a diminished carrying capacity, the villages could no longer support the entire population. Many thus turned to the government for aid, beginning a relationship of dependency that continues to this day (Forrest 1989).

Chama has continued to decline economically. There have been numerous government studies and efforts to revitalize the region, but most failed because they did not take into account the needs and desires of the local Hispano population (Knowlton 1964). In response to these economic conditions, emigration out of the area became an accepted solution again and intensified. Hispanos have not acquiesced to such conditions without a struggle, however. In fact, the area has a long history of resistance, beginning with the struggle against the first Anglo encroachment (Rosenbaum 1986). The region also garnered national attention in the 1960s when Reies Lopez Tijerina reignited the Hispanos' struggle to prevent further loss of their lands, much of which had been transferred to the U.S. Forest Service (Gardner 1970; Lopez Tijerina 1978).

Rio Arriba is presently one of the poorest counties in New Mexico, ranking 29 out of 33 (Bureau of Business and Economic Research 1989, p. 192). In 1979, 28 percent of the population was living below the poverty line (Bureau of Business and Economic Research 1989, p. 192). Since the 1960s, the area has attracted an increasing number of Anglos, who have come for both recreation and retirement (Carlson 1990). Because of the region's beauty and natural resources, including wildlife and fish, the state has promoted tourism as the primary means of developing the region.

This effort has yielded mixed results. On the one hand, tourism and recreation have created desperately needed jobs, although most are seasonal and low-wage. On the other hand, they have led to extreme land speculation. Now even fewer Hispanos can afford to buy land, and agriculture has become increasingly less viable (Miller and Potter

1986). Moreover, many Hispanos own parcels of land as small as one acre, due to their inheritance customs.

Agriculture no longer provides an adequate livelihood for several reasons: the lack of a land base, extremely small holdings, land speculation, competing land uses, and certain non-market-oriented attitudes Hispanos have towards resources (Weber 1991). Locals find jobs in tourism undesirable not only because of their economic drawbacks, but also because of the lack of dignity, meaningful work, and the erosion they cause in Hispano culture. Moreover, regional development has occurred in a highly unregulated manner, resulting in illegal subdivision, water contamination, and population pressures outstripping the infrastructure's capabilities (Schein 1991; *Rio Grande Sun* 1991a, b).

Although industry is not "beating a path" to Chama, even if it were, many Hispanos would hesitate to support it because of the potential pollution and ecological damage. In short, if they want an alternative to uncontrolled tourism, they must make agriculture viable once again. The lack of economic options produces a loss of hope. Families knew that their children would have no choice but to leave the area or scrape by on tourist jobs. Ideally, most families would like to make a living off the land. Ranching is part of Hispano history and tradition, and provides an opportunity to be close to nature in an authentic way (deBuys 1989, p. 296) but individual families can no longer make a living at it. First and foremost, Ganados provides a means to *collectively* gain a livelihood from the land through a vertically integrated business based on sheep. Sheep were chosen not only because they offer two sources of income, wool and meat, but also because they, the land, and weaving are part of Hispano history and tradition.

Ganados was born when two neighbors, Gumercindo Salazar and Maria Varela, began discussing "Gumi's" problems with his flock and ways to make ranching more profitable (Salazar 1991). As a school teacher, Salazar, like most Hispano ranchers in the area, could only devote part of his time to his flock. Another major problem he faced was protecting his sheep from predators. After considering various alternatives, they decided to implement a guard-dog program, which in due course dramatically reduced his losses. Soon another rancher, Antonio Manzanares (who owned a large flock) joined the group. By pooling their resources, they realized they could make ranching more productive. After the initial success of the guard-dog program, they began telemarketing their products, which enabled them to get a higher price for their lamb. In 1983, Ganados invited other locals to participate; and while many were hesitant, due to the failure of previous cooperatives, a few joined. Manzanares assumed the tasks of running the grazing operation and managing the flocks, while Varela engaged in fundraising (Salazar 1991).

During the early 1980s, local women took weaving lessons at the Los Ojos convent. For many it was their only source of recreation. Since the sheep cooperative had been expanding, Ganados soon identified new opportunities by using the coop's wool for weaving, thus providing new job possibilities for locals. Manzanares and Varela asked the women if they wanted to learn more about weaving and introduced them to Rachel Brown, a master weaver from Taos. She not only taught the local women a great deal about weaving, but also helped create an apprenticeship program so they could teach weaving to other community members. In 1983, Ganados incorporated its business and opened Tierra Wools, its first store for woolen goods. Within the first six months, it had sold $11,000 worth of merchandise. Ganados continued to grow rapidly in terms of size and breadth, eventually creating several new businesses, services, and related programs (see Table 1).

Members of the coop pay nominal dues and may participate in any of the programs. In addition, members of the weaving operation, including the managers, rotate their jobs, thus ensuring that everyone learns all facets of the enterprise. In 1990 the collective included approximately 25 weavers and 15 growers. While the latter own their individual flocks, which range greatly in size, Ganados also has its own flock. All the sheep are grazed together and managed cooperatively.

The weavers attract far more attention than the growers—not only because they are more visible, but also because they are more organized. Ganados did not intend to offer economic opportunities solely for women; but as it turned out, almost all the weavers are female, while growers tend to be either men or married couples. Ganados has been successful within the community not only because it is run by and for the community, but also because it built on the community's institutions and culture (Bauman 1973). Because Hispanos have very attractive cultural artifacts, and because the "Southwest" motif is so popular, they are able to make tourism work to their own advantage. By producing their own interpretations of Rio Grande designs, the weavers are reaffirming Hispano material culture, recognizing its evolving nature, and building a democratic workplace.

More importantly, however, the whole organization is structured in keeping with local ways. For example, in Hispano culture, women are very much the primary caretakers of children and the home. So in order for them to meet these obligations, their work schedules are kept flexible. Moreover, when school is not in session, women often take their children to work with them. The work area affords plenty of other children to play with and open space. The possibility of being with their children is crucial for many women. Toward this end, Ganados has instituted a program whereby women can buy a loom and weave at home. Several desired this, believing it would give them even more flexibility. While some people are critical of work at home, these women see it as ideal. Several commented that their husbands would not be as supportive of their involvement in Ganados if that meant neglecting their household or childcare responsibilities.

Building on another cultural trait, Ganados is cooperatively oriented. Hispanos have a long tradition of collaborative, communal undertakings, such as the traditional irrigation system, known as *acequias* (Crawford 1989). In both the weaving enterprise and the sheep cooperative, people usually work together. By working cooperatively, Ganados

---

Table 1
Businesses and Programs of Ganados

Businesses:

Tierra Wools: Ganados' weaving operation and store.

General Store: Opened in 1990, the store sells general goods and provides an outlet for local artisans to sell their crafts.

Pastores Lamb: This program markets specialty and *poquitero* lamb, grown without chemicals to gourmet restaurants in Santa Fe and Taos. All of the lambs come from Ganados' and its members' flocks.

Wool Washing Plant: Washes both Ganados' wool as well as wool from throughout the region.

Programs:

Churro Breeding Program: With the assistance of Dr. Lyle McNeal of Utah State University, Ganados is trying to increase the Churro flock through a breeding program. Churro is a sheep which the Spanish brought to America and which has almost become extinct.

Livestock Shares Program: This enables growers to increase their flock by "borrowing" lambs from Ganados, and then returning them. For each year of participation, the grower is assessed one lamb.

The Milagro Fund: This is a special fund designated to help other community groups develop their own cooperatives. The seed money was provided by hosting the opening of the movie "Milagro Beanfield War" with the cooperation of actor Robert Redford.

Summer Arts Program: Designed to serve local children, this program provides instruction on traditional arts and crafts during the summertime.

has enhanced community solidarity and strength. In short, it has built upon and reaffirmed local culture.

By most accounts, Ganados del Valle is an economic development miracle. It has thus captured national attention (Puleston Fleming 1985; Gullett 1988; Baker 1989; Charland 1989; Grauberger 1989; Horst 1990; Teltsch 1990; Jackson 1991; Chu and Linthicum 1991). In 1990, Tierra Wools grossed over $250,000, directly increased the income of more than 50 rural households, and became the fourth largest employer in the county. But what is most significant about Ganados, besides its economic success, is that it has allowed people to develop to their fullest potential. Women who previously saw themselves solely as housewives have acquired numerous other talents and skills and greatly expanded their horizons. Moreover, they now have a sense of ownership in Ganados, which more than anything, means they have hope for the future.

At this point, Ganados is continuing to expand. The demand for goods from Tierra Wools is so great that the coop finds it is difficult to keep up. The biggest problem is a lack of enough grazing land. During the summer, growers plant feed crops on their small plots, while the animals graze in the high country (Quintana n.d.). In the fall, the animals are brought down to the valley and fed the grasses grown during the summer.

If, for some reason, the food crop is lost or is insufficient, the growers must buy feed, which is quite expensive. Ideally, Ganados would like to have its own grazing land, but for now, buying a ranch is nearly impossible. As one ex-rancher explained, "If you went out to buy it now, you couldn't pay the interest on it if you lived a hundred years" (Puleston Fleming 1985, p. 40).

The Grazing Conflict

In response to the lack of regular grazing options, Ganados approached the New Mexico Department of Game and Fish (NMDGF) about the possibility of limited grazing on the three local WMAs: the Sargents, Humphrie, and Rio Chama (Ganados del Valle 1984; NMDGF 1985). After considering the situation, the department decided against it. For several years, Ganados pressed the issue, but the NMDGF continued to refuse (Schein 1985).

In the summer of 1990, Ganados found itself without land and decided, as a drastic measure, to commit an act of civil disobedience (Salazar 1989). On August 18, some of the members moved approximately 2,000 sheep on to a WMA. In a press release issued by Ganados, they explained,

Our greatest desire is to be a partner with New Mexico Game and Fish. We have the same goals. Inappropriate land development both hurts our agricultural economy and hurts the wildlife. We stand prepared to work out an ecologically sound management plan which would improve wildlife habitat, improve the local economy, and hopefully limit the growth of land development (Ganados del Valle 1989b).

The decision to trespass onto the WMA was not intended to expand the coop's rangeland but to force the NMDGF into action on their request (Flores 1989). The trespass action pressured the state into holding a town meeting on the issue and offering Ganados a temporary grazing site (see Peña 1992).

Eventually, the department appointed a task force to study the problem and to see if the limited grazing proposal could be incorporated into a research project. Scientists from New Mexico State University, NMDGF, members of Ganados, and environmentalists from the Nature Conservancy, Audubon Society, National Wildlife Federation, and the Wilderness Society were all appointed to the task force. Several proposals were generated, but all stumbled over the question of whether Ganados would be allowed to graze on the WMAs as part of the research design. Ultimately, the NMDGF not only rejected any plan that included such grazing but also voted unanimously to prohibit any future grazing on the WMAs. This action finally closed loopholes others had exploited in the past (NMDGF 1989).

Subsequently, Ganados became involved in mediation of its dispute with a group of environmentalists. Whatever future opportunity might present itself, Ganados wanted to find common ground with environmentalists so they could work together (Salazar 1991; Varela 1991). Progress has been made, on both sides. Each has gained a greater understanding of the other's needs and of the pressures each faces; while no solution to the coop's grazing problem has yet been found, several options are being considered (Varela 1991).

Biases in Environmental Policy

The reason the NMDGF, together with environmentalists and hunters, refused to allow Ganados to graze on a WMA is not because they are "bad" people. The truth is that the "Green Wall," as Varela (1990) calls the informal coalition of opponents, denied the coop's request because of the precedent it would set. The situation presents, in microcosm, the conflict of philosophies espoused by mainstream environmentalists and advocates of sustainable development.

More specifically, it shows how myopic is any view of nature that does not take into account the needs of low-income, minority communities. Furthermore, such a view only serves limited long-range environmental objectives because it does not incorporate environmentalism into everyday living. It is important, then, to explore how members of Ganados, the environmentalists, and the state's resource managers viewed the conflict and how the actions and attitudes of the two latter groups blocked the coop's efforts to achieve sustainable development.

Members of Ganados interpreted the actions of their opponents in various ways; but all agreed that if the Green Wall truly understood their situation, it would stop opposing them. Although a few members, such as Sophie Martinez and Gregorita Aguilar, saw the opposition as part of a larger plan to undermine the Hispanos, most interpreted it as simply a case of misguided policy that worked to the detriment of poor people. Members of Ganados were confident that their careful grazing practices would not harm wildlife (Ganados 1989a). Indeed, they felt the grasses needed improvement and limited grazing would provide it.

Asunción Maestas framed the issue in terms of outsiders "trying to take away the little we have." Santa Fe environmentalist Kenneth Cassutt admitted that the membership of his group was primarily from outside the region. "All of these outsiders from New York and California come to Santa Fe. I think what really draws them here is the diversity of cultures; that's something that doesn't exist in a vacuum."

Several weavers saw a contradiction in the environmentalists' desire for "cultural diversity" but their refusal to understand how dependent Hispano culture was on the land. Gumercindo Salazar (1991), while recognizing that the NMDGF did not want to alienate its environmental constituencies, believed that it opposed the grazing plan because it did not want to fight with northerners. Similarly, Maria Varela at one point stated that the department opposed the coop because it did not believe that Hispanics could devise a legitimate, well-conceived grazing plan. According to her, "They don't like our accusations of prejudice; but when you couple this decision with the information that for the past five years they have permitted other livestock grazing on two wildlife areas in the southern part of the state, prejudice against northern New Mexico communities is a plausible conclusion" (Varela 1989, p. A9).

In response to charges of racism, an official of the NMDGF stated:

> The charge of prejudice is of particular concern to me, not only because it is utterly baseless but because it damages the credibility of legitimate claims. It is clearly a case of crying wolf, when you consider that a Maestas of northern New Mexico chairs the Commission and a Montoya from

Las Cruces heads the Department; claims of prejudice by Ms. Varela strain credibility (Maestas 1990).

The fact that there are Hispanos in the department's leadership reveals the complexity of environmental racism. It forces us to look more critically at both the *accountability* of leaders and the philosophies underlying their policies on wildlife, environmentalism, and the development of rural communities. Just because a leader belongs to a disenfranchised racial or ethnic group does not mean he or she will represent the interests of that group. For an example of Maestas' identification and empathy with Ganados, note this statement from an interview, "If you want to maintain your culture, that's fine, just do it on your own hoof" (Maestas 1990).

Although grazing is allowed on other WMAs, the NMDGF insists it is being phased out. There is reason to believe this, given the close relationships among environmentalists, hunters, and the NMDGF. Originally devoted to providing hunting opportunities, the department is likely to preside over a decline in hunters as the state is increasingly urbanized. Moreover, as more and more middle-class Anglos move to New Mexico, the ranks of conventional environmentalists swell.

To ensure that it continues to have a constituency, the NMDGF has promoted an alliance between environmentalists and hunters. As the influence of preservationists grows, the department is adopting increasingly preservationist positions—such policies also reflect the wildlife managers' own growing concerns about ecosystems since the 1970s. The extreme anti-livestock, anti-grazing position regarding public lands is summed up by the slogan "Livestock Free by '93."

Certainly ranchers have done considerable damage in the West (Furguson and Furguson 1983). But environmentalists have refused to differentiate between Ganados and other livestock operations. Audubon member Thomas Jervis did not consider the coop's activities a threat to the environment. In his eyes, Ganados only became "an environmental issue because someone is trying to invade a wildlife area." Sierra Club member Samuel Cassutt actively supported Ganados, arguing to me that its case is an exception that needed to be made:

We have a lot of ranchers in the state who use public lands real cheaply, and sometimes they don't use it very wisely. But this is totally different; this is a situation where you have this incredible miracle that has happened. Ganados is a miraculous thing; and because of the history with the T.A. [Tierra Amarilla] land grant, just the whole history of the people there, there's just not that much land available to graze their sheep. An exception just has to be made.

While Cassutt supported Ganados on the merits of its project, he did not feel compelled to reconsider his overall approach to preservation. For members of the Sierra Club, Audubon Society, and Nature Conservancy, the only question is how much land can be protected in the form of "wilderness"—areas where no commercial activities are allowed, and humans only engage in camping, hiking, backpacking, and the like (Fish 1987).

But that agenda runs counter to the needs and desires of numerous indigenous communities, who do not see the land as "wilderness" (Peña 1991a) but as part of their "Homeland." The issue is politically difficult for environmentalists, for while it is easy for them to oppose a large, "nasty" corporation, it hurts their image to oppose a group of poor, struggling Hispanos. Not only are these people trying to "pull themselves up by the bootstraps," but many assert that the lands in question have been stolen from them.

While environmentalists voice sympathy for such groups, they oppose growth and economic activities on public lands. Moreover, they do not offer economic alternatives to poor communities hindered by environmental regulations. It is the height of hypocrisy for a preservationist to deny other people a livelihood when he or she enjoys a secure, middle-class existence in the city and consumes so many of the resources of the biosphere. Even worse, leaders of some organizations, such as the Nature Conservancy, did not acknowledge that their preservationist policies harmed local communities. Bill Waldman of the organization's Santa Fe office explained to me, "I would say no, we're not...organized in any way that is biased towards any segment of society, and we encourage as much support from all walks of society as we can get...In my interpretation of the Nature Conservancy projects that we have been associated with there has, in fact, been a benefit to the community, not any kind of deprivation."

In response to the Hispanos' demands for economic alternatives, New Mexico environmentalists have consistently suggested tourism, although several admitted that this was a poor option, since it is nearly impossible to raise a family on wages earned in the tourist industry. When I asked environmentalists whether they felt they should get more involved in promoting sustainable development, they all replied, "Yes, but we simply don't have the resources," or "Yes, but its not our primary focus. We're dedicated to preserving habitat."

State resource managers replied in a similar fashion. They said that, of course, they were concerned with local people, but development wasn't their job. One NMDGF commissioner explained,

My job is to have elk available for the public, whether it be for hunting, viewing aesthetics, or whatever. That's my job. I'd like to have lots of deer...I'd like to be accused of having too much wildlife. I'd like sportsmen to say, "Mr. Montoya, you have too many deer, too many elk, too many bears, too many peregrine falcons, and bald eagles." That would tickle me to death, because that's my job (Montoya 1990).

The racism and class bias evident in the grazing conflict is not primarily a product of mean, racist people. Rather, it stems from the nature of existing environmental policy and conflicting conceptions of the value of the natural world. The prevailing idea of nature among most preservationists has no place for people, even when they are historical component of the rural landscape and habitat. Wilderness preservation, narrowly defined, is particularly inappropriate in a rural context when it creates other ecological problems which are ignored (Peña 1992).

First, poor people will do what is necessary to sustain themselves and, in the process, can severely degrade the environment. For example, they may be forced to overgraze the areas they have access to, engage in wildlife poaching, or invite polluting industries to their area. Second, "wildlife don't read signs," as locals are fond of saying. Chama residents pointed out to the NMDGF that the elk often wandered into farm areas, thus underscoring the fact that the region is an ecosystem, not a piece of land defined by arbitrary property lines. Further, all agreed that Rio Arriba has a very large elk population. Some people interpreted the elks' wandering onto farms as evidence of the poor habitat on the WMAs, while others saw it simply as the result of overpopulation. A third problem with the preservationist position derives from its refusal to acknowledge that if the Hispanos cannot make a living in their homeland, they will be forced to move to the city, adding to increasing urban growth and further degrading the environment.

These problems epitomize the limitations of the current preservationist approach. Instead of working with a community that wants to conserve resources and operate in a sustainable fashion as it addresses its serious social problems, the preservationists opposed Ganados. Although they expressed slight variations of opinion, they all ended up opposing the Hispano coop because they believed their constituencies would otherwise feel betrayed. This is a legitimate concern, but the environmental leaders could have turned the situation into an educational opportunity. Certainly, in some cases, conventional wilderness preservation is the best policy, but the situation in Chama is not one of them. Elk are in no way endangered here, nor, as far as we know, are there any other rare or endangered species.

While preservation alone cannot serve as the basis for a sustainable society, neither can a complete return to traditional ranching and agriculture. While Chicano and Indian activists often suggest that their traditional grazing methods are both sustainable and protect the environment, this is, in fact, not always true. Certainly, many traditional grazing methods were sustainable, but they often depended on the large tracts of land that were available before the imposition of private property. But now in a different political and economic landscape, traditional methods by themselves are sometimes inadequate. Ganados has not hesitated to avail itself of modern scientific knowledge about range management or grazing techniques. At the same time, it continues to rely on the traditional knowledge of their experienced head shepherd, Martin Romero.

One of the misconceptions a displaced population, such as the Hispanos, can harbor is that regaining their land will solve all their problems. Few residents are fully aware of the complexities of the modern economy and of the near impossibility of ever becoming economically independent, even with a sizable land base. A majority have romantic views of the opportunities that regaining their lands would create. For one thing, many Hispanos in Rio Arriba currently lack the skills and knowledge necessary to effectively compete in today's market economy because of inadequate or nonexistent schooling, language barriers, and cultural differences.

The leaders of Ganados recognize this and have geared their programs toward helping their people develop their skills within their own cultural context. That also helps the business flourish. Although a development plan may on the surface appear simple and easy, its results will not materialize through good intentions alone. A great deal of skill, planning, and knowledge are necessary to implement what may appear to be a simple development strategy. This is certainly the case with Ganados del Valle. While Hispanos are drawing on their cultural heritage, they are also firmly rooted in the late 20th century.

Conclusion

The story of Ganados del Valle teaches valuable lessons about organizing sustainable development programs. First, it provides an excellent example of how a low-income community can manage its resources rather than just avoiding the effects of toxic wastes. Because Ganados operates in a nonindustrialized, rural area, it must cope with a far different set of circumstances than those of an inner-city community. Of course, both suffer from extreme poverty and discrimination. Because Ganados focuses on natural resource management, but acts within an environmental justice framework, it does not dismiss concerns about natural resources as a luxury. Instead, it sees them as linked to waste disposal problems and to many of the same social justice concerns as other environmental justice groups face. Likewise, Ganados points to a viable alternative to producing pollution and wastes that ravages other communities as well: manufacturing that consumes the fewest resources, relies on renewable ones, and employs careful production practices generates minimal waste.

The second contribution of Ganados is this focus on production. While radical preservationists typically consume a vast array of goods, they obstruct almost all forms of industry and manufacturing. Certainly industry must shoulder much of the blame for pollution, but we do need certain of its products. Some Deep Ecologists argue that our main problem is agro-industrialism per se and thus advocate a return to hunting and gathering (Manes 1990). Yet, this is not a realistic option. Instead, we must develop less environmentally degrading forms of production that still meet basic human needs. Ganados primarily produces clothing, blankets/rugs, and meat. Though on the high end of the market, it represent a step in the right direction.

The third issue Ganados has effectively addressed is providing labor opportunities. Traditionally, one of the most divisive issues between environmentalists and working-class communities has been over jobs. Workers feel their jobs are threatened by environmental programs, while most environmentalists provide no employment alternatives. Workers thus often refuse to recognize the very real environmental problems associated with their industries. Ganados shows how each local community might develop a plan appropriate to its own situation and work with its own strengths, rather than accept the imposition of a totally foreign plan. In addition to providing jobs, Ganados offers opportunities for broad human growth and development, all within the context of workplace democracy.

The environmental justice movement must assume leadership in such efforts by assisting communities interested in developing positive alternatives to the current development model. Our present production systems clearly produce unacceptable environmental and social consequences and disproportionately harm people of color. Numerous needs of low-income, minority communities can be met through sustainable development. Mainstream environmentalists, while acknowledging the need for both sustainable development and cultural diversity, still continue to underplay the various components of people's lives, including race, gender, class, and culture. Given the shortcomings of this approach, we in the environmental justice movement must offer more integrated models of community development that address racism, ecology, and culture.

Activists of color should take the lead in promoting sustainable development at home and abroad. They must appropriate this more holistic approach and apply it in a proactive manner. Many social justice activists have come to recognize that environmental justice goes beyond ensuring that the poor, the working class, and communities of color are not disproportionately harmed by environmental degradation.

Because many communities face serious problems on a number of fronts—from gangs, crime, poverty, racism, inadequate health care, and poor education—we must strive to meet their basic needs, while not losing sight of the environmental implications of our corrective actions. The record plainly shows that the results of unsound management and production eventually show up in the backyard of some already oppressed community. For this reason, we must act proactively as we fulfill our social justice and ecological agenda.

CHAPTER 9

Nature and Chicanos in Southern Colorado

Devon Peña and Joseph Gallegos

The exploitation of natural resources is a major cause of environmental degradation in this nation's rural, mountainous West (deBuys 1985; Worster 1985; Gottlieb 1988; Field and Burch 1988; Peña 1990a, 1991a, b, 1992). A hundred and twenty years ago, railroads opened up to rapid exploitation vast timber stands, gold and silver deposits, and grassland pastures in the Rocky Mountain region. The pace of this environmental and social disruption accelerated as the region was subjected to capitalist industrialization. In agriculture, this meant not just mechanization, but the increasing use of agro-industrial chemicals—for example, fertilizers, pesticides, and herbicides.

This chapter examines the ecological problems associated with industrial mining in rural southern Colorado's San Luis Valley. Rural industrialization here led to social displacement and long-term economic decline, particularly in areas subject to the boom/bust cycle of extractive industries like mining and timbering (Marston *et al.* 1989).

Rural Industrialization and Environmental Damage

Industrial agricultural systems have significantly increased surface and groundwater contamination. They have both accelerated the loss of topsoil and reduced the biotic diversity of the land, thus diminishing its long-term fertility and viability. Overgrazing, caused by the rise of large-scale commercial sheep and cattle industries, also has contributed to land degradation in the region (Westphall 1983; deBuys 1985; Peña 1991a, b; also see Jackson 1980; Jackson, Berry, and Colman 1984; National Research Council 1989). The mining industry, through the use of modern extractive and processing technologies, has seriously disrupted and damaged ecosystems in the intermountain West (Wentz

1974; Environmental Protection Agency 1986; Conservation Foundation 1987; Day 1989; Mineral Policy Center 1990, 1991; Gilles *et al.* 1991; Macalady *et al.* 1991).

Modern industrial mining involves the use of strip or pit mines, sometimes several miles long and thousands of feet deep. This results in more than just "mountain scarring," an aesthetic problem. It is also a hazard to the health of the entire eco-community, for these mines literally suck dry aquifers, entire water systems, and the wildlife dependent on them. Mine wastes and tailings also disrupt vadose zones (the natural groundwater filtration systems). Milling, processing, and disposing of mined ores are processes that mobilize heavy metals and other toxic substances, which then leach into the water and land (Environmental Protection Agency 1986; Day 1989; Jorgensen 1989; Stewart 1990; Haun 1991). This degrades water quality, reduces biological diversity, and harms all forms of life in the affected ecosystems.

Rural industrialization is often accompanied by a shift from native to external ownership and use of the land and water (Martinez 1987). As the indigenous resident population loses its land, a pattern of emigration out of the area often emerges. Severed from their land base, many rural youth in the intermountain West migrate to urban areas in search of better employment or educational opportunities. Thus, the industrialization of the countryside is as likely to displace the human inhabitants as the wetland willow. The long-term economic prospects of rural areas are also dimmed by the ravages of extractive industries. Reduced land, water, and air quality can stifle future economic development by making the affected regions less supportive of or attractive to farmers, artisans, and businesses built on tourism (Blaikie and Brookfield 1987; Marston 1989; Varela 1989).

Significant transfers of water rights, from agricultural to industrial and urban uses, often accompany rural development. So, increasingly, companies mine water for industrial and urban uses. Water mining and exportation is thus another important cause of environmental degradation and the social disruption of rural communities. The abandonment of the small family farm is primarily a consequence of the industrialization and commercialization of water (Gottlieb and Wiley 1982; Worster 1985; Brown and Ingram 1987; Gottlieb 1988; Marston 1989; Smith 1989; Reisner 1990).

This whole process is riddled with inequities. Usually based in urban areas, new investors and developers, political leaders, and government regulators are generally unresponsive to demands for environmental protection from the less powerful rural communities. Environmental degradation disproportionately harms low-income and ethnic minority communities in both urban and rural settings (Center for Third World Organizing 1986; Commission for Racial Justice 1987; Gilles *et al.* 1991; Goldman 1991; Peña 1992).

But rural ethnic communities often lack sufficient resources to engage in the expensive litigation that becomes inevitable when competing approaches to development and conservation clash. Isolation from the predominantly urban environmental organizations also places rural communities at a disadvantage. High poverty rates often divide rural communities when corporations engage in what Cynthia Hamilton (1990) calls "economic blackmail." The divide-and-conquer strategy works best when people are desperate for jobs. But sometimes communities can effectively organize to resist the economic bribery that offers jobs at the expense of a healthy environment. The struggle of the Chicano agropastoral community of San Luis against Battle Mountain Gold is a case in point. Despite overwhelming economic pressures, San Luis Chicanos have remained firmly opposed to the industrial mining that threatens their sustainable local culture with extinction.

The Natural, Cultural, and Social Context

The San Luis Valley (SLV) is a high, alpine desert plateau in southern Colorado surrounded by the 14,000-foot peaks of the Sangre de Cristo and San Juan mountains. Here lie the headwaters of the Rio Grande; the SLV collects much of the tributary flow that creates the river. The area, about the size of Connecticut, is considered one of the last relatively pristine, nonindustrialized rural valleys in the intermountain West. SLV streams have a higher percentage of "all aquatic life" classifications than watersheds in other regions of Colorado (Colorado Ground Water Association 1989). The relative absence of mining activities in the SLV till now is one reason for the high quality of the water in most of the mountain creeks and rivers that drain into the Upper Rio Grande. The valley's isolation and agropastoral character have slowed the pace of development.

Over a dozen peaks in these mountain ranges exceed 14,000 feet, and over 80 exceed 13,000 feet. The average elevation is 10,000 feet. This mountain barrier is a significant factor in maintaining the relatively undeveloped character of the SLV. The spring snow-melt runoff from the high peaks sustains the valley's agricultural economy. However, substantial mineral deposits underlie the rugged topography of the region. While gold lodes in the region were exhausted nearly a century ago, low-grade deposits remain today—concentrations of microscopic specks of gold dispersed in other geologic formations or in old mine tailings. The ruggedness of the mountains and the character of these remaining deposits have limited industrial mining in the SLV over the past 50 years.

Recent technological advances, however, have now made exploitation of the residual gold in microscopic mineral deposits economically feasible. The development of cyanide leach mining and milling technologies has revolutionized and revitalized the mining industry (see U.S. Department of Interior 1986; and EPA 1986). This has brought a new boom in the industrialization of the countryside, as extractive industries expand their use of long-standing, but idle, mining claims (Mineral Policy Center 1990, 1991; Southwest Research and Information Center 1990, 1991). While this may be good news for the mining corporations, it clearly menaces the rural environment near the sites of these new, high-tech mines (Peña forthcoming). Moreover, this boom poses a grave threat to the agropastoral communities because of the industrial uses and abuses of water and land that it entails. The destruction of the ecological balance has disrupted and altered indigenous land- and water-use patterns—in particular, agropastoral practices. Ecocide comes along with ethnocide.

In the southeastern part of the SLV lies the village of San Luis de la Culebra (St. Louis of the Water Snake). It is the oldest continuously inhabited agropastoral community in Colorado. It owns the oldest adjudicated water rights in the state. Under the doctrine of prior appropriation, the San Luis Peoples Ditch enjoys "priority one" in Colorado.

The Culebra microbasin has the largest number of "Centennial Farms" in the state, all owned by Chicano families. The Colorado "Centennial Farms" are so designated by the U.S. and Colorado Departments of Agriculture, the Colorado Historical Society, the Colorado State Fair, and the National Trust for Historic Preservation. To qualify, a farm or ranch must have been continuously owned and operated by the same family for at least a hundred years. In San Luis, the Corpus A. Gallegos Ranches, the Praxedis Ortega Ranch, and the Rio Culebra Ranch have all been so designated. Another five farms in the area will be eligible in the immediate future. Thirty-five irrigation ditch (acequia) associations, besides San Luis's, also have the oldest water priority dates in the state (State Engineers Office 1978).

The settlement of San Luis, through homesteading on the Sangre de Cristo Land Grant, dates back to 1851. Like other Chicano land-grant villages in the valley, it is an agropastoral community that relies on a safe and pure water supply to support subsistence agriculture, cash-crop farming, livestock raising, and hunting. These communities have inherited an agro-ecological tradition that spans three continents and more than 1,000 years, namely, the acequia madre (Ebright 1989; Clark 1987). The "mother ditch" gravity irrigation system has roots in both North

Africa and the upper Rio Grande. It is based on biological tractions, not mechanical efficiency. In contrast to the fossil-fuel-based center-pivot sprinkler systems favored by corporate agribusiness in the region, *acequias* work with the natural gravitational force of water. Thus, they are more energy efficient and enjoy the advantage of being based on the renewable use of water.

This interaction between water and land also increases biological diversity, since the irrigation ditches support wetlands along their earthen banks. *Acequia* irrigation systems have been shown to be ecologically sustainable and helpful in maintaining the cohesiveness and vitality of local cultures (Clark 1987, Ebright 1987, Peña forthcoming). But like other Chicano villages in southern Colorado and northern New Mexico, San Luis continues to combat the depletion of its land-base and water rights as well as the exodus of its native population.

The village serves as the county seat of the predominantly Chicano Costilla County. The 1990 U.S. Census reports that Chicanos comprise close to 78 percent of the county's population (U.S. Bureau of the Census 1991). The agropastoral villages in the Rio Culebra watershed are as much as 98 percent Chicano. While the unemployment rate in San Luis is approximately 27 percent of the economically active population (October 1989), county unemployment hovers in the 10- to 15-percent range. Close to 40 percent of the county population lives under federally defined poverty levels (Ogden *et al.* 1989; Division of Local Government, Demography Section 1987).

Costilla County has experienced steady loss of population due to emigration since the 1950s; nearly two-thirds of its native population have left (Division of Local Government, Demography Section 1987). According to one recent estimate, the population will decrease by an additional 3.4 percent (or 103 fewer residents) between 1980 and 2000 (Ogden *et al.* 1989, p. 8). Most of this emigration involves young, unemployed Chicanos who move to Colorado cities and towns such as Alamosa, Pueblo, Colorado Springs, and Denver, or to Wyoming, California, or even New Mexico (especially Albuquerque), in search of jobs and other economic opportunities. In this regard, San Luis is a typical western intermountain town experiencing steady depopulation.

The economic and social devastation of the past 40 years notwithstanding, San Luis survives as a viable enclave of rural Chicano culture. In fact, while emigration has depleted the local population, urban-based members of village families continue to support the farms and ranches (Deutsch 1987; Peña and Martinez 1991). This has created a "regional community" that unites families scattered among diverse rural and urban settings. Thus, emigration can actually increase the economic and cultural viability of the rural community as long as the urban members maintain close ties with the countryside. San Luis is currently experiencing economic revitalization based on an artisan crafts revival, low-impact tourism, and organic ranching and farming. But like many other Chicano communities in the Upper Rio Grande homeland, it faces a real struggle for cultural survival into the 21st century. Of particular significance is the battle against the environmental and social disruptions caused by rural industrialization (particularly mining).

Rural Chicanos are joining the growing movement of people of color against environmental racism. The struggle in San Luis pits the descendants of land-grant settlers—in particular, members of the *acequia madre,* or irrigation ditch associations—against Battle Mountain Gold (BMG), a transnational gold-mining corporation based in Houston, Texas, which operates in Canada, California, Nevada, Colorado, South America, and Indonesia. In December 1990, after a long struggle by the local community, BMG opened a strip-mine and cyanide-leach milling operation in the foothills above San Luis. Because the operation seriously threatens both the natural environment and the local culture, the community is fighting BMG, struggling for the preservation of its endangered agropastoral culture as much as its environment.

A Legacy of Land and Water Struggles

The environmental struggle in San Luis de la Culebra is not a recent development imported by the post-1960s white, middle-class activists who have settled nearby in places like Taos, Santa Fe, Chimayo, or Crestone. It is an indigenous struggle with roots in the Chicano land-grant movement that dates back to the mid-1800s. The Sangre de Cristo Land Grant was issued in 1843 to Narciso Beaubien and Stephen Lee, both naturalized Mexican citizens, who married into old New Mexican families (see Stoller 1985). At the time, the SLV, including the Rio Culebra microbasin, was part of the New Mexico Territory. The valley was a traditional spring and summer hunting ground for the Weminuche and Tabehuache clans of the Southern Mountain Utes, as well as for Apaches and other tribes from the high-plains country far to the east. Permanent Chicano settlement of the valley began in 1851 with the establishment of La Plaza de San Luis de la Culebra.

The land-grantees (Beaubien and Lee) never settled in the region; it is likely they never intended to do so. Instead, Beaubien and his heirs invited Chicano families to settle on their land. Most of the original families migrated from their villages in New Mexico, such as Socorro, Taos, and Abiqui. Thus, settlement of the Sangre de Cristo land grant followed the pattern of *community* and not individual land grants (Stoller

1985). The settlers received private riparian long-lots in the bottomlands of the seven major creeks in the Culebra microbasin; but the majority of the land, including the vast foothill woodlands and mountain forests and parks, was set aside as an *ejido,* a commons.

Trouble came after the SLV was officially detached from the rest of the upper Rio Grande homeland by the establishment of the Colorado Territory in 1859-1861. The first territorial governor of Colorado, Colonel William Gilpin, surreptitiously purchased a one-sixth interest in the land in 1858 from land speculator Joseph Pley. Thus began the long struggle by native Chicano settlers against land speculation and enclosure. Initially, the transfer of formal "ownership" of the land grant did not much affect the settlers. However, between 1864 and 1865, Gilpin hired mining experts to determine the mineral potential of his land. James Aborn, a mining geologist, reported the presence of 22 lodes and two "placers" of gold-bearing ore (Brayer 1974, p. 67). Before the turn of the century, mining exploration and exploitation in the Culebra Mountains above San Luis remained very limited. Gilpin's indulgence in speculation brought him no reward. And despite the legal maneuvering (which was to have grave consequences a hundred years later), the Chicano settlers remained the sole possessors and users of the common lands.

By the turn of the century, many speculators had traded in a variety of economic commodities in the Sangre de Cristo Land Grant. But not until the 1890s did speculators attempt to physically and legally enclose the common lands. The enclosure of the San Luis Commons at first proceeded mainly through the courts, as absentee "owners" filed lawsuits for trespassing against the locals who continued to use the lands for grazing, fuel-wood gathering, and hunting (see Peña 1991b). Despite these attempts at enclosure, Chicanos continued to settle on the disputed lands and to use the vast "Mountain Tract" common lands for pasturing and hunting. As early as 1906, squatters were reported moving up into the canyons of the Rio Culebra and San Francisco Creek. They would not be deterred in their attempts to expand the regional community (see Peña 1991b). During this period (from the 1890s through the early 1900s), absentee developers and speculators also tried to expropriate and manipulate water rights in the Culebra microbasin. This, too, was successfully resisted by the local Chicanos, who occupied land and utilized as much of the water as possible in order to avoid expropriations through abandonment proceedings (Peña 1991b).

Not until 1960, when a North Carolina lumberman by the name of Jack Taylor bought the "Mountain Tract," were the common lands of the Culebra basin effectively enclosed (Sandoval 1984). The Chicano struggle to reclaim the "Mountain Tract" intensified after 1960 and provoked armed skirmishes and the destruction of fences and barricades erected by the new "owners." This was part of the larger land-grant movement that flourished in northern New Mexico and southern Colorado throughout the 1960s and 1970s (Stoller 1985; Rosenbaum 1981).

After decades of litigation in state and federal courts, the Land Rights Council in San Luis lost its final appeal in 1991. But the descendants of the original land-grant settlers have not given up. Efforts are currently underway to establish a community land trust. Its goal, whose pursuit may involve the participation of a national environmental organization, is to purchase the "Mountain Tract" and restore its communal grazing, hunting, and timber rights. The commons would be managed as a protected natural and historical culture area (Peña forthcoming).

Clearly, the presence of BMG just north of the Tract has intensified local efforts to resolve the land-grant dispute. Villagers fear that mining will encroach on the old common lands and undermine efforts to restore communal access to the land grant. Thus, their efforts to promote and sustain environmental protection are closely wedded to the land-rights struggle.

Prelude to Struggle: Industrial Mining in the Rio Seco

In 1987, BMG announced plans to develop a strip-mine and cyanide leaching operation in the foothills of the Sangre de Cristo Mountains about three miles northeast of the town of San Luis. In December 1990, BMG opened the mine. The operation strip-mines microscopic specks of gold contained in the Santa Fe Conglomerate and crushes it to the consistency of beach sand. The gold-bearing ore is then processed by means of an enclosed cyanide-leaching vat system that extracts approximately 0.032 ounces of gold per ton of crushed conglomerate. The mining facility sits directly on top of the Rito Seco (Dry Creek) watershed, which feeds the San Luis Peoples Ditch which, in turn, provides irrigation water to the oldest farms and ranches in the state. It is hardly surprising that the BMG operation has generated sharp opposition from local farmers, ranchers, and other water users.

Earth Sciences, Inc. (ESI), a mining company based in Golden, Colorado, operated a cyanide-leaching facility in the same area until 1979. On April 6, 1975, a cyanide spill into the Rito Seco killed fish up to six miles downstream from the leach pad (Goforth 1975). The Colorado Department of Health issued a cease-and-desist order and EPA took similar action in October 1975. The department issued another cease-and-desist order in October 1979 along with a "Cleanup Order and Notice of Violation of Previous Order." Also in October 1979, the EPA prevailed in a lawsuit against ESI and ordered the company to reclaim the cyanide-leach pad area. To this date, neither the reclamation nor the cleanup has begun (Costilla County Committee for Environmental Soundness 1989, p. 1). BMG has bought the ESI mining claim and additional land and mineral rights in the Rito Seco watershed, about three miles northeast of San Luis.

In November 1988, concerned local residents organized the Costilla County Committee for Environmental Soundness (CES). It was established to:

> (1) protect the pristine and diverse ecology of Costilla County, (2) promote a healthy balance between agriculture, business, and the environment, and (3) encourage citizen involvement in efforts to keep the environment safe, beautiful, and conducive to the health of residents as well as plant and animal life…The CES is thus committed to protecting natural and cultural diversity by linking ecological concerns with issues of social justice and equity (CES 1990, p. 1).

The CES is comprised of local farmers, ranchers, members of the clergy, educators, businesspeople, and community planners. While it pursues a wide-ranging agenda, its principal present focus is on efforts to shutdown the BMG mine and to minimize environmental damage to the watershed on which the local *acequias* rely for their sustenance.

To prevent approval of the BMG proposal, the CES organized public participation in the hearings of the Mined Land Reclamation Board (MLRB), the Colorado state agency charged with issuing mining permits. At one hearing, in February 1989, the public expressed overwhelming opposition, and this led to rejection of the BMG proposal. However, the MLRB granted a mining permit to BMG at a second hearing held on March 22, 1989 (CES 1989, p. 1). Thus, the stage was set for a protracted struggle.

The next step by CES was to challenge the decision of the MLRB. On April 21, 1989, the committee joined several other opponents in filing a civil action in the District Court, City and County of Denver, against the MLRB and BMG. The CES sought to invalidate the permit and gain financial relief, arguing that the MLRB had failed to comply with its own regulatory guidelines by issuing a permit before completion of an environmental impact assessment (EIA) by the company and an Army Corps of Engineer study on the potential destruction of wetlands. The committee also contended that BMG had not provided a sufficiently objective environmental assessment. To those complaints, the MLRB responded that it was free to exercise administrative discretion in issuing mining permits. After a one-day hearing, the District Court ruled against the CES. Since BMG is on private land and no public lands are affected by the mining project, the CES could not cite the National Environmental Policy Act (NEPA) in support of its request for a full-blown environmental impact statement (EIS). After this ruling, the focus of the their strategy then shifted to the water courts, where CES sought to block BMG's acquisition and transfer of water rights from agricultural to industrial use. Without water, BMG could not operate its mine.

The Water Trial

On April 5, 1989, BMG filed a request for 700 acre-feet of water per year from underground sources. The claim was immediately opposed by the CES, the San Luis Peoples Ditch, and five other irrigation-ditch associations. By the end of the trial (November 1990), the company had increased its request to 1,400 acre-feet per year. Earlier, in March 1988, it had approached the Sanchez Ditch and Reservoir Company, asking for water rights to operate its mining facilities. Sanchez rejected the request. Then, in July 1990, a BMG subcontractor offered the San Luis Peoples Ditch $50,000 for use of water during a four-month construction project. That offer also was firmly rejected. During this period, the CES focused on maintaining solidarity among the various parties who owned water rights in the microbasin.

A united front against BMG's attempt to divide the water users through selective contract purchases held together largely as a result of efforts by the CES to educate local farmers and ranchers about the environmental and economic consequences of water-rights transfers. Therefore, the corporation was forced to look outside the community for water. It purchased the Columbian Ranch/Rocky Mountain Farms properties from absentee owners in Missouri. These properties, located about nine miles north of San Luis, include junior water rights tied to nine center-pivot irrigation wells and surface rights on the Trinchera Ditch.

The water trial (Colorado 89CW32) took place in Alamosa Water District Court Number Three in November 1990. It focused on BMG's proposal to transfer water rights from agricultural to industrial use. The corporation wanted to pipe over 1,000 acre-feet of water per year to the mine from its newly purchased properties. The transfer would involve nine center-pivot irrigation circles that were in agricultural use. With only 10 percent of the land in Costilla County under irrigation for agriculture, the possible transfer seriously alarmed the local farming and ranching community.

The trial proceedings provided a classic example of the "experts against the primitives" scenario (see Peña forthcoming). At its start, the judge made it clear that the opponents were not to "get emotional," or raise what he characterized as "fuzzy environmental issues." Water law, he declared, was a "strictly scientific and legal matter," and the water court was not the place to rehash environmental debates.

The opposition legal strategy was thus challenged from the start. Attorneys for the San Luis Peoples Ditch and the other opponents argued that issues of water quantity (transfer rights) could not be treated separately from issues of water quality. To no avail, they insisted that BMG wanted the judge to "stand here with one eye blind and not consider water quality." They pointed out that Section 404 of the Clean Water Act did not prohibit water courts from dealing with environmental concerns. To that contention, the judge responded, "we are not going to wipe-out any endangered species. I don't think there are any snail darters in there." In short, he was not ready to consider the possibility that Chicano agropastoralists are an endangered species.

This exchange brought into sharp relief the basic problem confronting indigenous local cultures when they come up against the power of the water courts. Western law defines water as a commodity and thus places it in the framework of property rights (Clark 1987). It is not treated scientifically, as part of a complex hydrological and ecological system. This was what BMG's opponents tried to say. But the law worked against them: your water rights do not include the right to have its quality protected against polluters.

This legal system is completely at odds with the centuries-old custom of water use in the Upper Rio Grande. For Chicanos and Native Americans, water is *not* a commodity. Instead, water rights are usufructuary: one has the right to use the water only as long as you do so responsibly (without infringing on the rights of others). Furthermore, the traditional system is based on "riparian" principles; that is, one cannot separate water from the adjacent land (Peña forthcoming). In contrast, under the current doctrine of "prior appropriation," water *can* be separated from the land. This is why BMG is permitted to dry out the center-pivot irrigation wells and pipe the water to the mine site. These legal realities mean that environmentalists are not very likely to emerge victorious from encounters with developers in water court.

As the trial progressed, the San Luis Peoples Ditch and other opponents developed a new strategy. If environmental evidence could not be introduced, they would negotiate with BMG to force some concessions regarding the community's primary concerns: Public health and their economic well-being.

Primary Concerns of the Community

The main controversies surrounding the BMG strip-mine and cyanide-leaching facilities center around these concerns. The strip-mine will eventually be about a mile long and over 500 feet deep. The most controversial aspect of the project is the "dewatering" of the Rito Seco aquifer. To reach the microscopic specks of gold, BMG must dewater the western and eastern pits. Since the ore-bearing stratum, known as the Santa Fe Conglomerate, is hydrologically connected to the aquifer, this will severely damage the sensitive wetlands of the Rito Seco. In fact, there is a high probability that the dewatering will destroy the wetlands, including various beaver ponds within the mine-site boundaries.

Water quality is another major communal concern. The construction activities have already visibly degraded it. The increased turbidity and sedimentation associated with construction activities have resulted in the death of at least one of the beavers living downstream from the site. The Colorado Division of Wildlife (DOW) will assist BMG in trapping and relocating the remaining beavers, an action opponents of the project view as strong evidence that the mining will seriously degrade their environment.

Thus, the project poses a very real, long-term threat to domestic and agricultural water supplies. Of particular concern to the villagers is the possible contamination of the *acequia madre* headwaters. Any polluting of the communal irrigation-ditch network will cause untold hardship and possible economic ruin. Opponents also fear that the mining operation will create a permanent toxic waste site.

The CES has also criticized BMG's reclamation plans. While the company claims that the San Luis Project will be the first fully reclaimed mining project in Colorado history, the CES has pointed out some fundamental flaws in the plan, principally its silence about the lack of irrigation water and its haphazard mixing of the "A" and "B" soil horizons. The CES voiced these concerns at the MLRB hearings, but was basically ignored. It repeated its argument during the trial. A CES member and local farmer, Joe Gallegos, warned that the replanting of piñon and juniper in the reclamation plots would prove useless unless an irrigation plan was implemented. BMG's demonstration plot did indeed fail: of the fifteen trees planted, all but one died within four months. The CES also criticized the company's grassland reclamation plan. The demonstration plot yielded little, largely because soil horizons were mixed and irrigation water was not provided. Residents also expressed their fears about the destruction of the sensitive wetlands of the Rito Seco, some of which are within a few hundred feet of the east mine pit.

The CES and other opponents went on to strongly decry the potential health hazards associated with the cyanide-leaching operation. Given the 1975 experience with the ESI cyanide spill, many local farmers and ranchers remain skeptical about BMG's assurances that the leach-vat operations are environmentally safe. The mining operation uses an average of 900 tons of sodium cyanide per year (one milligram is potentially fatal to an adult human). The number and types of heavy metals associated with the project are unknown. Of particular concern is the impact of cyanide or heavy-metal contamination on water used both for agriculture and domestic consumption. The local public health clinic and schools are located within two-and-a-half miles of the mine site, and the Rito Seco flows along the backside of the local schoolyards.

Finally, the CES, other BMG opponents, and the Costilla County Economic Development Council (EDC) also voiced concern at the trial about the impact the BMG mine will likely have on local efforts to promote economic development alternatives. The EDC is currently leading efforts to bring about an economic recovery based on an environmentally sound mix of an arts and crafts revival, bed and breakfast inns, art galleries, nature recreation, and sustainable agriculture. Local development planning leaders argue that the BMG mine is incompatible with their long-range plans for economic recovery and a cultural revival. Construction of the strip-mine required relocation of a county road through a thickly forested area. This encroached on one of the few county parks in the area, which is adjacent to and upstream from the mine site. Given the limited public access to nature recreation areas, many residents feel the mine has already made their environment much worse.

Gaining Concessions

Given all these serious concerns, BMG's opponents aimed at strengthening environmental standards in their negotiations with the company. Seven main groups participated. They decided that five of them would negotiate and the other two—CES and San Luis Peoples Ditch—would continue the coalition's legal opposition. This strategy appeared to provide a more legitimate basis for struggle in the future.

The negotiations did produce some important concessions. First, BMG agreed to increase its reclamation bond from $900,000 to $3.3

million. Second, it agreed to install a more expensive and reliable system to monitor leaks and spills (the vacuum lysimeter system). Third, it agreed to replace water losses in the Rito Seco immediately after they occurred, instead of only during the irrigation season. Fourth, BMG agreed to monitor air quality and not just water quality. Fifth, the company agreed to comply with right-to-know laws: to report the presence of all chemicals at the mine site and to help pay for equipment and training for local emergency-response teams. A sixth demand, for a 50-100 year indemnity bond, was rejected.

That demand was crucial, as it would have provided the community some protection should the corporation go bankrupt. Many water-quality problems associated with mining only emerge over years, even decades. The migration of heavy metals through groundwater aquifers is very slow-moving. BMG's opponents hoped to get the 50-100 year indemnity bond in order to cover the costs of a cleanup if the need ever arises. The objective was to protect future generations against pollution from the mine wastes and tailings.

A related problem had to do with the corporation's official name. When the trial started, BMG was filing its claim for the water rights and transfer using the name of Battle Mountain Resources (BMR). This, it turned out, was a "shadow" name. BMR simply did not exist. But that name could have complicated future litigation. Early in the trial opponents challenged BMG on this point and forced it to withdraw the BMR designation.

Political Aspects of the Struggle

Despite the broad organized opposition led by the CES and others, BMG and the media portrayed San Luis and surrounding villages as bitterly divided into pro-mine and anti-mine factions. Hence, a key aspect of the struggle became the effort to redefine public opinion. To enter the public debate effectively, the San Luis Peoples Ditch and the CES asked Devon Peña, a professor of sociology at Colorado College, to conduct a survey of environmental attitudes in Costilla County between late July and early August 1990. He took a random sample representing 15 percent of the voting-age population of the entire county. The survey results were clear: close to 78 percent of the respondents opposed the BMG mine; less than 18 percent supported it; and the remainder (5.4 percent) were undecided (see Peña and Martinez 1991).

The CES arranged for the regional newspaper, *The Valley Courier*, to make Professor Peña one of its environmental correspondents. This allowed BMG's opponents to shape local media coverage of the mining controversy. Peña wrote a series of investigative reports and editorials on the BMG controversy, the first of which was a lead report on the survey of environmental attitudes in the county (1990b, c, d, e, f, g, h). This reporting immediately shifted the terms of the public debate and enabled the CES to confront elected officials with the fact of solid opposition to the mine.

The newspaper reports, coupled with a series of protests and road blockades organized by environmental and Chicano student organizations at Colorado College, gave high statewide visibility to the struggle. Television, radio, and newspaper coverage increased after the publication of Peña's articles and the protests. For example, National Public Radio (NPR) broadcast a special report on the controversy, and several regional television stations followed suit. The effects of the media campaign were startling. BMG found itself on the defensive; it no longer controlled public opinion. Within a month of the first reports, the governor agreed for the first time to meet with BMG's opponents to discuss the issue. The CES had won the ideological battle, even if it had lost the legal battle. The political organization of the opponents will henceforth make it more difficult for corporations to gain mining permits in the SLV bioregion.

The CES also worked with Senator Tim Wirth (D-Colorado) to pressure the EPA and the United States Fish and Wildlife Service (USFWS) to meet with BMG's opponents. This led to meetings with Denver-based EPA mine-waste specialists and various officials from the USFWS. The discussions did not produce tangible results, although the EPA did visit the mine site for the first time and concluded that BMG would eventually have to ask for a Section 402 (Clean Water Act) "point discharge" permit. This confirmed the worst fears of the community that the mine was not a "zero-discharge" facility, as claimed by the corporation's experts and attorneys (see Peña forthcoming for further discussion). The EPA and USFWS also agreed to monitor the mine operation closely so as to be able to quickly shut it down if problems occur.

Finally, while San Luis battled against BMG, another environmental struggle was looming. The Citizens for San Luis Valley Water (CSLVW) was mobilizing its supporters to fight a water-development and exportation project planned for the northern end of the SLV by American Water Development, Inc. (AWDI). The CSLVW is a valley-wide organization of environmentalists, farmers, ranchers, businesspeople, and other citizens opposed to the mining and exporting of water to the Front Range and other urban areas. If the project were approved, the AWDI would export an annual average of 200,000 acre-feet of groundwater out of the SLV (Peña 1989).

The CSLVW wields tremendous resources (including a voter-approved mill levy). But when it was approached by the CES to join the fight against BMG, the water activists at first refused. It was only after the BMG water trial that CSLVW joined with the Chicanos of San Luis. This represented an important political development because it provided the Chicano community access to resources needed to give its campaign greater visibility and support.

Strategic Implications

The important struggles of agropastoral communities against the ecological damage and social displacement caused by rural industrialization have often been overlooked in discussions about the environmental justice movement. Isolated and easily forgotten, rural ethnic communities often find themselves at a disadvantage, politically, when compared to urban-based communities. In addition, since Chicanos are overwhelmingly urban-based, their struggles in rural communities are often overlooked by scholars and activists. But the battle San Luis waged against BMG provides important lessons to environmentally active ethnic communities in both rural and urban settings.

The first lesson is that corporate economic blackmail does not always succeed in dividing a community. Costilla County suffers from a very high unemployment rate; jobs are badly needed. Local residents nevertheless managed to achieve and maintain a high degree of solidarity against the mining developers. In part, this reflects the central role water plays in the economy and culture of the local bioregion. Many residents of San Luis are unemployed or underemployed and must rely on subsistence farming, gardening, and livestock raising to survive. Thus, even they have a strong interest in protecting water rights. The continuing importance of cash-crop farming and commercial livestock raising in the local economy also strengthens the resolve of residents to protect their water. While Chicanos have a long-standing emotional and cultural attachment to the land (Eastman *et al.* 1971), their practical need for clean water and land has also been a significant factor in building and sustaining their ecological awareness.

While some local residents eventually sought and gained employment at the mine, they remained ambivalent about the future of mining in the county. Many reported that they would rather have other options for employment and that they were appalled by the environmental destruction caused by mining (Peña and Martinez 1991). The CES recognized the value of maintaining good ties with the mine workers, many of whom are relatives of mine opponents.

The organization encouraged workers from the local community to organize a union and supplied them with information on workplace hazards and unionizing strategies. The ideas was to prevent BMG dividing the local "environmentalists" from the workers, as often occurs in mining controversies. Instead, the CES supported the need for jobs and for building a miners union. This organizing drive was actually strengthened by mine mismanagement. Safety hazards and accidents became a daily concern of workers and a source of conflict with management. Many of the local workers have since been fired, but the remaining ones are still agitating for union representation.

BMG had dispensed selective business contracts in its attempt to divide the community. For example, it gave a contract to provide diesel fuel for the mine to a local businessperson, who invested $60,000 in the equipment needed to meet the demands of the contract. After less than a year, BMG terminated the contract in favor of another fuel company in Alamosa, which submitted a lower bid. The local businessperson was outraged; he pointed out to BMG that he would not have made the investment if he had known that the contract would be so short-lived. He has become a major opponent of the mine.

Throughout the dispute, the CES maintained an open channel with the businessperson, so that when he was ready to join the opposition, the groundwork had already been prepared. The lesson for environmentalists is obvious: always keep communication channels open, especially with mineworkers, and even with businesspeople who may be benefiting from a relationship with the opponent. Opportunities for grassroots organizations to turn the "divide and conquer" strategy against corporations may eventually present themselves.

Perhaps the most important lesson has to do with the opposition's broader, long-term strategy to gain concessions. While the CES, San Luis Peoples Ditch, and other mine opponents would have preferred to prevent the opening of the mine altogether, they decided that gaining some concessions at least would strengthen their position should the mine eventually open, even if these initial concessions seemed insignificant.

But from an environmental point of view, some of the concessions will strengthen environmental protection and reclamation. However, the economic impact of the concessions is perhaps most critical. Operating costs at the BMG Rito Seco mine are the highest for the corporation globally: $350 per ounce of gold (compared to the global average of $280). The concessions have played a part in raising BMG's operating costs. For example, early opposition by the CES forced the company to abandon its plans for a cyanide-leach pad system. Instead, BMG was forced to adopt a safer and more expensive technology: the enclosed cyanide-leach vat system. In addition, the corporation underestimated the costs of operating this state-of-the-art milling technology.

With the price of gold declining in recent years, the mine operation in San Luis is not currently profitable. The situation became so serious that BMG asked the Costilla County Commissioners for a tax-rebate (under the Rural Enterprise Zone guidelines established by the state of Colorado). The CES learned of this move (from workers inside the company) and convinced the commissioners to reject the request.

The global gold market is likely to be saturated with Russian gold because of the breakup of the Soviet Union. In fact, these historic events will wreak havoc on the mineral market and devastate prices for years to come, as the newly independent republics expand gold production to improve their foreign exchange earnings. Given its high operating costs, BMG may be forced to close the Rito Seco mine much sooner than anticipated. It may turn out that the early concessions made by the corporation under protracted pressure from the CES, San Luis Peoples Ditch, and other opponents have hastened this closure and thus minimized the damage to the watershed.

The CES is preparing for the future. Its key objective at present is to gain passage of land-use and zoning regulations. The Colorado state constitution allows a certain degree of "home rule" under what is termed Section 1041 statutory authority. Those provisions permit county commissioners to enact local land-use and zoning regulations. Such regulations are particularly important in Costilla County, for the absence of public domain lands makes it difficult for citizens to get the EIS process started under NEPA. In such circumstances, a full, formal EIS is required only if federal actions or federal public lands are involved. Because Costilla is the only county in Colorado without public domain lands, it faces a high hurdle. However, Section 1041 land use and zoning regulations, if designed to protect water quality and promote land-use compatible with established practices, can place controls on mining.

The CES has been charged by the Costilla County Commissioners with the task of developing a draft of land-use and zoning regulations for the county. The committee is formulating regulations that will establish a citizen's review board with the power to demand complete Environmental Impact Statements as part of any future mining-permit review process. This will strengthen local participation in the process and will also add a regulatory hurdle, prior to review by the MLRB, that may dissuade mining corporations from considering Costilla County as a site for their operations. The establishment of local land-use and zoning regulations, which also grant citizen-review powers, creates an important protective mechanism for ethnic communities, particularly in rural areas where federal regulation is difficult or impossible.

Conclusion

The struggle against BMG concerns more than just environmental protection: long-term economic viability and cultural survival are also at stake. Rural Chicano communities and their culture are land-based. To protect water and land is to protect the local culture. The intensity of this struggle demonstrates the extent to which Chicanos are committed to a bioregional land ethic. As Joe Gallegos told us:

> We are not anti-development. But the form of development must be enduring, environmentally-sound, and respectful of our traditional cultural values and skills. My family has been farming the land here for five generations. I want to protect the land because it is the source of my livelihood. The land responds when you are good to it. I want to share this knowledge with younger generations so that we can keep the land in good health, and in so doing, keep our community full of the vitality and cultural heritage that has made it unique.

A long-term response to the threats posed by rural industrialization necessitates that San Luis resolve the status of the "Mountain Tract." Only by reclaiming the land-grant commons can the community prevent the future expansion of industrial mining into the Rio Culebra watershed. Throughout northern New Mexico and southern Colorado, for Chicano land-grant communities like San Luis, social justice and environmental struggles are inextricably linked.

Since November 1991, the tailings facility at BMG's Rito Seco mine has been responsible for the death of numerous waterfowl, mainly mallards and other duck species. Reports from observers in the field confirm that at least 100 ducks have died from exposure to the cyanide stew. Yet, when BMG approached the MLRB for a mining permit, it argued that the concentrations of "residual" cyanide in the tailings would never exceed the Clean Water Act (CWA) safety standard of 4 parts per million (ppm).

At last count, the cyanide in the tailings was pegged at 170 ppm: the range of 70 to 100 ppm is considered lethal to humans. The corporation, however, failed to report this to regulatory agencies until early April 1992, and six months transpired before it alerted officials and the local community. Upon notification, the MLRB issued a shutdown order. BMG has closed the mine and suspended operations until the problem can be solved (if this is possible). In the meantime, Joe Gallegos has been traveling to north-central Washington, where another local citizens group is organizing to block completion of another BMG strip-mine and cyanide-leach facility, scheduled to open on U.S. Forest Service land in 1993.

The CES is assisting the citizens of Washington in their battle against the proposed mine. These struggles continue and reflect a new level of organization and networking as the opposition to BMG expands nationwide. The corporation is also currently under indictment in Nevada for violations of the CWA: the tailings are leaking lethal doses of cyanide and heavy metals into the local watershed. Joining forces with grassroots groups in Washington and Nevada, the CES has launched a nationwide struggle to destabilize and undermine all of BMG's North American operations. They express hope for the future: the corporation is "running scared." All environmentally concerned citizens, people of color, and social justice activists would be wise to join this struggle.

CHAPTER 10

Farmworkers and Pesticides

Marion Moses

Widespread concern about pesticides was first sparked by the publication of Rachel Carson's now classic book *Silent Spring* (Carson 1962). The mainstream environmental movement has since focused considerable attention on the effects of pesticides on wildlife, food quality, and the health of the general public. Yet, far less attention has been focused on the members of our population most at risk from pesticides—the nation's farmworkers. This oversight is very troubling. Farmworkers labor under the worst conditions of any group of workers in the United States. They suffer from many kinds of toxic exposure and a paucity of legal protections. Their neglect by most mainstream environmental organizations is a political scandal.

The total number of U.S. farmworkers is not known. However, the Department of Agriculture (USDA) estimates there are two million hired workers and three million farmer owners and their families (unpaid) working on the two million farms in the United States. The leading states in number of hired farmworkers are California, Florida, and Texas (U.S. Department of Agriculture 1990). The largest amount of U.S. farm acreage is in field crops such as corn, wheat, soybeans, and cotton, whose cultivation and harvesting are almost completely mechanized. Yet, labor-intensive crops, primarily perishable fruits and vegetables, still require large numbers of workers for hand-cultivating and harvesting, the major work of the migrant and seasonal farmworker.

Work in agriculture poses many hazards, ranging from injuries and deaths caused by accidents with farm equipment—tractors, harvesters, ladders, irrigation devices, etc.—to heat stress, bee stings, snake bites, dust, airborne allergens, and noise. The most insidious hazard, however, is pesticide exposure. Almost all commercial crops are heavily and repeatedly sprayed with pesticides, and the great majority are toxic chemicals that pose acute and chronic health problems to exposed workers.

The largest single user of pesticides in the United States is agriculture, which accounts for 80 percent of total use: over one billion pounds of insecticides, herbicides, and fungicides are applied annually. In 1939 there were 32 pesticide products registered with the U.S. Department of Agriculture, while in 1989 there were 729 active-ingredient pesticide chemicals formulated into 22,000 commercial products (U.S. Environmental Protection Agency 1988). Pesticide use doubled every ten years between 1945 and 1985. Most of those used in agriculture are insecticides, herbicides, fungicides, and nematicides.

These pesticides frequently contain additional inert ingredients, which are not active as pesticides. These inert substances can be as toxic, or even more toxic, than the pesticide itself. Unlike the active ingredients, inert ones are neither required to be tested for their possibly acute and chronic health effects, nor listed by name on the pesticide label. They may comprise 90 percent or more of a registered pesticide product; but due to trade-secret provisions of the pesticide law, the Federal Insecticide Fungicide and Rodenticide Act (FIFRA), their identity cannot be released to the public by state or federal regulatory agencies (even in cases of serious poisoning).

Racism and the Development of Agriculture

The environmental threat to farmworkers is not just rooted in class exploitation: it is also firmly grounded in a racist occupational segregation that powerfully shapes the nature of the farm labor force. The harvesting of perishable food crops in the United States is disproportionately performed by ethnic and racial minorities. A 1990 national survey of farmworkers by the Department of Labor found that 77 percent identify themselves as part of an ethnic or racial minority group. Two-thirds were foreign-born: 92 percent Mexican, 4 percent other Latinos, 3 percent Asian, and 1 percent Caribbean. Of the one-third who were U.S.-born, 34 percent were Latinos, 5 percent were African Americans, and 1 percent were from other ethnic groups, including Native-Americans and Asians. The rest were non-Latino whites (Mines et al. 1991). In California, farmworkers are primarily Latinos of Mexican origin. They comprise over 90 percent of the workforce (Martin *et al.* 1985).

This racist pattern of occupational segregation has become a dominant feature of commercial agriculture in the United States. Tijuana, Mexicali, Matamoros, Ciudad Juarez, and other border cities in Mexico provide a pool for continuing importation of farmworkers. Recruitment, transportation, border crossing, and contractor hiring—with all its abuses, dangers, and degradations—keep the supply of labor in line with U.S. agribusiness demands and continue the exploitation of the poor and powerless on both sides of the border.

The exploitation of ethnic minorities in agriculture is deeply rooted in U.S. history, beginning with the period in which Africans were forced to work as slaves on plantations in the South. However, the defeat of the plantation system with its chattel slavery did not end the exploitation. It continued with the sharecropping system. And in time, many farm laborers were compelled to travel great distances from their homes to find work in agriculture, thus becoming part of a migrant labor pool subject to what has been aptly described in the 1962 CBS documentary as "The Harvest of Shame."

Exploitation of racial groups and agriculture's dependence on cheap labor are further exemplified by the development in California of large-scale, commercial agriculture, now called agribusiness. Carey McWilliams called farm labor California's "peculiar institution," and considered it "unique in malignancy, magnitude, and virulence." Cletus E. Daniel described the self-serving rationalization of agricultural employers, that white Americans wouldn't do farm work, as "an expedient racist folklore that would come to enjoy the status of a self-evident truth." Ernesto Galarza regarded the 1848 Treaty of Guadalupe-Hidalgo, which ended the war between the United States and Mexico, as one that "left the toilers on one side of the border, the capital and the best land on the other." These authors document the ongoing importation and exploitation of immigrant workers in U.S. agribusiness continuing search for cheap, docile wage labor. The brief summary that follows relies on their works (McWilliams 1976, 1976; Daniel 1981; Galarza, 1964, 1977).

Native Americans were one of the earliest groups to be used as a source of farm labor: as early as 1850 they were exploited through discriminatory vagrancy laws which pushed homeless Native Americans to move wherever labor was needed. With the completion of the transcontinental railroad in 1869, another large pool of cheap labor, Chinese "coolies," became available. In 1870, they made up 10 percent of the farm labor supply; by 1880 they were one-third, and by 1884, one-half. As their numbers increased so did racial bigotry, resulting ultimately in the passage of the federal Chinese Exclusion Act in 1882.

Japanese workers began arriving in the late 1890s and played an important role in agriculture until about 1910, by which time their numbers increased from slightly over 2,000 to more than 72,000. They were skillful farmers as well as wage laborers, who organized for better wages and eventually leased and bought land. They also became the target of bitter racial hostility, which resulted in the passage of restrictive immigration laws in 1907. Then, in 1913, California passed an alien land law that discriminated against Japanese ownership.

California growers also began to import Filipino workers, both from the Philippines and from Hawaii, where there was a surplus of plantation workers. The first exodus of Filipino men, from 1906 to 1919, was by indentured workers from Hawaii sugar and pineapple plantations. In the mid-1920s, they began arriving in the United States at the rate of 4,000 a year. As their numbers increased again, so did racial intolerance. In the 1930s, antimiscegenation laws were amended to include Filipinos, and federal law made them aliens overnight (formerly they were nonalien, noncitizens). They were forbidden to marry women of another race, and restrictions on immigration forbade them to bring wives or family from the Philippines. They were also forbidden to own land or engage in commercial transactions. By 1940, some 30,000 Filipinos, almost all single men (Pinoys), had joined in the migrant stream in California.

With the spread of World War II to the Pacific, the Filipinos' status as nonaliens was restored by the immigration service, and the discriminatory California laws were repealed in 1944. Thousands of Filipinos served in the U.S. Armed Forces, as part of the Allies' offensive. Young Filipinos now rarely enter the farm labor force, and many who remain are single, elderly men called Manong (elder brother), who came before World War II.

The Great Depression brought a temporary expansion of white farmworkers. White, dust-bowl migrants began to arrive in California in 1935, and by 1938 approximately 350,000 "Okies and Arkies" had entered the state. John Steinbeck immortalized these migrant workers in his 1939 novel *The Grapes of Wrath*. World War II, however, siphoned off many of them into shipyards and defense plants, leaving farm labor once again to racial and ethnic minorities.

The importation of workers from Mexico began after the Japanese exclusion and steadily increased until, by 1930, there were 75,000 Mexican workers in the migrant stream. Their migration was erratic from 1900 to 1942 as they arrived to supplement the Japanese, Filipinos, and those white Americans from the dust-bowl. Beginning in 1942, the importation of farm laborers from Mexico was organized and regulated through contractual agreements between the U.S. and Mexican governments. Because of labor shortages created by World War II, growers were permitted to import Mexicans to pick crops and then send them back to Mexico after the harvest was complete. These workers, all men, were known as *braceros* (Spanish for "arms" or field hands). The purpose of the program was to cope profitably with war-time farm labor shortages. However, after the war, farm interests pressured Congress to make the program permanent.

In 1951, the U.S. Congress passed Public Law 78, giving the importation of Mexican nationals for the profit of private industry the sanction of federal law. The *braceros* became dominant in the agricultural economy of California, Texas, New Mexico, Arizona, and Arkansas, and played minor roles in some 20 other states. Between 1950 and 1960, more than 3.3 million contracted Mexican nationals were employed in the United States, holding nearly one of two seasonal migrant labor jobs. Approximately 350,000 *braceros* were working annually in 1963 when the law was repealed.

Galarza calls the efforts of agribusiness interests to repeal Public Law 78 "panic in paradise." He also cites the agribusiness giants' dire predictions: "It would be a tale of East-of-Eden shaking as from an earthquake, the publicity mills of the agricultural corporations foretelling disasters: entire crops being lost, the price of food doubling, banks closing, canneries going bankrupt, family farming ruined, and communism erupting in Mexico." The reality, however, was simply the increased institutionalization of illegal importation of unprotected migrant labor to be ruthlessly exploited and poisoned.

The Health Effects of Pesticide Exposure

Farmworkers who handle the concentrated technical formulations, that is—pesticide mixers, loaders, and applicators—face the greatest exposure to pesticides. Flaggers, workers who guide crop-duster aircraft from the ground, are also heavily exposed, as are workers who clean and maintain pesticide spray rigs. Irrigators can also have high exposure when they are sent into recently sprayed fields to clean out filters and move pipes and other equipment that may be heavily contaminated. Field workers are also exposed to pesticide residues on leaf surfaces, on the crop itself, in the soil, or in the duff (decaying plant and organic material that collects under vines, trees, etc.). The highest exposure is from grapes, citrus fruit, peaches, apples, and other tree fruits that grow with a lot of leaves, or from crops that are sprayed often and close to harvest such as strawberries and tomatoes. Farmworkers are also exposed to pesticides and fumigants by ground application (Akesson 1964; Matthews 1982; Goldman *et al.* 1987; Ratner and Eshel 1986).

Farmworker children are also at high risk of pesticide exposure whether or not they work in the fields alongside their parents. Frequently, young children, including infants and toddlers, are taken to the fields by their parents because childcare is not available. The fetus is exposed as well when pregnant women work in the fields; most of the pesticides these women are exposed to pass through their skin very readily and can cross the placenta to affect the developing child. Children who are able to stay at home or in daycare are also exposed to pesticide residues brought home on their parents' work clothes. Contaminated soil is also tracked into vehicles and brought into the home. Many farmworkers live in or near fields that are heavily and repeatedly sprayed throughout the year. Because of drift from air and ground application of pesticides, workers and their families are exposed even when they are not working.

Pesticides are readily absorbed through the skin, by breathing them in, and by ingestion. They are also rapidly absorbed through the eyes, which can be a significant route of exposure in the case of splashes and spills. However, the skin is the major route for field workers—*not* the lungs as commonly believed. Pesticides can persist on the skin for many months after exposure ceases (Kazen *et al.* 1974). Fumigants, which are in the form of a gas, are the major exception since they are readily absorbed by breathing them into the lungs. This accounts, in part, for their greater toxicity. However, the skin is a route of absorption for fumigants as well.

The health effects of pesticide exposure include both immediate, acute problems and longer-range, chronic conditions (Moses 1989a, 1989b). Acute effects range from rashes, chemical burns, and other skin problems to systemic poisoning, which can lead to nausea, vomiting, and even death. Chronic effects can include cancer, sterility, spontaneous abortion, stillbirth, birth defects, and a variety of neuropathological and neurobehavioral disorders.

Workers in agriculture face an average risk of skin disease four times higher than workers in other industries. Most pesticide-related skin problems are primary irritant, or contact, dermatitis. Pesticides also can be "sensitizers," that is, cause allergic dermatitis. Some workers can be permanently disabled because they cannot tolerate exposure even to minute amounts of pesticides. Sunlight can aggravate the dermatitis, adding to the disability, even leading to convulsions and comas.

Perhaps the most lethal of pesticides used in agriculture is parathion, a nerve-gas type of insecticide first marketed in the United States in 1947. It is responsible for more occupational deaths throughout the world than any other single pesticide. The EPA parathion reregistration document states:

> [P]arathion causes poisonings among all categories of workers who use or come into direct contact with the pesticide. The risk extends not only to mixer/loaders and applicators, but to field workers and bystanders as well. In addition, these poisonings occur under the most stringent protective conditions and during use when in accordance with label directions. Little or no margin of safety exists for parathion use...

California poisoning incident data clearly show that... poisonings have continued to occur in spite of California's stricter control measures and restrictions...and there has been no apparent decline in ground applicator poisoning incidents... The California data also indicate that workers are being poisoned despite the use of protective clothing and adherence to label directions (U.S. Environmental Protection Agency 1986).

Parathion breaks down into leaf surfaces to a very poisonous chemical called paraoxon. Paraoxon is readily absorbed through the skin. It and Phosdrin, another highly toxic nerve-gas type pesticide, are responsible for the largest percentage of pesticide poisonings of agriculture workers in California (State of California Department of Health Services 1988; O'Malley 1992a, 1992b). These two toxins hardly exhaust the list of harmful pesticides, however. Harmful pesticides include Omite, sulfur, Roundup, Captan Orthocide, methyl bromide, creosote, triadimefon (Bayleton), and Cryolite (State of California Department of Health Services 1988). Pesticides known to cause allergic contact dermatitis include alachlor, benomyl, Botran, Captafol Folpet, Dazomet, anilazine, Maneb, Mancozeb, Zineb, Thiram Naled, PCNB, Propachlor, plyrethrums, and pyrethroids (Adams 1990). Other pesticides which are highly toxic and can cause severe poisoning include paraquat, Dinoseb, and methyl bromide.

Less is known about the extent or magnitude of pesticide-related chronic health problems in farmworkers that result from low-level exposure over a period of months or years. Appropriate studies have not yet been done. Because the period of time between the exposure and the development of a chronic health effect (called clinical latency) can range from 10 to 20 years or even longer, it is much more difficult and time consuming to document chronic effects than acute ones. However some important studies of farmworkers and others exposed to pesticides have been completed.

Epidemiological studies of workers exposed to pesticides reveal increased risk of developing several types of cancer, including: non-Hodgkin lymphoma, leukemia, multiple myeloma, testicular cancer, liver cancer, stomach cancer, pancreatic cancer, lung cancer, and primary brain cancer. (Complete citations for these studies can be found in an annotated bibliography: Moses 1989b.) Several studies have also suggested an association between pesticide exposure and increased cancer risk in children. A study in Baltimore, Maryland, of children with primary brain cancer found the risk of developing brain cancer was more than double if they had experienced pesticide exposure in the home (Gold et al. 1979). A study in Los Angeles of children with acute lymphocytic leukemia found that the risk of developing leukemia was almost four times greater if their parents used pesticides in the home and over six times greater if pesticides were used in the lawn and garden (Lowengart et al. 1987). Several agricultural communities in California's San Joaquin Valley of California have also reported much higher cancer rates among children than would be expected based on national averages (State of California Department of Health Services 1988b).

Pesticide exposure has also been studied as a risk factor for birth defects in farmers, farmworkers, and others living in areas subject to heavy use of agricultural chemicals. While not all studies have found an increased risk, definite correlations have been found for facial clefts, spina bifida, anencephaly, neural tube defects, and other congenital malformations (Balarajan 1983; Brender and Suarez 1990; Sever et al. 1988; White et al. 1988; Roeleveld et al. 1990). Limb-reduction defects have been correlated with farm work and living in an agricultural area (Kricker et al. 1986; Schwartz and LoGerfo 1988; Schwartz et al. 1986).

Many chemical pesticides are embryotoxic and fetotoxic in laboratory animals. The reason more birth defects are not found in the children of pesticide-exposed farmworkers may be that pesticides cause early fetal death resulting in spontaneous abortions. In the few studies available in humans exposed to pesticides in agriculture, spontaneous abortion and stillbirth have been consistently found. Farmworkers in Washington state as well as agriculture and horticulture workers in Denmark and Finland incurred an increased risk of spontaneous abortion or stillbirths (Vaughan et al. 1984; Heidam 1984; Hemminki et al. 1980). One study found a substantially increased risk for second-trimester spontaneous abortion in those exposed to pesticides (McDonald 1988). In a large U.S. study of 6,386 stillbirths, self-reported pesticide exposure of either parent increased the risk of stillborn offspring (Savitz et al. 1989).

Two pesticides are known to cause sterility in male workers—the fumigants DBCP (dibromochloropropane) and EDB (ethylene dibromide). In 1977, several men working in a northern California chemical plant that manufactured and formulated DBCP noticed that they had not recently fathered children. Five were found to have either no sperm whatsoever (azoospermia) or an abnormally low sperm count—less than 20 million/dl (oligospermia). All had been exposed to DBCP (Whorton et al. 1977). Further study of other DBCP-exposed workers at the plant found that almost half had abnormal sperm counts: 13 percent were azoospermic, 16.8 percent were oligospermic, and 15.8 percent had lower than normal sperm counts (between 20 to 39 million/dl).

While the acute toxic effects of exposure to many pesticides are well characterized and documented (Namba et al. 1971; State of California Department of Health Services 1988a; Tafuri and Roberts 1987; Morgan 1989; Hayes and Laws 1990), very little is known about neuropathological and neurobehavioral delayed or chronic effects in humans. Several early reports, however, describe cases of mental illness or severe psychological disturbance in pesticide applicators. Behavioral symptoms such as anxiety, difficulties in concentration, memory deficits, and other more subtle effects have also been widely reported (Dille and Smith 1964; Brown 1971; Rodnitzky et al. 1975; Levin and Rodnitzky 1976; Duffy et al. 1979). One recent study focused on the neuropsychological status of 100 persons poisoned by organophosphate pesticides (mainly parathion) an average of nine years after exposure. Compared with nonpoisoned controls, the poisoned subjects showed significant deterioration in memory, the capacity for abstraction, and mood. Twice as many of them had physical scores consistent with cerebral damage or dysfunction, and personality scores showing greater distress and an inclination to complain of disability (Savage *et al.* 1988).

Increased prevalence of Parkinson's disease has also been reported in agricultural areas of Quebec where there is high pesticide use (Barbeau *et al.* 1987), as well as cases in pesticide applicators (Bocchetta *et al.* 1986; Sanchez-Ramos *et al.* 1987). Investigators cite herbicide exposure as a possible risk factor because MPP—a metabolite of a street drug MPTP (1-methyl-4-phenyl-1,2,3,6-tetrahydropyridine) known to cause Parkinson's disease in drug abusers—resembles Paraquat. Furthermore, severe neurotoxic and behavioral effects, including toxic psychosis, can result from direct poisoning or chronic exposure to methyl bromide. Such changes can occur either after acute overexposure or from low-level chronic exposure, and can be progressive and irreversible (Hine 1969; Greenberg 1971; Prockop and Smith 1986; Anger *et al.* 1986).

Law, Government, and Public Policy

The first major piece of pesticide legislation, the Federal Insecticide Fungicide and Rodenticide Act (FIFRA), was passed in 1947. It was essentially a labeling law administered by the U.S. Department of Agriculture (USDA). In 1970, administration of FIFRA was transferred to the newly formed Environmental Protection Agency (EPA) due to the rising criticism of the USDA, the federal agency most hostile toward farmworkers and most resistant to any changes in policy that would ameliorate their harsh working conditions. Racism and other problems in the department, the fourth largest government agency, are well documented in a recent investigative report (McGraw *et al.* 1991).

Significant amendments to FIFRA were added with the passage of the Federal Environmental Pesticide Control Act of 1972. For the first time, there were provisions in the law for protection of human health and the environment. Pesticide manufacturers (called registrants) were required to submit toxicology data to the EPA on the pesticide's potential to cause chronic health problems, including cancer, birth defects, reproductive problems (spontaneous abortion, sterility, stillbirth), damage to the nervous system, and mutagenicity and other effects on DNA and chromosomes. The registrants were required to provide evidence that the pesticide would neither injure consumers, crops, livestock, or wildlife, nor damage the total environment.

Pesticides previously registered by the USDA had to meet the new standards. The EPA began the process of reevaluating and reregistering pesticides that did not meet the new standards, which turned out to be *all* of the pesticides then on the market. Because many registrants did not comply with the law in a timely and cooperative fashion, Congress amended FIFRA in 1975, 1978, and most recently in 1988, so as to extend the reregistration deadline for meeting the "new" standards. By 1989 only two active pesticide ingredients had been reregistered according to the new standards. At the current level of activity, it will take the EPA until well into the 21st century to evaluate the safety of all the pesticides now in use.

The toxicity data that registrants submitted to the EPA in support of the reregistration of their products were found to have enormous deficiencies and inadequacies. For some pesticides the data were simply fraudulent. In one laboratory, Industrial Biotest (IBT) in Illinois, the registrants were sent to jail for falsifying the results of animal studies of pesticide toxicology (Begley *et al.* 1983). The missing or inadequate toxicity data, called "data gaps," and the weaknesses and deficiencies of pesticide policies have profound implications for the health and safety of farmworkers, consumers, and the environment. Such concerns have been the subject of many reports highly critical of the EPA's administration and enforcement of FIFRA (U.S. General Accounting Office 1980, 1986b, 1991a, 1991b). It would appear that the EPA's administration of FIFRA is not significantly better than the USDA's. The EPA functions more as a pesticide-industry collaborator than as a regulator and protector of human health and the environment.

Agribusiness interests have long resisted any changes in pesticide laws and any other legislation that would give farmworkers the same benefits and protections provided workers in other sectors of the economy. This intransigence has been encouraged by the USDA and abetted by the EPA. In addition, congressional oversight of pesticide law is under the control of the Senate and House Agricultural Committees, not Committees on Environment and Labor. The resulting regulatory gridlock thwarts efforts to change the laws in ways that would benefit farmworkers.

Pesticide-use decisions have always been based on their economic impact on the agricultural and agrichemical industries, with almost no consideration of the impact on human health and the environment. Cost-benefit analyses focus almost exclusively on the benefits of pesticides in growing crops, the financial costs of alternative pesticides, the economic losses from a decrease in yield, and similar considerations.

Regulators have thus ignored the costs: to farmworkers from pesticide poisoning, disability, loss of income, and increased risk of chronic health effects; to society from pesticide pollution and contamination of the air, water, soil, and food; to wildlife from the killing of fish, birds, bees, and other species; and to the planet generally from the widespread environmental and ecological damage that continues unchecked because of the failure to develop safer, healthier, and more sustainable methods of growing crops.

Agribusiness interests further distort the farm-labor debate by refusing to accept responsibility for the consequences of failing to pay farmworkers a living wage—abysmal housing, lack of health care, malnutrition, and abject poverty. They mislead the public into believing that migrant farmworker problems are unsolvable and inevitable. They then expect the government to provide housing, health care, food stamps, and other benefits for the poverty-stricken workers. These benefits, while necessary, must be seen for what they are—an entitlement to the agricultural industry, a public subsidy that allows the exploitation of farmworkers to continue.

The massive failure of public policy and the resulting discrimination against farmworkers have been well documented for years in comprehensive hearings before Congress (U.S. Congress 1960, 1970). These historic patterns of injustice continue to persist (U.S. General Accounting Office 1992a). This pattern is particularly noticeable in a variety of federal laws. For example, farmworkers are for the most part excluded from the National Labor Relations Act, the Fair Labor Standards Act, and the Occupational Safety and Health Act.

The 1935 National Labor Relations Act, which gave workers the right to join a union and bargain collectively, excluded farmworkers, specifically stating that the law "shall not include any individual employed as an agricultural laborer." Fifty-seven years later they are still excluded. The 1938 Fair Labor Standards Act, which governs the minimum-wage and child-labor regulations, also excluded farm labor. Although some provisions have since been extended to cover farmworkers, the act still does not provide farmworkers the same protections as other workers. The minimum wage is lower for farmworkers, and they are excluded from the overtime provisions of the law: many work twelve to seventeen hours a day, often seven days a week, without any overtime pay.

Children are allowed to work in hazardous jobs at a younger age than is true in other industries, where the minimum age for hazardous work is eighteen years. In agriculture, sixteen-year-olds are permitted to operate hazardous farm machinery, such as tractors and harvesters; and if the farm is owned or operated by their parents, children of *any* age can do hazardous work. The minimum age at which children can work in nonhazardous jobs in other industries ranges from fourteen to sixteen. In agriculture, children younger than fourteen may work, and outside of school hours, twelve-year-olds can work with parental consent. A child of *any* age can work on the family farm.

The 1970 Occupational Safety and Health Act (OSHA), which governs standards of health and safety in the workplace, also excluded farmworkers. As of 1987, the Hazard Communication Standard, the Right-to-Know provisions of OSHA, were supposed to cover farmworkers. But OSHA decided that the EPA has prior jurisdiction and, because of a preemption clause in the act, will not enforce the standard for farmworkers. A small victory was won in 1988 when the OSHA field sanitation standard—which mandates that toilets, hand-washing facilities, and clean drinking water be provided by employers with more than ten employees—was expanded to include agricultural employers.

The failure of public policy is evident in state laws as well. One of the most important state laws that excludes farmworkers or denies them equal protection is Workers' Compensation Insurance. They are specifically excluded from coverage in 24 states; they are effectively excluded from six others since coverage depends on voluntary choice by the employer. Twelve states partially cover farmworkers. This usually means that a only very small number of year-round employees are covered. In only eight states are farmworkers fully covered.

In some states the law requires the farmworker to remain with the same employer for a specified amount of time in order to qualify for benefits. This period generally exceeds the length of the harvest season for the crops that migrant workers pick. Since they often work for more than one employer, and for very short periods of time, they are effectively denied coverage. Another state law that either excludes farmworkers outright or denies them effective coverage is the one governing unemployment insurance. Such laws make it so difficult to apply for or claim benefits that the worker often gives up in despair.

State housing and sanitation laws also discriminate against farmworkers, especially migrants. Many states do not require that running water and toilets be installed in migrants' housing units. Or flush toilets may not be required; and pit privies (latrines) are common even in recently constructed camps. Waivers and exemptions from building codes governing construction materials, the size of units, sanitation facilities, and maximum occupancy by square footage all result in migrant housing that is far below housing-industry standards. Most stables have more square footage per house than do farmworker housing units for people.

Another area of discrimination is health care. Farmworkers not under union contract rarely receive health benefits from their employers. State eligibility requirements for Medicaid vary enormously, and coverage is not transferable from state to state. The lack of affordable and accessible health care increases the potential for pesticide-related health problems, since workers having no access to a doctor also usually have no financial or legal recourse for getting a suspected pesticide-related illness documented, diagnosed, and treated.

State laws that regulate the use of farm-labor contractors are among the most egregious examples of exploitation of farmworkers. Instead of hiring their workers directly, many farmer/owners hire a labor contractor, who in turn hires the work crews. State law considers these contractors the legal employer, thus shielding the farmer/owner from any responsibility for the workers and any liability for violations of law.

Farmworkers hired by contractors are completely at their mercy, and the system is rife with abuse. Unscrupulous and dishonest contractors arbitrarily lower agreed-on wages (take it or leave it); deduct housing and transportation costs from the workers' pay, leaving them with very little money at the end of the season; make deductions for disability, taxes, and social security and keep the money for themselves; fail to pay liability or workers' compensation insurance; abscond at the end of the season leaving the workers helpless and bereft of any legal protection. This type of trade in human labor is legal in no other sector of the U.S. economy.

Underreporting of Pesticide-Related Illnesses

The biggest failure of federal and state regulatory agencies concerned with pesticides and farmworkers is in documenting the extent and nature of potential and actual pesticide-related illness and incidents.

No reliable data exist on the extent of pesticide-related illness among U.S. farmworkers. The wide range of EPA estimates—20,000 to 300,000 acute poisonings annually—attests to the need for a national reporting system. Efforts to mandate such a system have repeatedly failed because of the weak federal pesticide law (FIFRA), the timidity of the EPA, and the hostility of agricultural and agrichemical interests.

Most of the information on pesticide poisoning of U.S. farmworkers comes from California. That state's pesticide-illness reporting system, often touted as the best in the country, merits this reputation only because it is the best in a dismal field. While the California system has good points, its deficiencies and inadequacies should also be examined in detail since it is so often looked to as a model and its data are heavily relied on by the EPA.

California counties each have an agricultural commissioner responsible for an initial field investigation and a report of any suspected pesticide incident or illness. However, the commissioner's staff is not trained in public health, occupational health and safety, or toxicology. Yet, they often make decisions that require expertise in these fields. Their reports, in conjunction with the doctor's medical report for the Workers' Compensation board, determine whether or not an illness is considered pesticide-related, and should be listed in the annual pesticide-illness report. The cases that are rejected are classified as unrelated to pesticides, unlikely to be related, or unclassifiable, that is, inadequately investigated to determine the relationship to pesticide exposure.

An investigation by California Rural Legal Assistance (CRLA) revealed that between 1982 and 1988, 58 percent of medical reports of possible fieldworker pesticide illness were discounted by the California Department of Food and Agriculture (CDFA)—25 percent as unrelated, 13 percent as unlikely to be related, and 20 percent as unclassifiable. CRLA concluded that the high number of fieldworker cases reported by physicians but discounted as unlikely or unclassifiable by CDFA may be a result in part of poor investigations by county agricultural commissioners (Lightstone 1990). In 21 percent of the investigations conducted by the county agricultural commissioner's office that were examined by CRLA, either the name of the pesticide, the date of application, or both were missing. Yet, the CDFA rated 75 percent of these investigations as "adequate."

The CRLA investigation also found that law-enforcement actions remain weak. After a poisoning episode in 1985, the commissioners were given the authority to fine violators of pesticide laws. But they have rarely exercised this new authority. The great majority of violations of pesticide laws do not result in fines or sanctions. Between 1988 and 1989 some 5,766 warnings and notices of violations were issued, but only 8 percent of the agricultural and 3 percent of the nonagricultural violations resulted in fines. In the rural county of Kern, which leads the state in reported pesticide illnesses, only 4 percent of the violations resulted in a fine. But in the urban county of Alameda, 25 percent of the violations resulted in a fine (Lightstone 1990).

The ticket for entry into the California reporting system as a pesticide-related illness is a Workers' Compensation medical report (called the Doctor's First Report of Work Injury). The worker must see a doctor, the doctor must recognize the illness as pesticide-related and file a Workers' Compensation claim stating his or her diagnosis, and the California Department of Food and Agriculture must agree that the illness is related to pesticides.

Since many physicians fail to recognize pesticide poisoning or even to consider such a diagnosis, a large potential exists for underreporting. Furthermore, in mild and moderate poisoning, the signs and symptoms are nonspecific and easily confused with those of common illnesses such as gastroenteritis, upper respiratory disease, and other flu-like illness.

The problem of detection is actually worse, however. Workers ill from pesticide exposure may never see a doctor. There are strong disincentives to report illness for both the employer and the worker: the employer does not want to disrupt the harvesting of a perishable crop or pay increased Workers' Compensation insurance premiums, while many workers justifiably fear the loss of their jobs if they complain or ask to see a doctor. Because they must maximize income, they cannot afford to take time off from work or to pay for medical care. Since a farmworker family usually has only one vehicle and the whole family works, taking one person for medical care may mean that no one in the family earns any money that day. Furthermore, many workers are unaware of their rights under the law and so may not report the illness or may not realize they can see a doctor at their employer's expense (Kahn 1976; Wasserstrom and Wiles 1985). Undocumented workers are especially vulnerable because many do not know they are covered by the law and are very fearful of contact with authorities.

Another factor that contributes to the underreporting of pesticide-related illness is the large number of workers who return to Mexico for diagnosis and treatment if they become ill. No information on the extent or nature of these illnesses and on their relationship to pesticide exposure has been compiled.

All of these problems contribute to underreporting in the state with the *best* reporting system. And this is only for acute, observable, immediate illness. No attempt has been made in any state to document or monitor chronic health effects from pesticide exposure. And no other state's reporting system comes even close in quality to California's. Texas, Florida, Oregon, and Washington all have reporting systems that are rudimentary and/or poorly utilized. Therefore, farmworkers are caught in a no-win situation. Although no comprehensive and reliable pesticide-illness reporting systems exist anywhere in the country, the low number of *reported* illnesses is used to substantiate the claim that the country has no serious pesticide problem.

Farmworker Unions and Pesticides

The history of the unionization of U.S. farmworkers was one of bloodshed and failure until the mass nonviolent direct-action methods of Cesar Chavez and the United Farm Workers (UFW) brought success in the 1965 strike against California table-grape growers. In 1970, the growers signed collective bargaining agreements with the United Farm Workers union (UFW), an achievement in large part attributable to the support of the general public for a nationwide boycott against California table grapes (Matthiessen 1969; London and Anderson 1970; Taylor 1973, 1975; Levy 1975).

Because toxic-pesticide use has always been a major concern of Chavez, the union's first contracts with Delano area table-grape growers contained strong pesticide protections for farmworkers, including a prohibition on the use of DDT, Aldrin, Dieldrin, and parathion on union ranches. Baldemar Velasquez, the founder and president of the Farm Labor Organizing Committee (FLOC), based in Toledo, Ohio, has also made protection from pesticides a key platform in the committee's negotiations with pickle and tomato companies in northwest Ohio. The EPA lagged behind the UFW and FLOC, waiting until 1972 to ban all agricultural use of DDT and until 1974 to ban Aldrin and Dieldrin. But it still took no action against the highly toxic parathion.

In 1985, Chavez again called for a ban on parathion and four other pesticides used in grape production—Phosdrin, Dinoseb, Captan, and methyl bromide. Fifteen months later, the EPA suspended the registration of Dinoseb and, in 1988, banned it. The EPA also restricted some agricultural uses of Captan in 1988, but again failed to take any action against parathion. It is, however, considering restrictions on the use of methyl bromide due to its ozone depleting properties. After the parathion-related death of a farmworker in January 1990 recounted earlier, Chavez once again called for a total ban on the highly toxic pesticide. The CDFA characterized Chavez's request as "an overreaction to an emotional situation" (State of California Department of Food and Agriculture 1990). In 1992, the EPA took limited action against parathion, canceling authorization for 50 percent of its registered uses.

Farmworker unions in general favor 1) replacing of pesticides that pose grave threats to the health of workers with less toxic alternatives and 2) adopting more ecologically and environmentally sound methods of growing crops. The unions continue to play a key role in raising public awareness that the issue of pesticide-related health problems is vital to consumers and the environment, as well as to farmworkers.

Needed Action Strategies

A careful analysis of these problems suggests some very specific remedies. Here are some of the basic changes that would result in better protection for farmworkers, consumers, and the environment against the hazards of toxic pesticides:

- Laws should be enacted requiring that specific pesticide-use information be given immediately upon request to a farmworker, a farmworker's representative, a treating physician or other health-care worker, or anyone else needing the information because of a suspected or confirmed pesticide-related health problem.
- Mandatory reporting of all agricultural pesticide use should include the following: the specific pesticide used; the name of the owner/user; the commodity or crop involved; and the amount, method, and date of application. These reports should be maintained in the county and be readily and inexpensively available to workers and the general public upon request. Statistical summaries of the reports should be compiled promptly on an annual basis by crop/commodity and by pesticide, and they should be readily and inexpensively available to the general public upon request. These mandated reports should be retained for a minimum of 30 years and be readily available to governmental and nongovernmental researchers. These reports will be invaluable in providing data not now available for epidemiological studies of the human health effects of pesticides.
- The states should require mandatory reporting of all pesticide-related occupational incidents and illness to county or state health authorities. The data should also be reported to the CDC for use in compiling annual national summaries of occupational pesticide illness and incidents.
- In suspected cases of pesticide poisoning but where there is insufficient information to determine causation, the farmworker, not the pesticide, should get the benefit of the doubt.

- Posting should be required in all fields in which are used Toxicity Category I pesticides or those considered by the EPA to be probable human carcinogens, no matter what the length of the reentry interval.
- All pesticide regulations concerning the health and safety of farmworkers should be transferred from the USDA to more appropriate agencies.
- The authority over FIFRA should be transferred from the congressional committees on agriculture to the appropriate committees dealing with worker and environmental health and safety.
- Farmworkers should no longer be denied the equal protection of federal laws including OSHA, the Fair Labor Standards Act, and the National Labor Relations Act. These workers should be covered in the same manner as any others without restrictions, waivers, or exemptions.
- Finally, pesticide labels should include the name of all ingredients, both active and inert.

Conclusion

Agricultural and agrichemical interests, with the encouragement and support of the USDA, continue to block any changes in pesticide policy that would genuinely protect farmworkers. When confronted, they predict disaster, famine, the loss of farming as a way of life, skyrocketing food prices, and severe food shortages. The relentlessness of their opposition and their unremitting hostility toward the needs of farmworkers for protection thrive on the cowardliness and ineptness of the EPA.

Thirty years after the powerful indictment of pesticides by Rachel Carson, their use in the United States has actually increased, and the USDA remains the most conspicuous obstacle to changing toxic farming practices. Failures in public policy and leadership continue to undermine the many efforts of supporters and advocates of environmental justice, including progressive legislators, to decrease the burden of toxic pesticides that is borne so disproportionately by farmworkers and their children.

CHAPTER 11

Global Threats to People of Color

Dana Alston and Nicole Brown

Throughout the history of development, colonial powers and transnational corporations alike have exploited natural resources for their own profit and power with little regard for the social, political, and environmental impacts on local groups. While long overdue, mainstream environmental and conservation organizations have recently started to identify the global links among social, economic, and environmental problems. Slogans like "We are all in this together," "the circle of poison," and "everyone's backyard" are used with increasing frequency in their conversations.

Yet, this rhetoric does not quite get at the problem. It often seems to suggest the problems of environmental degradation are shared equally by all people. If we examine environmental issues internationally, the same domestic pattern of disproportionate exposure to environmental hazards and degradation exists worldwide among those who are nonwhite, poor, less educated, and politically less powerful. This international linkage between poverty, race, and environmental degradation can be even more clearly defined when exploring specific global issues such as the environmental impact of war, underground nuclear testing, and the exportation of hazardous industries and waste. The extractive nature of modernization and industrialization also contributes to the accelerated degradation of the environment around the world. Let's look at each of these problems in turn.

Ecological Impact of War

The war in the Persian Gulf demonstrated once again how international events are affected by domestic issues and vice versa. To find lasting solutions to the problem of environmental degradation at home, global issues must be addressed in many places simultaneously.

One reason for this is that ecological deterioration and warfare are inextricably linked. As warfare occurs, natural resources are destroyed and thus become more scarce. As this happens, competition for them becomes increasingly intense and sometimes even violent. Since World War II, all major conflicts in the world have been played out in developing countries. The roots of many of these conflicts are both historical and contemporary. They can be found in the colonial creation of artificial nation states and political boundaries in Africa, Asia, Latin America, and the Middle East. They can also be found in the politics and rivalries of the Cold War era, during which the United States and the Soviet Union fought a series of proxy wars in the Third World. Finally, they can be found in the exploitative economic policies promoted by countries of the North, as they attempt to retain control over, and access to, valuable natural resources in the South.

The word "ecocide" was coined after the war in Vietnam to describe the environmental devastation that took place in that country between 1968 and 1975 at the hands of the U.S. government. Vast areas of tropical forests, mangroves, and farmlands, as well as thousands of people, fell victim to intensive bombing and the use of chemical weapons and defoliants. Indeed, ecologists have shown that much of the damage caused by the war is irreversible. A document published by the Political Ecology Group reports that the thirteen million tons of bombs dropped on Vietnam pockmarked the land with 25 million craters and displaced three billion cubic meters of soil, causing water shortages and disease (Karliner *et al.* 1991). Undetonated bombs and shrapnel continue to maim and injure people and the land. Hundreds of thousands of Vietnamese suffer from cancer and other diseases; and thousands of children, both Vietnamese and American, are still being born with birth defects as a result of chemical poisoning.

When the oil fields in Kuwait began to burn in 1991, the world focused its attention once again on the environmental impact of war—this time in the Persian Gulf. The full extent of the ecocide in the Gulf is still unknown. What is known, however, is that the damage caused by the world's largest oil spill, vast burning oil fields, and millions of tons of explosives dropped on the area will adversely affect the ecosystems and economies of the entire Gulf region for decades to come.

One of the most ecologically deteriorated countries in the Americas is El Salvador, where civil war raged between 1980 and 1992. For twelve years, the Salvadoran army aggressively pursued intensive bombing and scorched-earth policies, patterned after those used by the United States in Vietnam. The objective was to destroy the physical environment that provided cover for the popular guerrilla forces. By 1989, the Salvadoran air force had dropped more than 3,000 tons of U.S.-made bombs on the countryside (Hall and Faber 1989; Faber 1989).

As a result of these policies, important wilderness areas and forests have been reduced to secondary-growth scrub, farmlands have been destroyed, virtual wastelands have been created, and the landscape remains scarred with bomb craters. According to Salvadoran environmentalists, bombing in the Chalatenango mountains destroyed at least 12,000 acres of valuable pines (Hall and Faber 1989; Faber 1989). This deforestation has led to soil erosion and will eventually affect the climate.

In Guatemala, the army's violent counterinsurgency campaign of the past few decades has resulted in the death or displacement of thousands of people and the devastation of the country's environment. As in El Salvador, the government army of Guatemala has been pursuing scorched-earth policies. For example, in the late 1980s, the government, with assistance from the U.S. Drug Enforcement Administration (DEA), launched a defoliation campaign under the guise of the "war on drugs."

The northwest highlands region—identified by the Guatemalan army as a "conflict zone"—was targeted supposedly for the eradication of marijuana and opium poppies. The intensive use of highly toxic defoliants such as glyphosate and paraquat has resulted in extensive ecological damage, as well as the poisoning of people and animals. As a direct result of the defoliation campaign, by mid-June 1987, "14 people had died and hundreds were poisoned after drinking contaminated water. People experienced nausea, skin irritation, vomiting, respiratory problems and diarrhea. Hundreds of cattle also died after drinking contaminated water" (Rossdeutcher 1987).

At the same time, the Guatemalan government has been actively encouraging colonization of the forests as an answer to social pressures for land reform. The country has the most inequitable system of land distribution in the Americas: 2 percent of the population owns 80 percent of the farmland (Dewart & Eckersley 1989). As part of their counterinsurgency strategy, however, the government army has designated much of the land colonized by peasants as "counterinsurgency zones."

Ranchers and military officers have been allowed to expropriate land in the name of national security and thereby expand their pastures and landholdings. Hence, the 1970s map of potential cattle-grazing areas is almost identical to the military map of counterinsurgency zones in the 1980s (Dewart and Eckersley 1989). The military campaign has thus helped the army and the Guatemalan elite to consolidate control over mineral-rich areas and the most arable lands.

In addition to the direct environmental impact of war, there are indirect consequences as well. Refugees and displaced persons put additional stress on the environment as they venture further into forests in search of cover or overpopulate preexisting settlements. For instance, after the U.S. invasion and bombing of Panama City in December 1989, some 30,000 people fled the capital to the nearby forests, where they cut down trees to build homes and plant crops. Certainly, deforestation due to colonization of the forests has been occurring in Panama for decades. However, as Stanley Heckadon-Moreno, former director of the Institute of Renewable Natural Resources, pointed out in a 1990 interview in the *Washington Post,* in the immediate aftermath of the invasion the rates of colonization and deforestation increased markedly.

The survival of the Panamanian tropical forest is crucial for the continued operation of the Panama Canal. The rainforests produce the water necessary for that operation. Yet, the felling of trees along the canal's watershed causes not only a drop in the canal's water level due to decreasing precipitation and lower groundwater tables, but also the erosion of exposed soils. This leads to the accumulation of silt, which threatens the canal and its reservoirs. It is estimated that "at current rates of siltation, the canal's cargo limits, revenue, and clientele will be reduced drastically by the year 2000" (Voelker 1988).

The ecological impact of warfare cannot be considered in a vacuum. War not only worsens the ecological crisis, but may increase the very poverty and inequity that may have led to the conflict. By themselves, cease-fire agreements and peace treaties are not lasting solutions to war. The social and economic structures that create the conditions for war and revolution must be replaced by a more equitable and just distribution of power, wealth, and resources. This equity must be achieved both between and within nations.

Trade, economic assistance, and military policies that reinforce inequities and promote underdevelopment in the name of multinational corporate interests must also be dismantled and replaced by more fair and just policies and practices. Military responses to economic and social problems—whether direct, as in the case of the United States in Vietnam, or indirect, as in El Salvador (75 percent of U.S. aid to El Salvador supported the war effort)—are not sustainable solutions. They do not address the underlying problems. Instead, they often exacerbate them.

Underground Nuclear Testing

Underground nuclear testing has long been a worrisome problem for Native Americans. While the testing has not fouled the land in immediately obvious ways, it has threatened the cultural survival of the people. As Western Shoshone Pauline Estevez told us about the events of January 27, 1951:

On that day we saw a flash of lightening. Then a dull clap of thunder followed and the earth beneath our feet trembled. We had no idea of what was going on; and the next day our mother took us to the desert to pray and to try to understand what we had seen and felt. But there was no answer, and we felt sad and empty when we got back home. It was much later when we heard that we had experienced the first atomic bomb test on the Nevada Test Site—right here on our land.

The militarism of the post-World War II era has promoted and encouraged the development and use of nuclear weapons and technology. That development—from the mining of uranium to the manufacture and testing of weapons—has had, and will continue to have, far-reaching and deleterious public health and environmental effects. Moreover, the shroud of secrecy around testing makes it difficult to assess its present and future impact. What is clear, however, is that testing has endangered the lives and livelihoods of thousands of indigenous peoples around the world. From the Aborigines in Australia to the Western Shoshone Indians in Nevada, from the inhabitants of the Central Asian Republic of Kazakhstan to the natives of the French Pacific, indigenous peoples throughout the world have witnessed the destruction of their lands by nuclear testing.

According to the Center for Defense Information (1991), since 1945 when the United States exploded the first atomic bomb at Alamogordo, New Mexico, six nations—the United States, the Soviet Union, Great Britain, France, China, and India—have detonated a combined total of at least 1,910 nuclear explosives at some 35 sites around the world. That's an average of one explosion every nine days. The United States has exploded nuclear weapons in Alaska, Colorado, Mississippi, New Mexico, and Nevada, as well as in Japan, the Marshall Islands, Christmas Island, the Johnson Atoll, and over the southern Atlantic Ocean. Since 1974, however, all U.S. nuclear tests have taken place on Western Shoshone lands at the Nevada Test Site. The Soviet Union exploded weapons in Semipalatinsk, Kazakhstan, and on the island of Novaya Zemlya. China tested its weapons at Lop Nur in Sinkiang province, home of the Uighur people, a national minority. Since 1962, Great Britain has been testing at the Nevada Test Site, having abandoned its former sites on aboriginal land in Australia and on southern Pacific islands. The French first exploded nuclear weapons in Algeria but, since 1966, have used the southern Pacific atolls of Mururoa and Fangataufa. India's single nuclear explosion took place in the Rajasthan desert near the Pakistani border.

Despite treaties and accords calling for the limitation of nuclear testing and committing the signatories to work toward its discontinuance, the world still awaits a treaty to ban nuclear testing. Both categories of nuclear tests, atmospheric and underground, spread radiation. The 1963 Partial Test Ban Treaty prohibited all but underground testing. This did not, however, eliminate the risk to the environment, for radiation has continued to leak into the atmosphere and groundwater. Moreover, serious geologic effects could result from the shock waves triggered by a nuclear explosion.

Many public health problems are associated with nuclear testing and radiation. The victims are not only test-site workers and military personnel directly involved. Civilians also may be exposed to airborne and waterborne contamination. While high levels of radiation result in severe injury and death in a short time, lower levels over a prolonged period also have damaging effects, of which the best known is cancer. For example, in southern Utah, communities downwind from the Nevada Test Site, suffer from rates of thyroid and bone cancers eight to twelve times higher, respectively, than the national average (Center for Defense Information 1991).

Because numerous South Pacific islands and the seas around them have been used for underground nuclear test sites, island women have been giving birth to deformed and critically ill children. Other women have developed cancer and cannot conceive at all. In some parts of the region, unusually high rates of poisoning from the ciguatera fish—the most common type of fish poisoning—may be connected with the ongoing U.S nuclear testing in the region. Whole islands have been destroyed. As a result, the inhabitants of these islands have become sick, have been killed, or have been displaced.

With the end of the Cold War and the disintegration of the Soviet Union, the geopolitical climate that led to the rapid development and buildup of nuclear arms no longer exists. Despite this, nuclear weapons and technology remain, and testing continues. Moreover, recent nuclear disarmament proposals raise grave questions about the monetary cost and the public health and environmental impacts of disposal. In particular, what will be the consequences of disposal for the minority, rural, and disenfranchised groups that bore the brunt of nuclear testing in the first place.

The International Waste Trade

With the increasing restrictions on toxic waste disposal in the United States and Western Europe, as well as public opposition to it, waste management companies and illegal waste traders are seeking alternative dump sites overseas. They target the politically and economically less powerful nations of the world, who have benefited the least from industrialization. The president of Zimbabwe, Robert Mugabe, has stated that "it is not fair that the poorest nations should suffer the worst effects of a progress in which they do not share" (Mpanya 1990).

The governments of developing countries are often lured by the large sums of money offered by waste-trading firms and the prospect of additional employment and development opportunities within their borders. This is simply an extension of the pattern of targeted dumping on communities of color in the United States.

Increasingly, however, governments in Africa, Asia, and Latin America are resisting the dumpers and have labeled the practice "toxic terrorism" and "economic extortion." In 1988, the Organization of African Unity (OAU) issued a resolution that called the dumping of nuclear wastes in Africa "a crime against Africa and African people." Now, after a strong campaign by African countries to impose a strict ban on the practice, in addition to stiff fines and prison sentences for violators, South Africa is the only country on the continent that still accepts toxic wastes. Evidence exists that the so-called "homelands" have been used as dumping sites for wastes from the United States.

With Africa becoming less accessible to them, international waste traders are increasingly targeting Central and South America, as well as the Caribbean, for dumping. Over the past few years, they have learned the value of presenting their proposals as development plans that promise employment, electricity, and social and technological progress. Wastes exported from the United States to Latin America range widely: asbestos, incinerator ash, municipal wastes and sewage, and industrial chemical toxics. By recently adopting a ban on waste imports as part of its new constitution, Colombia joined a growing number of Caribbean and Latin American countries who have said "no" to the waste trade.

Many environmental activists who focus on international waste trade issues strongly believe that Asia and the Middle East will now become targets. Cyprus, Lebanon, Turkey, China, and the Philippines have already suffered contamination from traded wastes. On the other hand, Central America is currently suffering from extreme environmental problems of a different source. Karliner (1991) asserts that they can be traced to "decades of development policies that have favored production for export over production for local needs, and the intensive exploitation of natural resources over the sustainable use of these assets."

In many cases, agricultural development has led to ecological and social disasters. Forests, wildlife habitats, and peasant villages have been cleared to make way for large plantations and roads. Forced to farm unsuitable land, displaced peasants and small farmers contribute to deforestation and soil erosion by clearing steep hillsides and tropical forests. All this has occurred in the name of agricultural development. Central America provides a case study of how misguided agricultural and development assistance policies have contributed to the degradation of the environment in developing countries. For the past 40 years, the aim of the prevailing development model in Central America has been to diversify the region's economies and integrate them into the world market. Economic growth through agricultural exports has been the theme. The agro-export model promotes the production and export of cash crops. Since the 1950s, the region's agro-export sector has been steadily expanding with the support of the U.S. Agency for International Development (USAID) and multilateral lending institutions such as the World Bank and the Inter-American Development Bank (IDB).

Beginning in the 1950s, when the emphasis was on cotton production, the development banks gave assistance to the local oligarchy, which expanded agricultural production at the expense of the *campesinos* who inhabited the fertile, volcanic Pacific plain. Then, in the 1960s and 1970s, monies from the World Bank, the IDB, and USAID financed the rapidly expanding cattle industry, as well as coffee and banana plantations. More recently, with the breakdown of the traditional agro-export market—characterized by falling prices for beef, sugar, coffee, and cotton—USAID and multilateral lenders have focused on nontraditional crops such as melons, snow-peas, broccoli, and flowers (Karliner *et al.* 1989).

The negative environmental impact of the agro-export model of development has been both direct and indirect. Direct degradation results from pesticide pollution and contamination, chemical depletion of soil nutrients, and deforestation; while indirect degradation follows from the displacement of large segments of the population to marginal lands where they settle and attempt to farm. This contributes to deforestation, soil depletion and erosion, and diminished water tables (Karliner *et al.* 1989).

These two categories of environmental destruction are interrelated. With the advent of large-scale cotton production in the 1950s, for example, thousands of *campesinos* were forced off their land in the Pacific lowlands to make way for the cotton plantations. Subsequently, they were encouraged to clear nearby forests for farming. After about two years, they were once again pushed out by the expanding cotton plantations. As a result, by the late 1960s, the forests of the Central American Pacific plain had been turned into large expanses of cotton (Karliner *et al.* 1989).

The intensive use of pesticides and chemical fertilizers leads to chemical dependency of the land. Since fertilizers permit year-round cultivation, the soil is not allowed to lie fallow and replenish itself. Moreover, the continuous harvesting of a single crop drains soil of its nutrients and reduces its regenerative capacities, thereby contributing to the dependency of the land on chemical fertilizers.

Pesticides kill parasites as well as their natural predators; and over time, many of the parasites build up a resistance to the chemicals. As a result, the continued and increasing use of pesticides becomes necessary. Furthermore, as farmers continue to plant traditional staples such as corn alongside pesticide-protected products for export, food crops that traditionally grew without chemical inputs become chemically dependent.

The nearly indiscriminate use of pesticides, which has characterized the agro-export industry in the region since the introduction of cotton cultivation in the 1950s, has serious deleterious effects on the land and the health of people and animals. Many of the chemicals, such as paraquat and DDT, are banned in the United States by the Food and Drug Administration. In fact, "an estimated 75 percent of the pesticides applied in Central America are either banned, restricted or unregistered in the U.S." (Faber et al. 1986).

Agrochemicals contaminate not only soil and produce, but also, as they flow into rivers and oceans, water supplies and fisheries. Farmer families who use pesticides also risk their health. The World Health Organization documented the highest concentration of carcinogenic DDT ever detected in human beings in the breast milk of mothers on the southern coast of Guatemala (Allamilla 1991).

Another negative consequence of the agro-export industry has been the unquantifiable loss of genetic material. This has also led to a loss of indigenous knowledge associated with the biodiversity of their region. In Guatemala, for example: "Indigenous farmers used to grow up to 130 types of maize depending on the exact soil quality of their land. Now they use hybrid seeds imported from the United States. The intercropping method of using the symbiotic qualities of maize, beans, and squash is rapidly disappearing" (Roth-Arriaza 1991).

The agro-export development model has helped to reinforce the social, political, and economic inequalities that characterize the nations of Central America. It has led to human and financial resources being diverted from the production of food for domestic consumption to the cultivation of crops for export. The new patterns of land tenure have pushed the majority of the population onto land unsuitable for farming and have increased destruction of the region's forests. The model has benefited large-scale commercial producers to the detriment of small subsistence farmers.

Attempts to incorporate small farmers into agro-exporting have proved unsustainable and almost always entrapped small farmers in a vicious cycle of indebtedness and dependency. Pesticide runoff, denuded hillsides, deforested lands, depleted soils, and contaminated rivers and seas—this is the environmental legacy of agricultural development in Central America gone awry.

Northern NGOs and the South

Over the last decade, tensions have been growing between developing countries and nongovernmental organizations (NGOs) of the North focused on environmental issues and wilderness conservation. Many Southern NGOs feel that those in the North are dictating economic and cultural policies to them and imposing their political views. Some have labeled this behavior "paternalistic." Others see it as an extension of the colonial attitudes of the past. Among the issues in contention are: diversifying the decisionmaking process for agenda and priority setting; achieving self-determination of indigenous peoples and national sovereignty; and redistributing financial resources.

Raising issues similar to those raised by communities of color in the United States, Southern NGOs have challenged the international conservation and environmental movements to build partnerships based on mutual respect, shared interests, and equity. They contend that a relationship with integrity is one in which the voices of developing countries are heard, their needs addressed adequately, and their cultures respected. If Northern NGOs are unwilling or unable to accept this kind of partnership, many Southern activists suggest that they should stay home. Hira Jhamtani of the People's Network for Forest Conservation in Indonesia addressed Northern NGOs this way: "Educate your own public. The time has come for you to put emphasis on action-oriented public education in the North rather than to continue supporting projects that maintain the status quo of oppression [in the South]" (Jhamtani 1991).

Debt-for-Nature Swaps

The first debt-for-nature swap took place in July 1987, when Conservation International (CI) raised money to buy $650,000 of Bolivian debt. Because the country was having difficulties repaying its loans, the original lending institution, Citibank, sold the debt to CI for about 15 cents to the dollar. In return, Bolivia's president agreed to set aside the value of the original debt for conservation purposes—to extend protection to 3.7 million acres of tropical forest and establish a fund for its management (Adam 1990).

To date, debt-for-nature swaps have been arranged or explored in a host of countries, including Ecuador, Argentina, the Philippines, Zambia, Poland, the Dominican Republic, Jamaica, Guatemala, Venezuela, Honduras, and Brazil. These swaps were promoted by the Nature Conservancy, Conservation International, World Wide Fund for Nature (WWF), and other conservation NGOs. Financial support has come from private and public financial institutions, the United Nations, and the governments of Norway, Sweden, and the United States. Kathryn Fuller, president of the U.S. branch of the WWF, says, "These arrangements have allowed conservationists to develop unprecedented relations with the international financial community. Now that these relations are in place, other novel ways of supporting conservation efforts may emerge" (Adam 1990).

Despite the potential benefits from protecting critical parts of the biosphere, the debt-for-nature strategy has undermined the efforts of indigenous peoples to achieve self-determination and ownership of the lands where they have lived for centuries. The Coordinating Body for Indigenous People's Organizations of the Amazon Basin (COICA)—representing 1.2 million Indian people in Peru, Bolivia, Ecuador, Colombia, and Brazil—addressed these issues in an open letter to the environmental and conservation community in 1990:

> We are concerned about the debt-for-nature swaps that put your organizations in a position of negotiating with our governments the future of our homelands. We know of specific examples of such swaps, which have shown brazen disregard for the rights of the indigenous inhabitants...
>
> We want to make it clear that we never delegated any power of representation to the environmentalist community nor to any individual or organization within the community.
>
> We propose joining hands with those members of the worldwide environmentalist community who recognize our historical role as caretakers of the Amazon Basin; support our efforts to reclaim and defend our traditional territories, and accept our organizations as legitimate and equal partners (COICA 1990).

COICA has come up with an alternative to the dept-for-nature deals: "debt-for-Indian-stewardship" swaps, where foreign debt would be traded for demarcation and protection of traditional territory. Indigenous peoples would play a leading role in arranging them and take responsibility for protecting and developing the preserved areas.

Although debt-for-nature swaps are growing in popularity among large conservation organizations in the United States, a growing number of Latin American organizations are expressing reservations. The Declaration of the Andes, which emerged from a meeting of 220 representatives of Latin American NGOs in 1991, called for suspension of all debt-for-nature swaps while national and regional policies on debt are elaborated. It also called for suspension of all debt-service payments and debt-for-nature negotiations until the principle of ecological debt is accepted and the amounts calculated.

During a September 1991 conference in Brazil organized by the Brazilian Institute for Economic and Social Analysis (IBASE), participants took a strong stand against debt-for-nature schemes. A statement summarizing the meeting declared that "such transactions are part of a more general strategy for converting debt, reaffirming the creditors' political and economic domination over the debtors within a development model which commercializes life in all its aspects" (IBASE 1991).

Biodiversity

The term "biodiversity" has often been used to describe the variety of biological life on the planet. However, according to the most recent working definition proposed by a consortium of international organizations, biodiversity comprises the vast global collection of genes, species, habitats, and ecosystems, as well as the cultural diversity that is its human expression. This broader definition is important because many Northern pharmaceutical and agricultural companies, as well as many conservation NGOs, have promoted various schemes to preserve biological diversity at the expense of cultural diversity. Perhaps the most controversial of these schemes involved the collection of plant materials for highly profitable biotechnology enterprises without any compensation to the source country.

An example of this general problem occurred in Madagascar, an island off the coast of southern Africa. According to a briefing document on biodiversity issued by the Panos Institute, three-quarters of the children of Madagascar who have had leukemia in recent years are alive thanks to the rosy periwinkle, the basis of two powerful anticancer drugs (vincristine and vinblastine). The people of Madagascar originally identified the medicinal properties of the plant, but earned nothing from the subsequent sales of the drugs. The Panos Institute (1992) documents that if Madagascar had received a reasonable share of the profits, rosy periwinkle would become the country's largest single source of income. This new revenue would also have provided a powerful incentive for environmental protection.

There has recently been an onslaught of Northern biologists eager to harvest the rich diversity of plants and study them for possible medicinal, industrial, or agricultural use. However, testing each individual plant species for its potential is time consuming. As Jon Tinker, president of the Panos Institute, so aptly put it, "If it takes 50 Amazonian peoples at least 10,000 years to identify 50 psychotropic [mind-affecting] plant-based drugs, how long would it take 50 transnational companies to rediscover them by checking through one million Amazonian plant species?" (Tinker 1991)

This logic has not escaped the eye of private industry. Of all the plant-based drugs in the modern medicine chest, three-quarters were discovered through ethnopharmacology, which draws on indigenous knowledge to help pinpoint useful plants (Panos Institute 1992). This has prompted Northern companies to send experts to the jungle to "harvest" native peoples' knowledge about the uses of various plants. Jason Clay (1990a, 1990b) of Cultural Survival calls this quest for indigenous knowledge "the last great resource rush."

In capitalist society and law, governments grant individuals, corporations, government agencies, and universities patents and copyrights to safeguard their knowledge and the products based on it. The question thus arises: What are the rights of indigenous peoples regarding the basic raw materials found on their ancestral lands and the knowledge that often unlocks their use? Organizations committed to indigenous self-determination have called for international agreements and laws to protect these rights.

In 1988, the International Society of Ethnobiology (ISE) also expressed concern by drawing up an eight-point plan based on the idea that "native peoples have been stewards of 99 percent of the world's genetic resources, and there is an inextricable link between cultural and biological diversity." At its second meeting, in China in 1990, the ISE resolved to work toward securing "the recognition of traditional and indigenous knowledge as inventive and intellectual, and, therefore, worthy of protection in all legal, ethical and professional frameworks" (Panos Institute 1992).

As they did in the debate over debt-for-nature swaps, indigenous people approach biodiversity as a question of land ownership, sovereignty rights, and cultural autonomy. Over the past two decades, numerous indigenous groups have formed organizations to protect these rights. The Kuna Indians of Panama organized the First Interamerican

Indigenous Congress on Natural Resources and the Environment. Some 70 groups from seventeen countries of the Western hemisphere were represented at the event. Other alliances have grown out of the work of the Mbuti of Zaire, the O'Odham of the Sonoran Desert in the United States and Mexico, the Pehuenche of Chile, the Mopawi of Honduras, and COICA of the Amazon Basin.

If Northern conservation organizations, universities, and industries continue to support the extraction of plant materials and the knowledge about their uses without compensation, such activities will continue to be seen by people everywhere as another form of cultural domination and an attack on the rights of indigenous people to sovereignty and self-determination.

The 1992 UNCED Meeting

In June 1992, the United Nations Commission on Environment and Development (UNCED) convened in Rio de Janeiro to consider the future of humanity as it struggles to balance development pressures against an increasingly imperiled global environment. Billed as the "Earth Summit," UNCED was called for in 1989 because of the interest by the international community in developing a "report card" on global progress in the area of the environment since the first Conference on the Environment in Stockholm in 1972. The UNCED process was expected to produce:

- several new treaties on climate change, global warming, biodiversity, forests, and biotechnology;
- a charter of rights (an Earth Charter);
- an agenda for the 21st century (Agenda 21); and
- a redefinition of the roles and responsibilities of various UN agencies.

As Northern governments and environmental organizations defined their narrow agendas, political positions, and priorities for UNCED, Southern NGOs became increasingly vocal about their concerns. The Conference of Non-Governmental Organizations in Consultative Status with the U.N. (CONGO) brought together organizations that collectively cover all regions of the world and all domains of human endeavor. Like communities of color in the United States, CONGO integrates environmental concerns into a broad agenda that emphasizes social and economic justice as well. These organizations deal with issues of poverty, peace, human rights, the status of women, health, education, and youth, among many others.

Dr. Sibusiso M. Bengu—a South African and CONGO's representative to the UNCED planning committee—expressed the concerns of many NGOs and other grassroots movements about the conference, which appeared to be focusing more and more on narrow conservation concerns to the neglect of the more challenging tension between environment protection and community development:

> NGOs involved in development are concerned that the West is using development as an excuse to discuss and bring in their environmental concerns at the expense of development issues. The UN conference must not be allowed to be hijacked by the Greens who do not care about underdevelopment, which has a claim on so many lives in the Third World (Bengu 1990).

Several initiatives and proposals from the South were offered to reduce the growing tensions between Southern and Northern NGOs prior to the Brazil meeting. One such initiative was the Proposal for NGO Interamerican Dialogue, which suggested cooperation among social movements, NGOs, and the indigenous peoples of the Americas. North American NGOs were asked to commit themselves to start campaigns, initiatives, and programs involving the South only after consultations with the largest possible number of Latin American and Caribbean social movements and NGOs. The proposal also recommended establishing a joint monitoring and solidarity-building system to avoid the destruction of the natural world and to prevent the imposition of measures that further promote poverty and powerlessness. Finally, the Latin American organizations outlined their current opposition to debt-for-nature swaps and the Enterprise for the Americas Initiative.

Despite this and other efforts toward relieving North-South tensions, fundamental disagreements continued to emerge. Among the issues in dispute were: 1) Who should pay the costs of global environmental programs? 2) How can North-South transfer of environmentally sound technologies be assured? 3) How can multinational control over natural resource exploitation be limited? 4) What is the role that population growth plays in environmental degradation? Poor nations say that the unbridled consumerism of the industrialized countries and a development model in which the only concern is economic growth are at the root of global environmental degradation. For their part, industrialized nations accuse developing countries of not making the environment a high priority and of not having a strong commitment to curbing population growth.

Conclusion

As we define and address the environmental issues that affect people of color globally, it is important to realize that they can be neither discussed nor dealt with effectively in isolation. Many of them are the outgrowth of the political, economic, and social imbalances inherent in the capitalist market system—imbalances which are manifested in policies and structures that work to the advantage of the Northern industrialized countries. Moreover, many of these same structures and policies are at the root of the inequities and injustices that face people of color in the United States today.

Rectifying this situation requires more than just political and economic will. It also requires the wholehearted, earnest commitment of the countries and institutions of the North to listen to, respect, and negotiate around the perspectives and recommendations of the South. A more complete and comprehensive analysis of the political and economic situation facing countries of the Southern hemisphere is needed. It should acknowledge the role that race and poverty play in the international system. The subsequent debate around these issues has to be led by voices from the South and should result in the development of alternative policies that eliminate the injustices and imbalances of the present system.

Chapter 12

Conclusion:
Environmentalism with Justice

Robert D. Bullard

This book documents the problem of environmental racism as well as the diverse environmental justice movement that has recently emerged in African-American, Hispanic, Native-American, and other minority communities to address it. Growing out of the work of scholars and activists at the First National People of Color Environmental Leadership Summit held in October 1991, this book speaks with both clarity and urgency. It offers the reader the chance to hear important voices of pain and resistance, voices from the grassroots.

The book thus stands in stark contrast to the report *Environmental Equity: Reducing Risk for All Communities,* published in February 1992 by the federal Environmental Protection Agency. That report, which took the EPA over eighteen months to complete, was written as a response to several scholars of color active in the environmental justice movement who wrote to the EPA's top administrator, William Reilly, asking that the agency finally address the disproportionately high environmental risks borne by people of color and low-income communities. Yet, despite more than eighteen months of study, the EPA failed to grasp the interplay of race and class biasing environmental decisionmaking. The weaknesses of the report are worth analyzing.

The EPA and Environmental Equity

The EPA's report is best seen as part of the EPA's "outreach strategy" to mount a public relations campaign to drive a wedge between grassroots environmental justice activists and mainstream civil rights and environmental groups rather than offer a substantive effort to address environmental problems that disproportionately harm people of color and low-income citizens. The agency's overall outreach plan was detailed in a confidential memorandum written by Lewis Crampton, an associate administrator of the EPA (see Weisskopf 1992, p. A15). Luckily, the memorandum was leaked to the press the same month as the EPA's equity report was officially released. The relevant points of Mr. Crampton's memorandum are as follows:

> Our goal is to make the agency's substantial investment in environmental equity and cultural diversity an unmistakable matter of record with mainstream groups before activists enlist them in a campaign that could add the agency to industry and local officials as a potential target. We propose a targeted, two-track strategy that concentrates our primary effort on a series of immediate steps to get our message to the mainstream groups—while continuing to give the more activist groups the attention they demand as part of a secondary effort.
>
> ...The goal of this strategy is to win the recognition the agency deserves for its environmental equity and cultural diversity programs before the minority fairness issue reaches the "flashpoint"—that stage in an emotionally charged public controversy when activist groups finally succeed in persuading the more influential mainstream groups (civil rights organizations, unions, churches) to take ill-advised actions. From what we've begun seeing in the news, this issue is reaching that point.
>
> ...[W]e should continue meeting with the activist groups driving the minority fairness issue. Because, like many activist movements, these groups need more recognition and visibility, they are not as receptive to a straightforward presentation of evidence. But we may be able to deflect some of their hostility from the agency by taking the initiative to grant them respect and the access they want and by finding some common ground on which we can agree. Talking with and listening to these groups is the second track of the strategy (Crampton 1991, pp. 2-3).

Contrary to the EPA's self-serving claim of "substantial investment in environmental equity and cultural diversity," their environmental equity report reveals itself as a public relations ploy to diffuse the issue of environmental racism. The EPA staff that produced the *Equity Report* did not produce one piece of original research or develop a single piece of new information. More importantly, the report appears to reflect a half-hearted and less-than-serious treatment of its own subject matter. The report contains, for instance, a very selective, biased, and superficial review of the literature on the nature and severity of environmental problems faced by low-income populations and communities of color in the United States. The systematic omission of important works that document the impact of discriminatory land-use planning, differential enforcement of regulations and laws, and inequitable facility siting is quite glaring, in fact.

The report only makes passing reference to a handful of studies that document the relationship between the sociodemographic characteristics of communities and the quality of their physical environment. Some of the books ignored by the EPA date back to the early 1970s; others are more recent but widely available. The report failed, for example, to cite Allen V. Kneese and Blair T. Bower, *Environmental Quality Analysis* (1972); D. K. Newman and D. Day, *The American Energy Consumer* (1975); Michael Greenberg and Richard Anderson, *Hazardous Waste Sites: The Credibility Gap* (1984); Louis Blumberg and Robert Gottlieb, *War on Waste* (1989); Robert D. Bullard, *Dumping in Dixie: Race, Class, and Environmental Quality* (1990); and Benjamin Goldman, *The Truth about Where You Live* (1991). The EPA's problem with these books, of course, is that they document the greater health and environmental risks faced by people of color, a contention that the EPA is trying to downplay. The report also omits most of the voluminous literature on environmental politics generally. A growing body of multidisciplinary environmental research (sociology, political science, economics, planning, law, ethics, engineering, natural resource management, human ecology, etc.) is beginning to focus on equity concerns. Increasingly, the claim of a "value-free" science, environmental policy, and application of technology is being challenged within these circles. Significantly, the EPA fails to cite more than a handful of the studies challenging the idea that waste facility siting is typically based on scientific, nonpolitical criteria. Instead, the report emphasizes the EPA's and other agencies' heavy reliance upon scientific risk-based decisionmaking when it comes to health and environmental problems.

Perhaps most absent from its analysis is any mention of the 1984 report *Political Difficulties Facing Waste-to-Energy Conversion Plant Siting*, written by Cerrell Associates, a private consulting firm, for government planners in California. Many environmental activists have called the Cerrell report a "smoking gun" of environmental injustice. The government-sponsored study confirmed what many people had suspected all along: Cerrell Associates had in fact advised the California Waste Management Board to place waste-to-energy facilities (incinerators) in areas least likely to express opposition—specifically older neighborhoods and those with low-income populations. (Cerrell Associates 1984).

Some important studies of environmental racism are mentioned in the report, but it is interesting to see how they are presented. While the *Equity Report* does cite the U.S. General Accounting Office study *Siting of Hazardous Waste Landfills and Their Correlation with Racial and Economic Status of Surrounding Communities,* it fails to mention that this study was only initiated after massive civil disobedience protests in predominantly African-American Warren County, and a special request by District of Columbia delegate Walter Fauntroy (see U.S. General Accounting Office 1983). It also fails to mention that the pattern of siting inequities uncovered by the GAO in 1983 has only worsened since then. Instead, the EPA report criticizes the *Toxic Wastes and Race* study published in 1987 by the United Church of Christ's Commission for Racial Justice, while, at the same time, offering no research of its own on the questions explored in the UCC-CRJ's study. (Even the Centers for Disease Control [CDC] and the Agency for Toxic Substances and Disease Registry [ATSDR] have backed several minority environmental-health initiatives along similar lines—including a health study and a national conference.)

Trying to find "some common ground" with its critics, the study does admit that lead poisoning is a real problem in communities of color. Citing the 1988 ATSDR study, *The Nature and Extent of Lead Poisoning in Children in the United States: A Report to Congress,* the EPA points out the glaring racial and class dimensions of the lead problem. Its report also concurs with the ATSDR study that there is "sufficient" scientific evidence available on lead and human health risks.

Tellingly though, the EPA report implies that lead poisoning is the only environmental hazard for which clear and unambiguous evidence exists of differential exposure due to race and class differences. At the same time, it does not explain why the EPA has done so little to protect those who are "most vulnerable" to lead poisoning. The agency has consistently delayed and dragged its feet on the problems posed by lead-contaminated paint, soil, and drinking water. Even being armed with sufficient facts and documented "proof" is not a strong enough incentive for the EPA to tackle the environmental and health problems involving mostly people of color. For millions of lead-exposed, inner-city children, the agency's delaying tactics are tantamount to a life sentence in lead-contaminated environments.

The report specifically fails to mention some of the EPA's most questionable decisions regarding lead abatement in communities of color. A case in point is the EPA's actions in West Dallas, Texas, a community whose residents still do not understand why the agency scrapped a 1983 voluntary cleanup plan proposed by the local lead smelter company. At least three government studies documented the threat from lead in the neighborhood. Yet, the EPA not only scrapped the industry-initiated cleanup plan, but it waited seven more years to launch a comprehensive cleanup.

This pattern of obscuring environmental racism is consistent throughout the report. For example, the report glosses over the pesticide problem faced by farmworkers and those who live in migrant labor camps. The selection of reference literature in the farmworker section is grossly inadequate. For example, it does not include a single piece of research by Dr. Marion Moses, who heads the Pesticide Education Center and has written extensively on the problem. Instead of hard research, the authors of the report rely on their intuition. As they put it: "Intuitively, one would expect that ethnic minorities who make up a large part of the documented and undocumented farm work force might experience higher pesticide exposures" (Environmental Protection Agency 1992, p. 19).

The report denies, however, that this situation is an example of environmental racism. The report suggests that it is not racist for the majority of migrant farmworkers (people of color) to be poisoned as long as some few white farmworkers are poisoned along with them. This, of course, ignores the fact that the very ethnic composition of today's migrant farmworkers is rooted in a historic pattern of racial occupational segregation. More than 90 percent of migrant farmworkers are persons of color (African-American, Afro-Caribbean, Latino, and Asian). Perhaps that is why farmworkers are still waiting to be treated as "first-class" workers.

The case of migrant farmworkers is a classic example of the double standards in environmental and health protection. The report, at this point, reemphasizes the agency's "risk-based" decisionmaking. However, it fails to explain (using its own "science") its quick actions on the chemical Alar "scare" and its painfully slow action on the pesticide Parathion. Action on Alar came in about three weeks, while action on Parathion was delayed for five years after the agency reached the conclusion that it should cancel its use. Environmental justice demands that the EPA do something about the different value assigned to the health of farmworkers (who are exposed to pesticides in the fields) and white-collar office workers (at risk from contaminated air chemicals in a "sick" building).

The EPA report also fails to discuss the inequitable and discriminatory decisions of state and local governments or the EPA's collusion with these practices. The EPA's current position of relegating facility siting to private industry and the states actually creates and perpetuates environmental inequities. The EPA sanctions discriminatory local government and industry siting by granting the necessary operating permits without consideration of equity issues. The agency has done little to encourage local and state governments to adopt equitable facility siting plans. Its argument is that it should not involve itself in local land-use and facility siting controversies in granting permits. Unfortunately, defining the problem as a "local" land-use issue will not make it disappear. By backing away from federal equity requirements, the agency seems perfectly willing to allow the Houstons and the King and Queen Counties of the nation to selectively dump on communities of color.

As mentioned before, the EPA's use of "scientific" risk assessment/management procedures in authorizing incinerator plants justifies and favors projects being pushed by both industry and local policymakers. Even William Ruckelshaus (a two-time chief of the EPA and current CEO of Browning-Ferris Industries) described risk analysis as "a kind of pretense" (see Blumberg & Gottlieb 1989, p. 104).

One of the key problems is that the EPA refuses to examine *aggregate* risks in deciding on permits. For example, it should view comprehensively a neighborhood like Chicago's Southeast side, which is "saturated" with toxic waste dumps, steel mills, municipal landfills, hazardous waste incinerators, salvage yards, grain elevators, and oil refineries. And it should assume responsibility for protecting the Southeast side Chicago community from the further risks of siting still another waste facility in the area. By not figuring the aggregate, cumulative, and synergistic risks, certain neighborhoods become "sacrifice zones." Furthermore, "impacts" must figure in permit decisions. Surely, the agency can develop methodologies to assess multiple exposure in "contamination-saturated" communities.

The report also ignores the fact that the federal government is blocking initiatives to end inequitable practices in the interstate transport and storage of hazardous wastes. Few states want to become the dumping ground for another's garbage or hazardous waste, and some have even resorted to outright bans and restrictions. In response, the U.S. Supreme Court on June 1, 1992, struck down certain state laws that would ban the transport of wastes across state borders or differential fees imposed on out-of-state shipments. The high court ruled that the Constitution forbids discrimination against interstate commerce— even if the material is household garbage or hazardous chemicals. This ruling affected nineteen states that had erected such barriers (Savage 1992, p. A12).

Instead of focusing on this problem, the report creates the impression that communities are actively recruiting noxious facilities: "[T]here are numerous examples of poor communities seeking a waste site or industrial facility to increase the tax base and create jobs" (Environmental Protection Agency 1992, p. 24). Interestingly, the report fails to cite any of these "numerous examples." Nor does it explore *who* in the community is actually doing this inviting. As we have seen in this book, it is usually a community's business and political elites (not the ordinary residents of the community) who seek waste facilities as an economic development program (Bullard 1990).

This is particularly true in Native-American reservations. They have become prime targets for waste-disposal firms. The leaders of more than a hundred reservations have been approached in recent years by such firms (Angel 1992). Nearly all of the proposals were defeated through grassroots opposition. The threat to Native lands hovers from Maine to Alaska. Both the U.S. Department of Interior and the Bureau of Indian Affairs are promoting the construction of waste facilities on Native lands as a form of economic development. Native Americans, however, are not beating down the doors to recruit polluting industries for the reservations. The EPA's report, however, attempts to blame the victims.

Beyond Government Denial and Public Relations Ploys

Long-time civil rights activist Reverend Benjamin Chavis described the EPA's communication strategy as an "attempt to seduce certain members of the community." He further argues that "if the EPA had a genuine concern about improving its relationship with the civil rights community, it would engage in dialogue with the community on some of its critical issues" (quoted in Weisskopf 1992, p. A15). It should come as no particular surprise, then, that the residents of West Dallas, Texarkana, Kettleman City, East Los Angeles, South Central Los Angeles, Richmond (CA), West Harlem, East St. Louis, Chicago's Altgeld Gardens, and Houston's Northwood Manor tend to view the EPA as the "enemy" rather than a "protector." These communities realize that environmental racism and injustice is real. They live with it every day of their lives. They also realize that the EPA and other governmental agencies typically favor industry and well-organized white communities in disregard of both justice and basic democratic accountability.

The environmental justice movement that is emerging in African-American, Latino, and Native-American communities is thus led by residents who refuse to wait for the protection provided by corporate "good neighbor" policies and governmental regulatory agencies. They realize their communities must defend themselves and that they need to create a social movement powerful enough to force needed change.

Such activists are typically well-integrated into the existing local protest organizations and social networks. Many of these organizations have a long history of fighting institutional racism. In addition, new groups are springing up. Whether old or new, these grassroots groups have adopted environmental justice as their goal and mobilizing theme. This approach seems to be succeeding where the mainstream environmental movement and regulatory agencies have historically failed. As this book attests, evidence is growing that this new movement can produce important changes. Moreover, progress has been made in broadening the agenda of the social justice and environmental movements to include environmental equity. This bodes well for forging needed alliances in the future.

A great deal of work remains to be done, however—in mobilizing people of color who are members of churches, fraternal organizations, civic clubs, and professional groups. Moreover, the environmental justice movement could better utilize the expertise of students and faculty at the historically black colleges and universities (HBCUs) and other minority institutions—many of which are located in the heart of the minority community. A number of useful devices to support mobilization could be designed at colleges and universities, including student-community internships, environmental education components in inner-city schools, workshops on environmental justice for local public officials and administrators, and mechanisms for closer monitoring and enforcement of environmental regulations in communities of color.

It is also necessary for the movement to increase its sharing of information and personnel both nationally and globally. After years of public hearings, court battles, direct action campaigns, information gathering, and on-the-job training, thousands of community residents have become exceptionally knowledgeable on some very technical subjects. These resident "experts" could help other communities that have less expertise in dealing with environmental problems. Moreover, endangered communities need to be informed about the strategies of communities that have resisted—and prevailed against—industrial polluters and unresponsive government agencies.

Simply put, African Americans and other people of color must be empowered through their own organizations and institutions if they are to effectively address the problem. The key challenge ahead for the environmental justice movement, then, is to deepen its self-reliance and self-organization while, at the same time, winning outside support and allies.

It is certainly time for the mainstream environmental movement to diversify and reach out to the "other" America. This does not mean, of course, that the Big Ten environmental organizations should swallow up the grassroots efforts and take over their campaigns. Rather, the 1990s offer mainstream environmentalists challenging opportunities to embrace coalition work, social justice, and redistributive politics. Certainly, if mainstream environmental organizations are to increase their credibility on global issues, they must add to their agenda issues that directly affect the poor and people of color in this country and around the world. Building a powerful movement with an integrated program and genuine racial-ethnic and social-class diversity is the first step in changing the elitist image traditionally projected by the environmental movement in this country.

A Model Environmental Justice Framework

The question of environmental justice is not anchored in a debate about whether or not decisionmakers should tinker with the EPA's risk-based management paradigm. Distribution of burdens and benefits is not random. Reliance solely on "objective" science for environmental decisionmaking, in a world shaped largely by power politics and special interests, often masks institutional racism. A national environmental justice framework is needed to begin addressing environmental inequities that result from social oppression.

The environmental justice framework implicit throughout this book rests on an ethical analysis of strategies to eliminate unfair, unjust, and inequitable conditions and decisions. The framework also seeks to prevent the threat before it occurs. It does so by incorporating the concerns of social movements that seek to eliminate harmful, discriminating practices in housing, land use, industrial planning, health care, and sanitation services. Thus, the environmental justice framework attempts to uncover the underlying assumptions that contribute to and produce unequal protection. This framework brings to the surface the blunt questions of "who gets what, why, and how much." To be specific, the environmental justice framework:

- incorporates the principle of the right of all individuals to be protected from environmental degradation;
- adopts a public health model of prevention (that eliminates the threat before harm occurs) as the preferred strategy;
- shifts the burden of proof to polluters/dischargers who do harm, discriminate, or who do not give equal protection to racial and ethnic minorities, and other "protected" classes; and
- redresses disproportionate impact through "targeted" action and resources.

The lessons from the civil rights struggles around housing, employment, education, and public accommodations over the past four decades suggest that environmental justice will need to have a legislative foundation to ensure its principle of across-the-board environmental rights. It is not enough to demonstrate the existence of unjust and unfair conditions; the practices that caused the conditions must be made illegal. In cases where applicable laws already exist, the environmental justice framework demands that they are enforced in a nondiscriminatory fashion. Yet, much more is needed than better enforcement of existing laws. Unequal protection needs to be attacked via a federal Fair Environmental Protection Act that moves protection from a "privilege" to a "right."

A Fair Environmental Protection Act would need to address both the *intended* and *unintended* effects of public policies, land-use decisions, and industry practices that have a disparate impact on racial and ethnic minorities, and other vulnerable groups. The purpose of this act would be to prohibit environmental discrimination based on race and class. The precedents for this framework are the Civil Rights Act of 1964, which attempted to address both *de jure* and *de facto* school segregation, the Fair Housing Act of 1968 and as amended in 1988, and the Voting Rights Act of 1965.

The struggle for new legislation will also need to be directed at the state level. Since many of the decisions and problems lie with state actions, states will need to model their legislative initiatives (or even develop stronger initiatives) on the needed federal legislation. States that are initiating "fair share" plans to address *interstate* waste conflicts (siting equity) need also to begin addressing *intrastate* siting equity concerns being raised by impacted local communities.

The public health principle of our framework suggests further that impacted communities should not have to wait until conclusive "proof" of causation is established before preventive action is taken. For example, the framework offers a solution to the lead problem by shifting the primary focus from *treatment* (after children have been poisoned) to *prevention* (elimination of the threat via abating lead in houses). Overwhelming scientific evidence exists on the ill-effects of lead on the human body. However, very little action has been taken to rid the nation of lead poisoning in housing.

This suggests the need for the burden-of-proof principle. Under the current system, individuals who challenge polluters must "prove" that they have been harmed, discriminated against, or disproportionately impacted. Few impacted communities have the resources to hire lawyers, expert witnesses, and doctors needed to sustain such a challenge.

The environmental justice strategy would require that entities applying for operating permits (landfills, incinerators, smelters, refineries, chemical plants, etc.) prove that their operations are not harmful to human health and will not disproportionately impact racial and ethnic minorities and other protected groups. This principle would also require proven statistics of disparate impact to constitute proof of discrimination in legal proceedings instead of using "intent" as the relevant criteria. Proving intentional or purposeful discrimination in a court of law is next to impossible. Yet, numerous empirical studies point to disparate public and private waste facility siting where African Americans and Latino Americans are disproportionately impacted. These statistical analyses should be given the greatest weight in legal decisionmaking.

The targeted resources principle of the environmental justice framework would also mean providing the most resources where environmental and health problems are greatest. Reliance solely on "objective" science disguises the exploitative way the polluting industries have operated in some communities and condones a passive acceptance of the status quo. The federal EPA already has geographic targeting that involves pollution prevention, multimedia enforcement, research into causes and cures of environmental stress, stopping habitat loss, education, and constituency building. Examples of such geographic initiatives underway include the Chesapeake Bay, Great Lakes, Gulf of Mexico, and the Mexican Border programs.

Environmental justice targeting would channel resources to the "hot spots," communities that are burdened with more than their "fair share" of environmental problems. For example, the EPA's Region VI has developed a Geographic Information System and comparative risk methodologies to evaluate environmental equity concerns in the region. The methodologies combines susceptibility factors (i.e., age, pregnancy, race, income, pre-existing disease, and lifestyle) with chemical release data (i.e., Toxic Release Inventory and monitoring information), geographic and demographic data (i.e., site-specific areas around hazardous waste-sites, census tracts, zip codes, cities, and states), and state health department vital statistics data for its regional equity assessment.

Region VI's 1992 Gulf Coast Toxics Initiatives project is an outgrowth of its equity assessment. The project targets facilities on the Texas and Louisiana coast. Inspectors will spend 38 percent of their time in this multimedia enforcement effort. In order for this project to move beyond the "first-step" phase and begin addressing real inequities, it will need to channel *most* of its resources (not just inspectors) to the areas where *most* of the problems occur.

An environmental justice framework would allow us to identify such communities nationally. Yet, as we have seen, a key question

remains resource allocation—the level of resources that will be chan-
neled into solving the pollution problem in communities that have a
disproportionately large share of poor people, working-class people,
and people of color. This will be an important arena of struggle in the
coming decades.

Conclusion

Environmental philosophy and decisionmaking has often failed to
address the "justice" question of who gets help and who does not; who
can afford help and who cannot; why some contaminated communities
get studied while other get left off the research agenda; why industry
poisons some communities and not others; why some contaminated
communities get cleaned up while others do not; and why some communities are protected and other are not protected.

The grassroots environmental justice movement chronicled in
this book seeks to strip away the ideological blinders that overlook
racism and class exploitation in environmental decisionmaking. From
this critical vantage point, the solution to unequal environmental protection is seen to lie in the struggle for justice for all Americans. No
community, rich or poor, black or white, should be allowed to become
an ecological "sacrifice zone."

Saying "NO" to the continued poisoning of our communities of
color is the difficult first step in this struggle. Yet, our long-range vision
must also include institutionalizing sustainable and just environmental
practices that meet human needs without sacrificing the land's ecological integrity. If we are to succeed, we must be visionary as well as
militant. Our very future depends on it.

Contributors

Dana Alston has been active on social, economic, and racial justice issues for 20 years. She is presently the director of the Environment, Community Development and Race project of the Panos Institute. Ms. Alston served on the planning committee for the first National People of Color Environmental Leadership Summit.

Conner Bailey is an associate professor in the Department of Agricultural Economics and Rural Sociology at Auburn University. His research interests include the sociology of natural resources and the sociology of the environment. He has been involved in research in the social and political aspects of hazardous waste disposal for the past six years.

Nicole Brown joined the Panos Institute in October 1990 and has worked on the Central America and Caribbean Regional Program. A native of Jamaica, she holds an M.A. in International Studies, with an emphasis in Latin American Studies, from the Johns Hopkins University School of Advanced International Studies (SAIS).

Robert D. Bullard is a professor of sociology at the University of California, Riverside. For over a decade, he has conducted research and worked on urban land use, housing, community development, industrial facility siting, and environmental justice. His book *Dumping in Dixie: Race, Class, and Environmental Quality* (Westview) has become a standard text in the field.

Benjamin F. Chavis, Jr., an ordained minister and a 25-year veteran of the civil rights movement, is Executive Director of the United Church of Christ Commission for Racial Justice. Under his leadership, the Commission issued its landmark study *Toxic Wastes and Race* and helped coordinate the First National People of Color Environmental Leadership Summit.

Robert W. Collin is an assistant professor in the Department of Urban and Environmental Planning, School of Architecture, at the

University of Virginia. He holds Masters degrees in Law, Planning, and Social Work. He teaches housing and community development.

Charles E. Faupel is an associate professor in the Department of Sociology at Auburn University. Over the last fifteen years, he has done extensive research in the sociology of disaster and the sociology of drug use. For the past six years he has been researching the management of hazardous waste as a social and political issue.

Joseph Gallegos has a degree in mechanical engineering with a focus on energy systems and environmental design from Colorado State University. He is a rancher and leader in sustainable agriculture in northern New Mexico and southern Colorado. He has lectured extensively throughout the country on agriculture and the environmental and economic effects of industrial mining.

James H. Gundlach is an associate professor of sociology and the director of the College of Liberal Arts Computer-Assisted Learning Laboratory at Auburn University. He received his Ph.D. from the University of Texas at Austin. His current research is on the effects of cultural and social conditions on premature death.

Cynthia Hamilton has been active in grassroots organizing for almost 20 years. She is currently an associate professor in the Pan African Studies Department at California State University, Los Angeles, and a lecturer in the Graduate School of Architecture and Urban Planning at UCLA. She has conducted research on urban restructuring and its consequences for African-American communities.

William M. Harris, Sr., is a professor in the University of Virginia's Department of Urban and Environmental Planning, in the School of Architecture. His major teaching and research areas include housing, economic development, and planning theory.

Charles Lee is the research director for the United Church of Christ Commission for Racial Justice. His pioneering work has helped to define issues of environmental racism and environmental justice. He directed the Commission's landmark *Toxic Wastes and Race in the United States,* the first national study of the demographic patterns associated with the location of hazardous waste sites. In 1991, he helped coordinate the First National People of Color Environmental Leadership Summit in Washington, D.C.

Marion Moses, M.D., is a board-certified physician in occupational medicine, with many years experience treating pesticide-related health problems in farmworkers. She worked with the United Farm Workers union for several years, and is the principal investigator for a health study of migrant farmworkers in Ohio and Florida. She is also the founder of the Pesticide Education Center, a nonprofit organization based in San Francisco.

Devon Peña is an associate professor of sociology at Colorado College and serves as a consultant to a variety of grassroots environmental justice organizations in northern New Mexico and southern Colorado. He is editor of a forthcoming special thematic issue of the journal *New Scholar*, entitled "Subversive Kin: Chicano Studies and Ecology." He is also author of the forthcoming book, *The Terror of the Machine* to be published by the University of Texas and the Center for Mexican American Studies.

Janet A. Phoenix, M.D., M.P.H., is the director of health education for the Alliance to End Childhood Lead Poisoning, a national nonprofit organization. Before joining the Alliance, she worked with the District of Columbia's Childhood Lead-Poisoning Prevention Program. She is currently a doctoral candidate at Johns Hopkins University's School of Hygiene and Public Health.

Laura Pulido recently earned her Ph.D. in urban planning at the University of California, Los Angeles. She is currently an assistant professor of geography at California State University at Fullerton, where she teaches classes on environmentalism and Chicano issues. She is an active member of the Labor/Community Strategy Center in Los Angeles.

Dorceta E. Taylor, a recent graduate of Yale University, is an assistant professor of sociology in the School of Natural Resources at the University of Michigan. Her current postdoctoral research is on the emergence of environmental justice groups in the United States, Britain, and Canada.

References

Adair, Margo. "Embracing Diversity: Building Multicultural Alliances." Pp. 42-46 in Brad Erikson, ed., *Call to Action: Handbook for Ecology, Peace and Justice.* San Fransisco: Sierra Club Books, 1990.

Adam, Nigel. "Banking on Nature." *Newsweek,* 21 May 1990.

Adams, R.M. *Occupational Skin Disease.* 2nd ed. Philadelphia: Saunders, 1990.

Agency for Toxic Substances and Disease Registry, *The Nature and Extent of Lead Poisoning in Children in the United States: A Reprint to Congress.* Atlanta: U.S. Department of Health and Human Services, 1988.

Akesson, N.B. and Yates, W.E. "Problems relating to application of agricultural chemicals and resulting drift residues." *Annual Review of Entomology* 9 (1964): 285-318.

Alabama Blackbelt Defense Committee. *The Accused Speak.* Gainesville, AL: Alabama Blackbelt Defense Committee, n.d.

Alabama Department of Economic and Community Affairs. *Alabama County Data Book 1984.* 1984.

Alabama Department of Economic and Community Affairs. *Alabama County Data Book 1988.* 1989.

Alexander, Edward. *Approaches to Planning.* New York: Gordon and Breach, 1986.

Allamilla, Ileana. "Ecological Terrorism as a Pacification Strategy in Guatemala." *Guatemala Review,* April 1991.

Allenby, C. and Kizer, K.W. *Childhood Lead Poisoning in California, Causes and Prevention: Interim Report to the California Legislature.* June 1989.

Alliance to End Childhood Lead Poisoining. *Childhood Lead Poisoning Prevention: A Resource Directory.* 2nd ed. Washington, D.C.: National Center for Education in Maternal and Child Health, 1991.

Alonso, William. "Beyond the Inter-Disciplinary Approach to Planning." *American Institute of Planners Journal* 37 (1971): 196-273.

Alston, Dana. *We Speak for Ourselves: Social Justice, Race, and Environment.* Washington, D.C.: The Panos Institute, 1990.

Anderson, Bob. "Plant Sites: Is Racism an Issue?" *Baton Rouge Morning Advocate,* 12 May 1992: A1, A5.

Anderson, Bob; Dunn, Mike; and Alabarado, Sonny. "Prosperity in Paradise: Louisiana's Chemical Legacy." *Morning Advocate,* 25 April 1985.

Angel, Bradley. *The Toxic Threat to Indian Lands: A Greenpeace Report.* San Francisco: Greenpeace, 1992.

Anger, W.K.; Moody, L.; Burg, J.; *et al.* "Neurobehavioral evaluation of soil and structural fumigators using methyl bromide and sulfuryl fluoride." *Neurotoxicology* 7 (1986): 137-156.

Australian Government. *Australian Veterans Health Studies.* Case-control study of congenital anomalies and Vietnam service (birth defects study). 1983.

Bachrach, Kenneth M. and Zautra, Alex J. "Coping with Community Stress: The Threat of a Hazardous Waste Landfill." *Journal of Health and Social Behavior* 26 (June 1985): 127-141.

Baghurst, P.A.; Robertson, E.F.; and McMichael, A.J. "The Port Pirie Cohort Study: Lead Effects on Pregnancy Outcome and Early Childhood Development." *Neurotoxicology* 8 (1987): 395-401.

Bailey, C.; Faupel, C.E.; and Holland, S.F. "Hazardous Wastes and Differing Perceptions of Risk in Sumter County, Alabama." *Society and Natural Resources* 5 (1992): 21-36.

Bailey, C.; Faupel, C.E.; Holland, S.F.; and Waren, A. *Public Opinions and Attitudes Regarding Hazardous Waste in Alabama: Results from Three 1988 Surveys.* (Rural Sociology Series No. 14). Auburn, AL: Auburn University, Alabama Agricultural Experiment Station, 1989.

Baker, James. "A Land Battle in New Mexico: Sheep War." *Newsweek* 114 (1989): 39.

Balarajan, R. and McDowall, M. "Congenital malformations and agricultural workers." *Lancet* 1 (1983): 1112-1113.

Barbeau, A.; Roy, M.; Bernier, G.; *et al.* "Ecogenetics of Parkinson's Disease: Prevalence and environmental aspects in rural areas." *Canadian Journal of Neurological Science* (1987): 1436-1441.

Bauman, Zygmunt. *Culture as Praxis.* London: Routledge & Kegan Paul, 1973.

Beasley, Conger, Jr. "Of Pollution and Poverty: Keeping Watch in Cancer Alley." *Buzzworm* 2 (July/August 1990a): 39-45.

Beasley, Conger, Jr. "Of Poverty and Pollution: Deadly Threat on Native Lands." *Buzzworm* 2 (September/October 1990b): 39-45.

Begley, S.; Rotenberk, L. and Hager, M. "Scandal in the testing lab." *Newsweek,* 30 May 1983: 83.

Behrens, R.H. and Dukes, D.C.D. "Fatal methyl bromide poisoning." *British Journal of Industrial Medicine* 43 (1986): 561-562.

Bengu, Sibusiso. "Statement of the Preparatory Committee on the United Nations Commission on Environment and Development." Nairobi, Kenya (August 1990).

Bethell, T.N. *Sumter County Blues: The Ordeal of the Federation of Southern Cooperatives* (report to the National Committee in Support of Community Based Organizations). Washington, D.C.: Center for Community Change, 1982.

Bittner, E.; King, D.T.; and Holston, I. "Fracturing in the Upper Cretaceous Selma Group Chalky Marls, Inner Coastal Plain of Alabama: Stratigraphic (Facies) Control of Joint Development and Regional Joint-Strike Orientations. *Transactions-Gulf Coast Association of Geological Societies* XXXVIII (1988): 277-282.

Blaikie, Piers and Brookfield, Harold. *Land Degradation and Society.* London: Methuen, 1987.

Blauner, Robert. *Racial Oppression in America.* New York: Harper and Row, 1972.

Blumberg, Michael and Gottlieb, Robert. *War on Waste: Can America Win Its Battle with Garbage?* Washington, D.C.: Island Press, 1989.

Bocchetta, A. and G.U. Corsini, "Parkinson's disease and pesticides," (Letter) *Lancet* 2 (1986): 1163.

Bonacich, Edna. "A Theory of Ethnic Antagonism: The Split Labor Market." *American Sociological Review* 37 (October 1972): 547-549.

Bookchin, Murray. *Remaking Society: Pathways to a Green Future.* Boston: South End Press, 1990.

Bornschein, R.L.; Hammond, P.B.; and Dietrich, K.N. "The Cincinnati Prospective Study of Low-Level Lead Exposure and Its Effects on Child Development: Protocol and Status Report." *Environmental Research* 38 (1986): 4-18.

Bramwell, Anna. *Ecology in the 20th Century: A History.* New Haven: Yale University Press, 1989.

Brayer, Herbert O. "William Blackmore: The Spanish-Mexican Land Grants of New Mexico and Colorado, 1863-1878." In *Spanish and*

Mexican Land Grants, edited by Carlos E. Cortes. New York: Arno Press, 1974.

Brazilian Institute for Social and Economic Analysis (IBASE). "Debt for Nature Conversion in Debate." Rio de Janeiro, 1991.

Brender, J.D. and Suarez, L. "Paternal occupation and anencephaly." *American Journal of Epidemiology* 131 (1990): 517-521.

Brown, F. Lee and Ingram, Helen M. *Water and Poverty in the Southwest.* Tucson: University of Arizona Press, 1987.

Brown, H.W. "Electroencephalographic changes and disturbance of brain function following human organophosphate exposure." *Northwest Medicine* 70 (1971): 845-846.

Brown, Michael H. *Laying Waste: The Poisoning of America by Toxic Chemicals.* New York: Pantheon Books, 1980.

Brown, Michael H. *The Toxic Cloud: The Poisoning of America's Air.* New York: Harper and Row, 1987.

Brundtland, Gro Harlem. "Chairman's Foreword." *Our Common Future,* by The World Commission on Environment and Development. New York: Oxford University Press, 1990. Pp. ix-xv.

Bryant, Bunyan and Mohai, Paul. *Race and the Incidence of Environmental Hazards.* Boulder, CO: Westview Press, 1992.

Bullard, Robert D. "Solid Waste Sites and the Black Houston Community." *Sociological Inquiry* 53 (Spring 1983): 273-288.

Bullard, Robert D. "Endangered Environs: The Price of Unplanned Growth in Boomtown Houston." *The California Sociologist* 7 (Summer 1984): 84-102.

Bullard, Robert D. *Invisible Houston: The Black Experience in Boom and Bust.* College Station, TX: Texas A & M University Press, 1987.

Bullard, Robert D. *Dumping in Dixie: Race, Class, and Environmental Quality.* Boulder, CO: Westview Press, 1990.

Bullard, Robert D. "Environmental Racism." *Environmental Protection* 2 (June 1991b): 25-26.

Bullard, Robert D. "Environmental Justice for All." *EnviroAction,* Environmental News Digest for the National Wildlife Federation (November 1991a).

Bullard, Robert D. *Directory of People of Color Environmental Groups 1992.* Riverside, CA: University of California, Riverside, Department of Sociology, 1992a.

Bullard, Robert D. "Urban Infrastructure: Social, Environmental, and Health Risks to African Americans." In *The State of Black America 1992*, edited by Billy J. Tidwell, pp. 183-196. New York: National Urban League, 1992b.

Bullard, Robert D. and Feagin, Joe R. "Racism and the City." In *Urban Life in Transition,* edited by M. Gottdiener and C.V Pickvance, pp. 55-76. Newbury Park, CA: Sage, 1991.

Bullard, Robert D. and Wright, Beverly H. "Environmentalism and the Politics of Equity: Emergent Trends in the Black Community." *Mid-American Review of Sociology* 12 (1986): 21-37.

Bullard, Robert D. and Wright, Beverly H. "The Politics of Pollution: Implication for the Black Community." *Phylon* 47 (1986): 71-78.

Bullard, Robert D. and Wright, Beverly H. "Blacks and the Environment." *Humboldt Journal of Social Relations* 14 (1987): 165-184.

Bullard, Robert D. and Wright, Beverly H. "The Quest for Environmental Equity: Mobilizing the African American Community for Social Change." *Society and Natural Resources* 3 (1991): 301-311.

Bureau of Business and Economic Research. *New Mexico Statistical Abstract.* 1989.

Buttel, Frederick and Flinn, William, L. "The Structure and Support for the Environmental Movement 1968-1970." *Rural Sociology* 39 (1974): 56-69.

Buttel, Frederick and Flinn, William L. "Social Class and Mass Environmental Beliefs: A Reconsideration." *Environment and Behavior* 10 (September 1978): 433-450.

Calpotura, Francis. "PUEBLO (People United for a Better Oakland) and Lead Poisoning." Excerpts from speech presented at the National Conference on Preventing Childhood Lead Poisoning, Washington, DC (October 7, 1991).

Carlson, Alvar. "New Mexico's Sheep Industry, 1850-1900: Its Role in the History of the Territory." *New Mexico Historical Review* 44 (1969): 25-49.

Carlson, Alvar. *The Spanish-American Homeland: Four Centuries in New Mexico's Rio Arriba.* Baltimore: The Johns Hopkins Press, 1990.

Carmichael, S. and Hamilton, C.V. *Black Power.* New York: Vintage, 1967.

Carson, Rachel. *Silent Spring.* Boston: Houghton Mifflin, 1962.

Casey, P.H. and Collie, W.R. "Severe mental retardation and multiple congenital anomalies of uncertain cause after extreme parental exposure to 2,4-D." *Journal of Pediatrics* 104 (1984): 313-315.

Catton, William. *Overshoot: The Ecological Basis of Revolutionary Change.* Chicago: University of Illinois Press, 1982.

Center for Defense Information. *Defense Monitor* 19 (September 1990).

Center for Defense Information. *Defense Monitor* 20 (March 1991).

Center for Defense Information. *Defense Monitor* 20 (April 1991).

Center for Demographic and Cultural Research. *Alabama Population Data Sheet.* Montgomery, AL: Auburn University, 1991.

Center for Investigative Reporting and Bill Moyers. *Global Dumping Grounds: The International Trade in Hazardous Waste.* Washington, D.C.: Seven Locks Press, 1990.

Centers for Disease Control. "Preventing Lead Poisoning in Young Children." Atlanta: Centers for Disease Control Statement, October 1991.

Center for Third World Organizing. *Toxics and Minority Communities.* Oakland: Center for Third World Organizing, 1986.

Cerrell Associates, Inc. *Political Difficulties Facing Waste-to-Energy Conversion Plant Siting.* California Waste Management Board, Technical Information Series. Prepared by Cerrell Associates, Inc. for the California Waste Management Board. Los Angeles, CA: Cerrell Associates, Inc., 1984.

Charland, Bill. "Economic Development Isn't Just Numbers; It's Ideas." *Rocky Mountain News,* 24 July 1989: 44.

Chase, Steve, ed. *Defending the Earth: A Dialogue Between Murray Bookchin and Dave Foreman.* Boston: South End Press, 1991.

Chemical Waste Management, Inc. *Solid and Hazardous Waste: A Basic Study Guide.* Livingston, AL: Chemical Waste Management, Inc., 1989.

Chemical Waste Management, Inc. *1989 Annual Report.* Oak Brook, IL: Chemical Waste Management, Inc., 1990.

Children's Defense Fund. *A Children's Defense Fund Budget: An Analysis of the FY 1987 Federal Budget and Children.* Washington, D.C.: Children's Defense Fund, 1986.

Chu, Dan and Linthicum, Leslie. "MacArthur Grant Winner Maria Varela Shepherds a Rural New Mexico Community Toward Economic Rebirth." *People* 35 (1991): 115-117.

Citizens for a Better Environment. *Richmond at Risk: Community Demographics and Toxic Hazards from Industrial Polluters.* San Francisco: CBE, 1989.

Citizens' Clearinghouse for Hazardous Waste. *Everyone's Backyard* 9 (May 1991): 2.

Clark, Ira G. *Water in New Mexico: A History of Its Management and Use.* Albuquerque: University of New Mexico Press, 1987.

Clay, Jason W. "Editorial: Genes, Genius, and Genocide." *Cultural Survival Quarterly* 14 (April 1990a).

Clay, Jason W. *Indigenous Peoples and Tropical Forests.* Cambridge: Cultural Survival, Inc., 1990b.

Cole, Charles. "Triple Jeopardy: Race, Poverty and Toxic Waste." *Response,* April 1990.

Collette, Will. "Institutions: Citizens Clearinghouse for Hazardous Waste." *Environment* 29 (September 1987): 44-45.

Collin, Robert and Morris, Robin. "Race and the American City: An Interdisciplinary Critique." *The National Black Law Review* 11 (1989): 177.

Collins, Daniel; Baum, Andrew; and Singer, Jerome E. "Coping with Chronic Stress at Three Mile Island: Psychological and Biological Evidence." *Health Psychology* 2 (1983): 149-166.

Colorado Groundwater Association. *Water in the Valley.* Lakewood, CO: Colorado Groundwater Association, 1989.

Commoner, Barry. *Making Peace with the Planet.* New York: Pantheon, 1990.

Conservation Foundation. *State of the Environment: A View Towards the Nineties.* Washington, D.C.: Conservation Foundation, 1987.

Coordinating Body for Indigenous People's Organizations of the Amazon Basin (COICA). "It's Our Rain Forest." *Mother Jones,* (April/May 1990).

Corwin, Miles, "Unusual Allies Fight Waste Incinerator." *Los Angeles Times,* 24 February 1991: A1, A36.

Costilla County Committee for Environmental Soundness. *BMG: A Chronology.* San Luis, CO: CES, 1989.

Costilla County Committee for Environmental Soundness. *Sustainable Regional Development and the Conservation of Rural Resources: A Strategy for Environmental and Social Justice in Ethnic Farming Communities.* Proposal submitted to The Tides Foundation. San Luis, CO: CES, 1990.

Crampton, Lewis. "Environmental Equity Community Plan." Confidential EPA Memorandum to Gordon Bender, Chief of Staff. 15 November 1991.

Crawford, Stanley. *Mayordomo: Chronicle of an Acequia in Northern New Mexico.* New York: Anchor Books, 1989.

Cunningham, A.B. "Indigenous Knowledge and Biodiversity: Global Commons or Regional Heritage?" *Cultural Diversity Quarterly* (Summer 1991).

Cutter, Susan C. "Community Concern: Social and Environmental Influences." *Environment and Behavior 13* (1981): 105-124.

Daly, Herman and Cobb, Jr., John B. *For the Common Good.* Boston: Beacon Press, 1989.

Daniel, Cletus E. *Bitter Harvest, A History of California Farm workers 1870 - 1941.* Ithaca, NY: Cornell University Press, 1981.

Daschle, Thomas. "Dances with Garbage." *Christian Science Monitor,* 14 February 1991.

Davis, Morris E. "The Impact of Workplace Health and Safety on Black Workers: Assessment and Prognosis." *Labor Studies Journal* 4 (Spring 1981): 29-40.

Day, Janet. "Gold Leaves Legacy of Poison," *Rocky Mountain News,* 26 November 1989: 131.

deBuys, William. *Enchantment and Exploitation: The Life and Hard Times of a New Mexico Mountain Range.* Albuquerque: University of New Mexico Press, 1989.

Denton, Nancy A. and Massey, Douglas S. "Residential Segregation of Blacks, Hispanics, and Asians by Socioeconomic Class and Generation." *Social Science Quarterly* 69 (1988): 797-817.

Deutsch, Sarah. *No Separate Refuge: Culture, Class and Gender on an Anglo-Hispanic Frontier in the American Southwest, 1880-1940.* New York: Oxford University Press, 1987.

Devall, Bill and Sessions, George. *Deep Ecology: Living as If Nature Mattered.* Salt Lake City, UT: Gibbs Smith, 1985.

Dewart, Tracey and Eskersley, Michael. "Guatemala: The Political Roots of Deforestation." *Links* (Fall 1989).

Dietrich, K.N.; Kraft, K.M.; and Bornschein, R.L. "Low-Level Fetal Lead Exposure Effect on Neurobehavioral Development in Early Infancy." *Pediatrics* 80 (November 1987): 721-730.

Dille, J.R. and Smith, P.W. "Central nervous system effects of chronic exposure to organophosphate insecticides." *Aerospace Medicine* 35 (1964): 475-478.

Division of Local Government, Demography Section, State of Colorado. *Local Government Survey.* 1987.

Dolan, Maura. "Toxic Waste Incinerator Bid Abandoned." *Los Angeles Times,* 24 May 1991.

Dolin, Eric J. "Black Americans' Attitudes Toward Wildlife." *Journal of Environmental Education* 20 (January 1988): 17-21.

Donahoe, R.J. and Groshong, R.H. *Hazardous Waste Disposal in the Upper Cretaceous Selma Group.* Guidebook for Field Trip IV, April 4, 1990. Tuscaloosa, AL: Alabama Geological Society, 1990.

Douglas, Gordon. "The Meanings of Agricultural Sustainability." In *Agricultural Sustainability in a Changing World Order,* edited by G. Douglas. Boulder, CO: Westview, 1984.

Duffy, F.H.; Burchfiel, J.L.; Bartels, P.H.; *et al.* "Long-term effects of an organophosphate upon the human electroencephalogram." *Toxicology and Applied Pharmicology* 47 (1979): 161-176.

Dunlap, Riley E. "Public Opinion on the Environment in the Reagan Era: Polls, Pollution, and Politics." *Environment* 29 (1987): 6-11, 31-37.

Eastman, Clyde; Caruthers, Garrey; and Leifer, James A. "Contrasting Attitudes Toward Land in New Mexico," *New Mexico Business,* 24 (March 1971).

Eaton, M.; Schenker, M.; Whorton, D.; *et al.* "Seven-year follow-up of workers exposed to 1,2-dibromo-3-chloropropane." *Journal of Occupational Medicine* 28 (1986): 1145-1150.

Ebright, Malcolm. *The Tierra Amarilla Grant: A History of Chicanery.* Santa Fe, NM: Center for Land Grant Studies, 1985.

Ebright, Malcolm. "New Mexican Land Grants: The Legal Background." In *Land, Water and Culture: New Perspectives on Hispanic Land Grants,* edited by C. Briggs and J. Van Ness, pp.15-64. Albuquerque: University of New Mexico Press, 1987.

Ebright, Malcolm. *Spanish and Mexican Land Grants and the Law.* Manhattan, KS: Sunflower University Press, 1989.

Eckersley, Robyn. *Environmentalism and Political Theory: Toward an Ecocentric Approach.* Albany: State University of New York Press, 1992.

Edelstein, Michael R. *Contaminated Communities: The Social and Psychological Impacts of Residential Toxic Exposure.* Boulder, CO: Westview Press, 1987.

Elling, Ray. *The Struggle for Workers' Health: A Study of Six Industrialized Countries.* New York: Baywood Publishing Company, Inc., 1986.

Environmental Defense Fund. *Legacy of Lead: America's Continuing Epidemic of Childhood Lead Poisoning: A Report and Proposal for Legislative Action.* March 1990.

Environmental Information Ltd. *Industrial and Hazardous Waste Management Firms.* Minneapolis: Environmental Information Ltd., 1986.

Epstein, Samuel; Brown, Lester O.; and Pope, Carl. *Hazardous Waste in America.* San Francisco: Sierra Club Books, 1983.

Erickson, J.D.; Mulinare, J.; McClain, P.W.; *et al.* "Vietnam veterans' risks for fathering babies with birth defects (Summary Report)." *Journal of the American Medical Association* 252 (1984): 903-912.

Faber, Daniel, *et al.* "Central America: Roots of Environmental Destruction." The Environmental Project on Central America (EPOCA), Green Paper, 1986.

Falk, W.W. and Lyson, T.A. *High Tech, Low Tech, No Tech: Recent Industrial and Occupational Change in the South.* Ithaca, NY: State University of New York Press, 1988.

Faupel, C.E. and Bailey, C. "Contingencies Affecting Emergency Planning for Hazardous Wastes. *International Journal of Mass Emergencies and Disasters* 6 (February 1989): 131-154.

Faupel, C.E.; Bailey, C.; and Griffin, G. "Local Media Roles in Defining Hazardous Waste as a Social Problem: The Case of Sumter County, Alabama. *Sociological Spectrum,* 11 (1991): 293-319.

Feagin, Joe R. *Free Enterprise City: Houston in Political and Economic Perspective.* Englewood Cliffs, NJ: Prentice Hall, 1988.

Feagin, Joe R. and Feagin, Clairece B. *Discrimination American Style: Institutional Racism and Sexism.* Malabar, FL: Robert E. Krieger, 1986.

Furguson, Denzel and Furguson, Nancy. *Sacred Cows at the Public Trough.* Bend, OR: Maverick Publications, 1983.

Field, B. and Kerr, C. "Herbicide use and incidence of neural-tube defects." *Lancet* 1 (1979): 1341-1342.

Field, Donald and Burch, William R. *Rural Sociology and the Environment.* Westport, CT: Greenwood Press, 1988.

Fish, Jim, ed. *Wildlands: New Mexico BLM Wilderness Coalition Statewide Proposal.* New Mexico Bureau of Land Management Wilderness Coalition. Courtesy of Rio Grande Chapter, Sierra Club, 1987.

Fitzgerald, G.R.; Barniville, G.; Black, J.; *et al.* "Paraquat poisoning in agricultural workers." *Journal of the Irish Medical Association* 71 (1989): 336-342.

Flores, Camille. "Committee Backs Sheep-Grazing Project." *Albuquerque Journal,* 20 August 1989: A3.

Forrest, Suzanne. *The Preservation of the Village.* Albuquerque: University of New Mexico Press, 1989.

Fox, Stephen. *The American Conservation Movement: John Muir and His Legacy.* Madison, WI: University of Wisconsin Press, 1985.

Fowler, John *Sheep Grazing on Wildlife Areas.* Commission Action Narrative. Agenda No. 7. Minutes to 15 December 1989. New Mexico Department of Game and Fish files, pp. 13-16.

Freeman, Myrick A. "The Distribution of Environmental Quality." In *Environmental Quality Analysis,* edited by Allen V. Kneese and Blair T. Bower. Baltimore: Johns Hopkins University Press for Resources for the Future, 1971.

Freudenberg, Nicholas. "Citizen Action for Environmental Health: Report of a Survey of Community Organizations." *American Journal of Public Health* 74 (1984): 444-448.

Freudenberg, Nicholas and Steinsapir, C. "The Grass Roots Environmental Movement: Not in Our Backyards." Paper presented at the Annual Meeting of the American Association for the Advancement of Science, New Orleans, February 1990.

Furuseth, O. "Community Sensitivity to a Hazardous Waste Facility." *Landscape and Urban Planning* 17 (1989): 357-370.

Mines, R.; Gabbard, S.; and Boccalandro, B. Findings from the *National Agricultural Workers Survey (NAWS): A Demographic and Employment Profile of Perishable Crop Workers.* Washington, D.C.: U.S. Department of Labor, 1991.

Galarza, Ernesto. *Merchants of Labor: The Mexican Bracero Story.* Santa Barbara: McNally and Loftin, 1964.

Galarza, Ernesto. *Spiders in the House and Workers in the Field.* Terre Haute, IN: University of Notre Dame Press, 1970.

Galarza, Ernesto. *Farm Workers and Agri-business in California, 1947-1960.* Terre Haute, IN: University of Notre Dame Press, 1977.

Gale, Richard P. "The Environmental Movement and the Left: Antagonists or Allies." *Sociological Inquiry* 53 (Spring 1983): 179-199.

Ganados del Valle. "A Proposal to Cooperatively Graze the Humphries and Sargents Game Lands." Ganados' Files, 30 May 1984.

Ganados del Valle. "A Proposal to Improve Wildlife Habitat on the Rio Chama, Humphries and Sargent Wildlife Areas." Ganados' Files, 1989a.

Ganados del Valle. Ganados' Files. Press Release dated 18 August 1989b.

Ganados del Valle. "The Grazing Proposal and the Issues." Ganados' Files, n.d.

Gardner, Richard. *Grito! Reies Tijerina and the New Mexico Land Grant War of 1967*. Indianapolis: Bobbs-Merrill, 1970.

Geiser, Ken and Gerry Waneck. "PCBs and Warren County." *Science for the People* 15 (1983): 13-17.

Gelobter, Michel. "The Distribution of Air Pollution by Income and Race." Paper presented at the Second Symposium on Social Science in Resource Management, Urbana, Illinois, June 1988.

George, Alan and Smith, Patrick. "The Dumping Grounds." *South* 1 (August 1988): 4.

Gianessi, Leonard; Peskin, H.M.; and Wolff, E. "The Distributional Effects of Uniform Air Pollution Policy in the U.S." *Quarterly Journal of Economics* (May 1979): 281-301.

Gibbs, Lois M. *Love Canal, My Story*. Albany: State University of New York Press, 1982.

Gilles, Cate, Lena Bravo, and Don Watahomigie. "Uranium Mining at the Grand Canyon: What Costs to Water, Air, and Indigenous People?" *The Workbook* 16 (Spring 1991): 1.

Goforth, Bruce. *Rito Seco Fish Kill, Costilla County*. Unpublished report. Colorado Division of Wildlife, Ft. Garland District. Ft. Garland: DOW 1975.

Gold, E.; Gordis, L.; Tonascia, J.; *et al.* "Risk factors for brain tumors in children." *American Journal of Epidemiology* 109 (March 1979): 309-319.

Goldfield, David R. *Promised Land: The South Since 1945*. Arlington Heights, IL: Harlan Davidson, 1945.

Golding, J. and Sladden, T. "Congenital malformations and agricultural workers." (Letter). *Lancet* 1 (1983): 1393.

Goldman, Benjamin. *The Truth about Where You Live: An Atlas for Action on Toxins and Mortality*. New York: Random House, 1991.

Goldman, L.R.; Mengle, D.; and Epstein, D.M. "Acute symptoms in persons residing near a field treated with the soil fumigants methyl bromide and chloropicrin." *West Journal of Medicine* 147 (1987): 95-98.

Goldsmith, J.R.; Potashnik, G.; and Israeli, R. "Reproductive outcomes in families of DBCP-exposed men." *Archives of Environmental Health* 39 (1984): 85-89.

Gorz, Andre. *Ecology as Politics.* Boston: South End Press, 1980.

Gottdiener, Mark. *The Social Production of Space.* Austin: University of Texas Press, 1988.

Gottlieb, Robert. *A Life of Its Own: The Politics and Power of Water.* New York: Harcourt, Brace, Jovanovich, 1988.

Gottlieb, Robert and Ingram, Helen. "The New Environmentalists." *The Progressive* 52 (1988): 14-15.

Gottlieb, Robert and Wiley, Peter. *Empires in the Sun.* New York: Putnam, 1982.

Grauberger, Janice. "Ganados del Valle: Regional Marketing at its Best." *National Wool Grower,* December 1989: 24-25.

Green, Stephen G. "Second Thoughts about Debt Swaps." *The Chronicle of Philanthropy* 4 (5 November 1991).

Greenberg, J.O. "The neurological effects of methyl bromide poisoning." *Industrial Medicine* 40 (1971): 27-29.

Greenberg, Michael R. and Anderson, Richard E. *Hazardous Waste Sites: The Credibility Gap.* New Brunswick, NJ: Rutgers University Center for Urban Policy Research, 1984.

Greenpeace. *The International Trade in Wastes: A Greenpeace Inventory.* Washington, D.C.: Greenpeace, USA, 1990.

Greenpeace. "The 'Logic' Behind Hazardous Waste Export." *Greenpeace Waste Trade Update* (First Quarter, 1992): 1-2.

Grossman, Karl. "Environmental Racism." *Crisis* (April 1991): 14-17, 31-32.

Grossman, Karl. "From Toxic Racism to Environmental Justice." *E: Environmental Magazine* 3 (June 1992): 28-35.

Guha, Ramachandra. "Radical American Environmentalism and Wilderness Preservation: A Third World Critique." *Environmental Ethics* 11 (1989): 71-83.

Guha, Ramachandra. *The Unquiet Woods: Ecological Change and Peasant Resistance in the Himalaya.* Berkeley: University of California Press, 1990.

Gullet, Scott. "Robert Redford's New Mexico Love Affair." *New Mexico Monthly* 1 (1988): 12-16.

Hacker, Andrew. *Two Nations: Black and White, Separate, Hostile, Unequal.* New York: Scribner's Sons, 1992.

Hall, Bill and Faber, Daniel. "El Salvador: Ecology in Conflict." The Environmental Project on Central America (EPOCA), Green Paper, 1989.

Hall, William and Ayers, Tyrone. *Survey Plans and Data Collection and Analysis Methodologies: Results of a Pre-Survey for the Magnitude and Extent of the Lead-Based Paint Hazard in Housing.* 1974.

Hamburger, T. "Thousands Forced to Leave Land." In *Change in Rural America: Causes, Consequences, and Alternatives,* edited by R.D. Rodefeld, J. Flora, D. Voth, I. Fujimoto, and J. Converse, pp. 28-29. Saint Louis, MO: The C.V. Mosby Company, 1978.

Hamilton, Cynthia. "Women, Home, Community." *Race, Poverty, and the Environment Newsletter* 1 (April 1990).

Hanify, J.A.; Metcalf, P.; Nobbs, C.L.;, *et al.* "Aerial spraying of 2,4,5-T and human birth malformations: An epidemiological investigation." *Science* 212 (1981): 349-351.

Harding, Vincent. *The Other American Revolution.* Los Angeles, CA: Center for Afro-American Studies and the Institute of the Black World, 1980.

Harris, William. *Black Community Development.* San Francisco, CA: R & E Press, 1976.

Haun, J. William. *Guide to the Management of Hazardous Waste.* Golden, CO: Fulcrum, 1991.

Hayes, W.J., Jr. and Laws, E. eds., *Handbook of Pesticide Toxicology.* 3 vols. San Diego: Academic Press, 1990.

Hecht, Susanna and Cockburn, Alexander. *The Fate of the Forest.* London: Verso, 1989.

Hegel, Georg W.F. *Philosophy of History.* New York: Dover, 1956.

Heidam, L.Z. "Spontaneous abortions among dental assistants, factory workers, painters, and gardening workers: A follow up study." *Journal of Epidemiology and Community Health* 38 (1984): 149-155.

Hemminki, K.; Niemi, M.L.; Saloniemi, I.; *et al.* "Spontaneous abortions by occupation and social class in Finland." *International Journal of Epidemiology* 9 (1980): 149-153.

Henderson, Hazel. *The Politics of the Solar Age: Alternatives to Economics.* New York: Anchor Press/Doubleday, 1981.

Higginbotham, A. Leon. "An Open Letter to Justice Clarence Thomas from a Federal Judicial Colleague," *University of Pennsylvania Law Review* 140 (January, 1992): 1005-1028.

Hine, C.H. "Methyl bromide poisoning." *Journal of Occupational Medicine* 11 (1969): 1-10.

Hong, Peter. "The Toxic Mess Called Superfund." *Business Week,* 11 May 1992, 32-34.

Horst, Shannon. "A Gentler Grip on the Earth." *Christian Science Monitor,* 27 March 1990.

Infante, P.F.; Epstein, S.S.; and Newton, W.A., Jr. "Blood dyscrasias and childhood tumors and exposure to chlordane and heptachlor." *Scandinavian Journal of Work and Environmental Health* 4 (1978): 137-150.

International Physicians for the Prevention of Nuclear War (IPPNW). *Radioactive Heaven and Earth: The Health and Environmental Effects of Nuclear Weapons Testing, in, on and above the Earth.* New York: Apex Press, 1991.

Jackson, Donald. "Around Los Ojos, Sheep and Land are Fighting Words." *Smithsonian* 22 (1991): 37-47.

Jackson, Wes. *New Roots for Agriculture.* Lincoln: University of Nebraska Press, 1980.

Jackson, Wes; Berry, Wendell; and Colman, Bruce, eds. *Meeting the Expectations of the Land: Essays in Sustainable Agriculture and Stewardship.* San Francisco: North Point Press, 1984.

Jacobs, H.M. "Social Equity in Agricultural Land Protection." *Landscape and Urban Planning* 17 (1967): 21-23.

Jaimes, M. Annette, ed. *The State of Native America: Genocide, Colonization, and Resistance.* Boston: South End Press, 1992.

Jaynes, Gerald D. and Williams, Robin M., Jr., *A Common Destiny: Blacks and American Society.* Washington, D.C.: National Academy Press, 1989.

Jhamtani, Hira. "The Imperialism of Northern NGO's." *Panoscope,* no. 24. London: The Panos Institute, 1991.

Joint Center for Political Studies. "Fourth National Policy Institute, the Environment: State and Local Concerns." *Focus* 12 (1984): 9.

Jones, J.M. *Prejudice and Racism.* Reading, MA: Addison-Wesley, 1972.

Jones, J.M. "The Concept of Racism and Its Changing Reality." In *Impact of Racism on White Americans,* edited by Benjamin P. Bower and Raymond G. Hunt, pp. 27-49. Beverly Hills: Sage, 1981.

Jorgensen, Eric P. *The Poisoned Well: New Strategies for Groundwater Protection.* San Francisco: Sierra Club, 1989.

Kahn, E. "Pesticide-related illness in California farm workers." *Journal of Occupational Medicine* 18 (1976): 693-696.

Kaplan, R. and Talbot, J. "Ethnicity and Preference for Natural Settings: A Review of Recent Findings." *Landscape and Urban Planning* 15 (1988): 107-117.

Karliner, Joshua, *et al.* "Central America's Other War," *World Policy Journal* 6 (4) (Fall 1989).

Karliner, Joshua *et al.* "War in the Gulf: An Environmental Perspective." *Political Ecology Action Paper* (January 1991).

Kay, Jane. "Fighting Toxic Racism: L.A.'s Minority Neighborhood is the 'Dirtiest' in the State." *San Francisco Examiner,* 7 April 1991a: A1.

Kay, Jane. "Indian Lands Targeted for Waste Disposal Sites." *San Francisco Examiner,* 10 April 1991b: A10.

Kazen, C.; Bloomer, A.; Welch, R.; *et al.* "Persistence of pesticides on the hands of some occupationally exposed people." *Archives of Environmental Health* 29 (1974): 315-318.

Kazis, Richard and Grossman, Richard. *Fear at Work: Job Blackmail, Labor, and the Environment.* Philadelphia: New Society Publishers, 1983.

Kennedy, Ellen, ed. *The Negritude Poets.* See "Return to My Native Land," by Aime Cesaire, and "Prayer to the Masks," by Leopold Senghor. New York: Viking Press, 1975.

Kernberger, Karl. "The Quiet Ones." Video produced by KNME-TV, Albuquerque, 1975.

King, Coretta. *The Words of Martin Luther King, Jr.* New York: New Market, 1984.

Klein, Julie. *Interdisciplinarity.* Detroit, MI: Wayne State University Press, 1990.

Kneese, Allen V. and Bower, Blair T. *Environmental Quality Analysis.* Baltimore: Johns Hopkins University Press for Resources for the Future, 1972.

Knowles, L.L. and Prewitt, K. *Institutional Racism in America.* Englewood Cliffs, NJ: Prentice-Hall, 1969.

Knowlton, Clark. "Land-Grant Problems Among the State's Spanish Americans." *New Mexico Business* 20 (1967): 1-13.

Knowlton, Clark. "Causes of land Loss Among the Spanish Americans in North New Mexico." In *The Chicano,* edited by G. Lopez y Rivas, pp. 111-1121. New York: Monthly Review Press, 1973.

Kozol, Jonathan. *Savage Inequalities: Children in America's Schools.* New York: Crown Publishers, 1991.

Kreger, Janet. "Ecology and Black Student Opinion." *The Journal of Environmental Education* 4 (March 1973): 30-34.

Kricker, A.; McCredie, J.; Elliott, J.; and Forrest, J. "Women and the environment: A study of congenital limb anomalies." *Community Health Studies* 10 (1986): 1-11.

Kunreuther, Howard. "A New Way to Site Hazardous Facilities." *Wall Street Journal,* 27 December 1985: 8.

Kushner, J.A. *Apartheid in America: An Historical and Legal Analysis of Contemporary Racial Segregation in the United States.* Frederick, MD: Associated Faculty Press, 1980.

Kutsche, Paul and Van Ness, John. *Canones: Values, Crisis, and Survival in a Northern New Mexico Village.* Albuquerque: University of New Mexico Press, 1981.

LaBalme, Jenny. "Dumping on Warren County." In *Environmental Politics: Lessons from the Grassroots,* edited by Bob Hall, pp. 23-30. Durham, NC: Institute for Southern Studies, 1988.

Landrigan, Philip J. and Gross, Richard L. "Chemical Wastes: Illegal Hazards and Legal Remedies." *American Journal of Public Health* 71 (1981): 985-987.

Lappe, Frances Moore and Collins, Joseph. *World Hunger: Ten Myths.* San Francisco: Institute for Food and Development Policy, 1979.

Lazarus, Richard E. and Launier, Raymond. "Stress-Related Transactions between Persons and Environment." In *Perspectives in International Psychology,* edited by Lawrence A. Pervin and Michael Lewis, pp. 279-327. New York: Plenum, 1978.

Lee, Bill Lann. "Environmental Litigation on Behalf of Poor, Minority Children: *Matthews v. Coye:* A Case Study." Paper presented at the Annual Meeting of the American Association for the Advancement of Science, Chicago, April 1992.

Lee, M.H. and Randsell, J.F. "A farmworker death due to pesticide toxicity: A case report." *Journal of Toxicology and Environmental Health* 14 (1984): 239-246.

Letz, G.A.; Pond, S.M.; Osterloh, J.D.; *et al.* "Two fatalities after acute occupational exposure to ethylene dibromide." *Journal of the American Medical Association* 252 (1984): 2428-2431.

Levin, H.S. and Rodnitzky, R.L. "Behavioral effects of organophosphate pesticides in man." *Clinical Toxicology* 9 (1976): 391-405.

Levine, Adeline. *Love Canal: Science, Politics, and People.* Lexington, MA.: D.C. Heath and Co., 1982.

Levy, Jacques. *Cesar Chavez, Autobiography of La Causa.* New York: W.W. Norton, 1975.

Lightstone, R. "Pesticide poisoning and environmental data in California." *Rural California Report* 2 (March 1990): 6-7.

Limerick, Patricia Nelson. *The Legacy of Conquest: The Unbroken Past of the American West.* New York: W.W. Norton & Company, 1987.

Loftis, Randy Lee. "Louisiana OKs Dumping of Tainted Soil." *Dallas Morning News,* 12 May 1992: A1, A30.

Logan, John and Molotch, Harvey. *Urban Fortunes: The Political Economy of Place.* Berkeley: University of California Press, 1987.

London, J. and Anderson, H. *So Shall Ye Reap, The Story of Cesar Chavez and the Farm Workers' Movement.* New York: Thomas Y. Crowell, 1970.

Lopez Tijerina, Reies. *Mi Lucha Por La Tierra.* Mexico: Fondo de Cultura Económica, 1978.

Lowe, G.D.; Pinhey, T.K.; and Grimes, M.D. "Public Support for Environmental Protection: New Evidence from National Surveys." *Pacific Sociological Review* 23 (October 1980): 423-445.

Lowengart, R.A.; Peters, J.M.; Cicioni, C., *et al.* "Childhood leukemia and parents' occupational and home exposures." *Journal of the National Cancer Institute* 79 (January 1987): 39-46.

Macalady, Donald L.; Ranville, James F.; Smith, Kathleen S.; and Daniel, Stephen R. "Absorption of Copper, Cadmium, and Zinc on Suspended Sediments in a Stream Contaminated by Acid Mine Drainage: The Effect of Seasonal Changes in Dissolved Organic Carbon." *Completion Report,* vol. 159, Colorado Water Resources Research Institute. Ft. Collins, CO: Colorado State University, 1991.

Maestas, Gerald. "Sheep Grazing Has No Place in New Mexico's Wildlife Areas." *Albuquerque Journal,* 12 January 1990: A7.

Manes, Christopher. *Green Rage: Radical Environmentalism and the Unmaking of Civilization.* Boston: Little, Brown and Co., 1990.

Mann, Eric. "Environmentalism in the Corporate Climate." *Tikkun* 5 (1990): 60-65.

Mann, Eric. *L.A.'s Lethal Air: New Perspectives for Policy, Organizing, and Action.* Los Angeles: Labor/Community Strategy Center, 1991.

Manzanares, Antonio. "Grazing Plan Presentation," Commission Action Narrative. Agenda no. 10. Minutes, 25 July 1985, from New Mexico Department of Game and Fish files, pp. 12-13.

Marable, Manning. *How Capitalism Underdeveloped Black America.* Boston: South End Press, 1983.

Maraniss, David and Weisskopf, Michael. "Jobs and Illness in Petrochemical Corridor." *Washington Post,* 22 December 1987.

Marcuse, Herbert. *Eros and Civilization, A Philosophical Inquiry into Freud.* New York: Vintage, 1961.

Marcuse, Peter. "Professional Ethics and Beyond: Values in Planning." *Journal of the American Institute of Planners* 42 (1976): 274.

Marston, Ed, ed. *Reopening the Western Frontier.* Washington, D.C.: Island, 1989.

Martin, P.; Mines, R.; and Diaz, A. "A profile of California farm workers." *California Agriculture* (May-June 1985): 16-18.

Martinez, Ruben. "Chicano Lands: Acquisition and Loss," *Wisconsin Sociologist* 24 (1987): pp. 2-3, 89-98.

Matthews, G.A. *Pesticide Application Methods.* New York: Longman, 1982.

Matthiessen, Peter. *Sal Si Puedes: Cesar Chavez and the New American Revolution.* New York: Random House, 1969.

McCaull, Julian. "Discriminatory Air Pollution: If the Poor Don't Breathe." *Environment* 19 (1975): 26-32.

McDonald, A.D.; McDonald, J.C.; Armstrong, B., *et al.* "Fetal death and work in pregnancy." *British Journal of Industrial Medicine* 45 (1988): 148-157.

McGraw, M.; Taylor, J.; Reeves, G.; and Mansur, M. "Failing the Grade, Betrayals and Blunders at the Department of Agriculture: A Special Report." *Kansas City Star,* December 8-14, 1991.

McHarg, Ian. *Design with Nature.* New York: Natural History, 1969.

McNeely, Jeffrey and Miller, Kenton. *National Parks, Conservation, and Development: The Role of Protected Areas in Sustaining Society.* Proceedings of the World Congress on National Parks, 1982. Washington, D.C.: Smithsonian Institution, 1984.

McQuaid, Kevin L. "Norris McDonald: Bridging the Gap between Green and Black." *E: The Environmental Magazine* 2 (January/February 1991): 55.

McQueen, Rod. "Canada's 'Green' Invasion of U.S. Begins." *Financial Post,* 4 December 1991: 11.

McWilliams, Carey. *Factories in the Field, the Story of Migratory Labor in California.* Santa Barbara: Peregrine Press, 1976. (First published in 1939).

McWilliams, Carey. *California, the Great Exception*. Santa Barbara: Peregrine Press, 1971. (First published in 1949).

Meadows, Donella; Meadows, Dennis; Randers, Jorgen; and Behrens, William. *The Limits to Growth*, a Report for the Club of Rome's Project on the Predicament of Mankind. New York: Universe Books, 1972.

Merchant, Carolyn. *The Death of Nature*. San Francisco: Harper & Row, 1981.

Midtling, J.E.; Barnett, P.G.; Coye, M.J., *et al.* "Clinical management of field worker organophosphate poisoning: Case report." *Western Journal of Medicine* 143 (1984): 168-172.

Miller, Anita and Potter, Earl. *Land Use in Rio Arriba County: Problems and Opportunities*. Santa Fe: Potter & Kelly Law Firm, 1986.

Mineral Policy Center. *Clementine: Journal of Responsible Mineral Development*, 1 (Spring/Summer 1990): 1.

Mineral Policy Center. *Clementine: Journal of Responsible Mineral Development*, 2 (Spring/Summer 1991): 1.

Mitchell, Robert C. *Public Opinion on Environmental Issues, Results of a National Public Opinion Survey*. 1980.

Mohai, Paul. "Public Concern and Elite Involvement in Environmental Conservation." *Social Science Quarterly* 66 (December 1985): 820-838.

Mohai, Paul. "Black Environmentalism." *Social Science Quarterly* 71 (April 1990): 744-765.

Mollenkopf, John. "Community and Accumulation." In *Urbanization and Urban Planning in Capitalist Society,* edited by Michael Dear and Allen Scott. New York: Methuen, 1981.

Montague, Peter. "What We Must Do: Grassroots Offensive Against Toxics in the 90's." *The Workbook* 19 (March 1990): 90-114.

Montoya, Bill. New Mexico Department of Game and Fish. Interview with author. Santa Fe, New Mexico, August 7, 1990.

Morell, David. "Siting and the Politics of Equity." In *Resolving Locational Conflict,* edited by Robert W. Lake, pp. 117-136. New Brunswick, NJ: Rutgers University Center for Urban Policy Research, 1987.

Morgan, D.P. *Recognition and Management of Pesticide Poisoning.* 4th ed. Washington, D.C.: U.S. Environmental Protection Agency, 1989.

Morrison, Denton E. "The Soft Cutting Edge of Environmentalism: Why and How the Appropriate Technology Notion is Changing the Movement." *Natural Resources Journal* 20 (April 1980): 275-298.

Morrison, Denton E. "How and Why Environmental Consciousness has Trickled Down." In *Distributional Conflict in Environmental Resource*

Policy, edited by Allan Schnaiberg, Nicholas Watts, and Klaus Zimmermann, pp. 187-220. New York: St. Martin's Press, 1986.

Morrison, Denton E. and Dunlap, R. "Environmentalism and Elitism: A Conceptual and Empirical Analysis." *Environmental Management* 10 (1986): 581-589.

Moses, M. "On Another Subject: Agricultural Workers and Pesticides." *EPA Journal* (July/August 1988): 44-46.

Moses, M. "Pesticide related health problems in farm workers." *American Association of Occupational Health Nurses Journal* 37 (1989a): 115-130.

Moses, M. "Cancer and occupational and environmental exposure to pesticides, an annotated bibliography." *American Association of Occupational Health Nurses Journal* 37 (1989b): 131-139.

Mpanya, Mutomobo. "The Dumping of Toxic Waste in African Countries: A Case of Poverty and Racism." In *The Proceedings of the Conference on Race and the Incidence of Environmental Hazards,* edited by Bunyan Bryant and Paul Mohai. Ann Arbor, MI: University of Michigan School of Natural Resources, 1990.

Murrow, Edward R., *The Harvest of Shame.* Documentary. New York: CBS Television News, 1962.

Namba, T.; Nolte, C.T.; Jackrel, J., *et al.* "Poisoning due to organophosphate insecticides: Acute and chronic manifestations." *American Journal of Medicine* 50 (1971): 475-492.

Nash, Roderick. *Wilderness and the American Mind.* 3rd ed. New Haven: Yale University Press, 1982.

National Research Council, Committee on the Role of Alternative Farming Methods in Modern Production Agriculture, Board on Agriculture. *Alternative Agriculture.* Washington, D.C.: National Academy Press, 1989.

National Urban League. *The State of Black America 1987.* New York: National Urban League, 1987.

Nauss, D.W. "The People vs. the Lead Smelter." The *Dallas Times Herald,* 17 July 1983.

Needleman, H.L.; Schell, A.; Bellinger, D.; Leviton, A.; and Allred, E.N. "The long-term effects of exposure to low doses of lead in children: an 11-year follow-up report. *New England Journal of Medicine,* 322 (1992): 83-88.

Nelkins, D. and Brown, M.S. *Workers at Risk: Voices from the Workplace.* Chicago: University of Chicago Press, 1984.

Nelson, C.J.; Holson, J.F.; Green, H.G.; and Gaylor, D.W. "Retrospective study of the relationship between agricultural use of 2,4,5-T and cleft palate occurrence in Arkansas." *Teratology* 19 (1979): 377-384.

New Mexico Department of Game and Fish, *Annual Report.* Santa Fe: New Mexico Department of Game and Fish. 1976

New York State Joint Legislative Commission on Toxic Substances and Hazardous Wastes. *Lead Contamination in New York State.* Albany, NY: New York State Senate, 1992.

Newman, Dorothy K. and Day, Dawn. *The American Energy Consumer.* Cambridge, MA: Ballinger, 1975.

Newman, Oscar. *Design Guidelines for Creating Defensible Space.* Washington, D.C.: National Institute of Law Enforcement and Criminal Justice, Law Enforcement Assistance Administration, U.S. Department of Justice, 1970.

Noble, Kenneth B. "U.S. Told to Set Sanitation Rule for Field Hands." *New York Times,* 7 February 1987.

O'Connor, James. "Uneven and Combined Development and Ecological Crisis: A Theoretical Introduction," *Race and Class* 30 (3) (January-March 1989).

O'Hare, Michael; Bacow, Lawrence; and Sanderson, Debra. *Facility Siting and Public Opposition.* New York: Van Nostrand Reinhold, 1983.

O'Malley, M. *Systemic Illness Associated with Exposure to Parathion in California, 1982-1989.* Report No. HS-1625. Sacramento, CA: Department of Pesticide Regulation, Worker Health and Safety Branch, 1992a.

O'Malley, M. *Systemic Illness Associated with Exposure to Mevinphos in California, 1982-1989.* Report No. HS-1626. Sacramento, CA: Department of Pesticide Regulation, Worker Health and Safety Branch, 1992b.

Office of Technology Assessment. *Technologies and Management Strategies for Hazardous Waste Control.* Washington, D.C.: Government Printing Office, 1983.

Office of Technology Assessment. *Superfund Strategy Summary.* (1985): 253.

Ogden, J.R. and Associates. *Baca Water Project's Economic Impact on the San Luis Valley.* Alamosa, CO: Ogden and Associates, 1989.

Omi, Michael and Winant, Howard. *Racial Formation in the United States: From the 1960's to the 1980's.* New York: Routledge, Kegan and Paul, 1986.

Ong, Paul and Blumenberg, Evelyn. "Race and Environmentalism." Paper read at Graduate School of Architecture and Urban Planning, 14 March 1990, at UCLA.

Osorio, A.M. and Ames, R. *Investigation of a Fatality Among Parathion Applicators: Kern County, California.* Berkeley, CA: State of California Department of Health Services, HESIS and Pesticide Unit, 1990

Paehlke, Robert. *Environmentalism and the Future of Progressive Politics.* New Haven: Yale University Press, 1989.

Panos Institute. "Cultural and Biological Diversity: Toward the Edge of the Cliff." Panos Media Briefing No. 1. London: The Panos Institute, 1992.

Pardo, Mary. "Mexican American Women Grassroots Community Activists: Mothers of East Los Angeles." *Frontiers: A Journal of Women's Studies* 11 (January 1990): 1-6.

Peña, Devon. "The Saguache County Community Council: A Chicana-Led Political Revolution." Unpublished manuscript. Department of Sociology, Colorado College, Colorado Springs, CO., 1989.

Peña, Devon. "The Green Marx: Capitalism and the Destruction of Nature." Unpublished manuscript. Department of Sociology, Colorado College, Colorado Springs, CO, 1990a.

Peña, Devon. "Environmental Impacts of BMG Cited." *Valley Courier,* 18 September 1990b.

Peña, Devon. "Poll Shows San Luis Against BMG Mine." *Valley Courier,* 21 September 1990c.

Peña, Devon. "Problems Alleged in Construction of Tailings Facility." *Valley Courier,* 23 November 1990d.

Peña, Devon. "Labor Conditions and Safety at BMG Criticized." *Valley Courier,* 24 November 1990e.

Peña, Devon. "Why Judge Ogburn Should Rule Against BMG." *Valley Courier,* 28 November 1990f.

Peña, Devon. "Why Judge Ogburn Should Rule Against BMG." *Valley Courier,* 29 November 1990g.

Peña, Devon. "If Judge Ogburn Decided to Make a Bit of History." *Valley Courier,* 1 December 1990h.

Peña, Devon. "An American Wilderness in a Mexican Homeland." Paper presented at the 33rd Annual Meetings of the Western Social Science Association, Reno, Nevada. 1991a.

Peña, Devon. "San Luis Vega and Garrett Hardin: The Commons in Cross-Cultural Perspective." Paper presented at the 33rd Annual

Meetings of the Western Social Science Association, Reno, Nevada. 1991b.

Peña, Devon. "The 'Brown' and the 'Green': Chicano and Environmental Politics in the Upper Rio Grande." *Capitalism, Nature & Socialism* 3 (1992): 1-25.

Peña, Devon. "A Gold Mine, an Orchard, and an Eleventh Commandment," in *New Scholar,* vol. 13: And in *Subversive Kin: Chicano Studies and Ecology,* forthcoming.

Peña, Devon and Martinez, Ruben. "Rural Chicano Communities and the Environment: An Attitudinal Survey of Residents of Costilla County, Colorado." Field Report Series, vol. 1, Rio Grande Bioregions Project, Hulbert Center for Southwestern Studies, Colorado College, Colorado Springs, CO, 1991.

Peoples, S.A. and Maddy, K.T. Organophosphate pesticide poisoning. *Western Journal of Medicine* 129 (1978): 273-277.

Pepper, David. *The Roots of Modern Environmentalism.* London: Croom & Helm, Ltd., 1986.

Perry, David C. and Alfred J. Watkins. *The Rise of the Sunbelt Cities.* Beverly Hills: Sage, 1977.

Pollack, Sue and Grozuczak, JoAnn. *Reagan, Toxics and Minorities.* Washington, D.C.: Urban Environment Conference, 1984.

Portney, Kent E. "The Potential of the Theory of Compensation for Mitigating Public Opposition to Hazardous Waste Siting: Some Evidence from Five Massachusetts Communities." *Policy Studies Journal* 14 (1985): 81-89.

Potashnik, G. and Abeliovich, D. "Chromosomal analysis and health status of children conceived to men during or following dibromochloropropane-induced spermatogenic suppression." *Andrologia* 17 (1985): 291.

Potashnik, G. and Yanai-Inbar, I. "Dibromochloropropane (DBCP): An 8 year reevaluation of testicular function and reproductive performance." *Fertility and Sterility* 47 (1987): 317-323.

Potashnik, G.; Yanai-Inbar, I.; Sacks, M.I.; *et al.* "Effect of dibromochloropropane in human testicular function." *Israel Journal of Medical Science* 15 (1979): 438-442.

Prabhakar, J.M. "Possible relationship of insecticide exposure to embryonal cell carcinoma." (Letter) *Journal of the American Medical Association* 240 (1978): 288.

Pratt, C.B.; George, S.L.; O'Connor, D.; *et al.* "Adolescent colorectal cancer and dioxin exposure." (Letter) *Lancet* 2 (1987): 803.

Pratt, C.B., Rivera, G., Shanks, E., *et al.* "Colorectal carcinoma in adolescents, implications regarding etiology." *Cancer* 40 (1977): 2464-2472.

Prockop, L.D. and Smith, A.O. "Seizures and action myoclonus after occupational exposure to methyl bromide." *Journal of the Florida Medical Association* 73 (1986): 690-691.

Puleston Fleming, Jeanie. "Ganados del Valle: A Venture in Self-Sufficiency." *New Mexico Magazine* (September 1985): 39-42.

Pye, Veronica I.; Patrick, Ruth; and Quarles, John. *Groundwater Contamination in the United States.* Philadelphia: University of Pennsylvania Press, 1983.

Quintana, Patricia. "Agricultural Economic and Market Potential for the Chama Valley." Unpublished manuscript. Ganados' files, n.d.

Ratcliffe, J.M.; Schrader, S.M.; Steenland, K.; *et al.* "Semen Quality in Papaya Workers with Long Term Exposure to Ethylene Dibromide." *British Journal of Industrial Medicine* 44 (1987): 317-326.

Ratner, D. and Eshel, E. "Aerial pesticide spraying: an environmental hazard." (Letter) *Journal of the American Medical Association* 256 (1986): 2516-2517.

Rawls, John. *A Theory of Justice.* Cambridge, MA: Harvard University Press, 1971.

Reed, Dan. "Jackson to Chevron: Clean Up." *West County Times,* 8 May 1990: A1.

Rees, William. "The Ecology of Sustainable Development." *The Ecologist* 20 (1990): 12-16.

Reisner, Marc. *Overtapped Oasis: Reform or Revolution for Western Water.* Washington, D.C.: Island, 1990.

Rensenbrink, John. "What Marx Forgot, Liberals Have Never Known and Conservatives Find Frightening: The Ecology of Democracy." Paper delivered at American Political Science Association meeting. Washington D.C., 1988. Mimeographed.

"State Issues Boil Order." *Rio Grande Sun,* 11 April 1991a: B1.

"State Cites Village for Violations at Landfill." *Rio Grande Sun,* 20 June 1991b: B1, B2.

R.I.S.E. (Residents Involved in Saving the Environment) v. Kay, 768 F. Supp. 1141 (E.D. Va. 1991).

Rita, P.; Reddy, P.P.; and Reddy, S.V. "Monitoring of workers occupationally exposed to pesticides in grape gardens of Andhra Pradesh." *Environ Res* 44 (1987): 1-5.

Roan, C.C.; Matanoski, G.E.; McIlnay, C.Q., *et al.* "Spontaneous abortions, stillbirths, and birth defects in families of agricultural pilots." *Archives of Environmental Health* 39 (1984): 56-60.

Robertson, James. *The Sane Alternative.* Saint Paul: Riverbasin Press, 1983.

Rodnitzky, R.L.; Levin, H.S.; and Mick, D.L. "Occupational exposure to organophosphate pesticides, a neurobehavioral study." *Archives of Environmental Health* 30 (1975): 98-103.

Rodriguez, Sylvia. "Land, Water, and Ethnic Identity in Taos." In *Land, Water and Culture: New Perspectives on Hispanic Land Grants,* edited by C. Briggs and J. Van Ness, pp. 313-403. Albuquerque: University of New Mexico Press, 1987.

Roeleveld, N.; Zielhuis, G.A.; and Gabreels, F. "Occupational exposure and defects of the central nervous system in offspring: review." *British Journal of Industrial Medicine* 47 (1990): 580-588.

Romero, P.; Barnett, P.G.; and Midtling, J.E. "Congenital anomalies associated with maternal exposure to oxydemeton-methyl." *Environmental Research* 50 (1989): 256-261.

Rosenbaum, Robert. *Mexicano Resistance in the Southwest: The Sacred Right of Self-Preservation.* Austin: University of Texas Press, 1981.

Rossdeutcher, Daniele. "Bizarre Spraying Campaign Haunts Guatemala." *Earth Island Institute Journal* (Fall 1987).

Rostow, W.W. *Getting From Here to There.* New York: McGraw-Hill, 1987.

Roth-Arrriaza, Naomi. "The Politics of Environmental Destruction." *Report on Guatemala* (Summer 1991).

Ruffins, Paul. "Blacks and Greens: What Can the Environmental Movement Do to Reach Out to Minorities?" *Race, Poverty and the Environment* 1 (February 1990): 5.

Russell, Dick. "Environmental Racism: Minority Communities and Their Battle against Toxics." *Amicus Journal* 11 (Spring 1989): 22-32.

Russell, Dick. "Environmental Racism." *Amicus Journal* 11 (February 1989): 22-32.

Salazar, Gumercindo. Testimony before the U.S. House Interior Oversight Subcommittee. Taos, NM: Ganados' files, 29 July 1989.

Salazar, Gumercindo. Member of Ganados del Valle. Interview with author. Chama, NM, 12 August 1991.

Sanchez, Jesus. "The Environment: Whose Movement?" *California Tomorrow* 3 (1988): 10-17.

Sanchez, Roberto. "Health and Environmental Risks of the Maquiladora in Mexicali." *Natural Resources Journal* 30 (Winter (1990): 163-186.

Sanchez-Ramos, J.R.; Hefti, F.; and Weiner, W.J. "Paraquat and Parkinson's Disease." (Letter) *Neurology* 37 (1987): 728.

Sanders, Hank. "Defending Voting Rights in the Alabama Black Belt." Interview with Hank Sanders by Frances M. Beal, *The Black Scholar* (June 1986): 25-34.

Sandifer, S.H.; Wilkins, R.T.; Loadholt, C.B., *et al.* "Spermatogenesis in Agricultural Workers Exposed to Dibromochloropropane (DBCP)." *Bulliten of Environmental Contamination and Toxicology* 23 (1979): 703-710.

Sandoval, Ron. "San Luis Vega." In *La Cultura Constante de San Luis*, edited by Randall Teeuwen. San Luis, CO: San Luis Museum and Cultural Center, 1984.

Saunders, D.; Ames, R.G.; Knaak, J.B., *et al.* "Outbreak of Omite-CR Induced Dermatitis Among Orange Pickers in Tulare County, California." *Journal of Occupational Medicine* 29 (1987): 409-413.

Savage, David G. "High Court Rejects Curbs on Waste Dumps." *Los Angeles Times,* 2 June 1992: A12.

Savage, E.P.; Keefe, T.J.; Mounce, L.M., *et al.* "Chronic Neurological Sequelae of Acute Organophosphate Poisoning." *Archives of Environmental Health* 43 (1988): 38-45.

Savitz, D.A.; Whelan, E.A.; and Kleckner, R.C. "Self-reported exposure to pesticides and radiation related to pregnancy outcome—Results from national natality and fetal mortality surveys." *Public Health Report* 104 (1989): 473-477.

Schein, Maureen. "Sheep Grazing Proposal Nixed." *Rio Grande Sun,* 12 September 1985.

Schein, Maureen. "Lodgers Say Water Shortage Hurt Weekend Business." *Rio Grande Sun,* 4 April 1991: B1.

Schnaiberg, Allan. *The Environment: From Surplus to Scarcity.* New York: Oxford University Press, 1980.

Schnaiberg, Allan. "Redistributive Goals Versus Distributive Politics: Social Equity Limits in Environmentalism and Appropriate Technology Movements." *Sociological Inquiry* 53 (Spring 1983): 200-219.

Schwartz, D.A. and LoGerfo, J.P. "Congenital limb reduction defects in the agricultural setting." *American Journal of Public Health* 78 (1988): 654-657.

Schwartz, D.A.; Newsum, L.A.; and Heifitz, R.M. "Parental occupation and birth outcome in an agricultural community." *Scandinavian Journal of Work and Environmental Health* 12 (1986): 51-54.

Schwartz, Joel and Levin, Ronnie. "Lead: An Example of the Job Ahead." *EPA Journal* 18 (March/April 1992): 42-44.

Serrano, Angie. Ganados del Valle. Interview with author, Los Ojos, NM, 17 August 1990.

Sever, L.E.; Hessol, N.A.; Gilbert, E.S., *et al.* "The prevalence at birth of congenital malformations in communities near the Hanford site." *American Journal of Epidemiology* 127 (1988): 243-254.

Sharp, D.S.; Eskenazi, B.; Harrison, R., *et al.* "Delayed health hazards of pesticide exposure." *Annual Review of Public Health* 7 (1986): 441-471.

Shiva, Vandana. *Staying Alive: Women, Ecology and Development.* London: Zed, 1988.

Shiva, Vandana. "Global Resource Distribution." In *Call to Action: Ecology, Peace and Justice,* edited by Brad Erikson, pp. 70-73. San Francisco: Sierra Club Books, 1990.

Siler, Julia Flynn. "Environmental Racism? It Could Be a Messy Fight." *Business Week,* 20 May 1991: 116.

Simon, Marlise. "North-South Divide Is Marring Environment Talks." *New York Times,* 17 March 1992.

Sklar, Holly, ed. *Trilateralism: The Trilateral Commission and Elite Planning for World Management.* Boston: South End Press, 1980.

Smith, A.H.; Fisher, D.O.; and Pearce, N., *et al.* "Congenital defects and miscarriages among New Zealand 2,4,5-T sprayers." *Archives of Environmental Health* 37 (1982): 197-200.

Smith, Kerry. *Presidents Reagan's Executive Order.* Chapel Hill, NC: University of North Carolina, 1986.

Smith, Zachary. *Groundwater in the West.* New York: Academic Press, 1989.

South Boston Gazette-Virginian Editorial. "More than 60 Speakers Say 'No' to Dump." *South Boston Gazette-Virginian,* 28 March 1986: 10-14.

South Carolina Department of Health and Control. "Status of Governor Campbell's Executive Order No. 89-03." April 5, 1989.

State of California Department of Food and Agriculture, Worker Health and Safety Branch. *Summary of illnesses and injuries reported in*

California by physicians as potentially related to pesticides. Issued Annually. Sacramento, CA: 1975-1988.

State of California Department of Food and Agriculture. Sacramento, CA. Press release dated 8 February 1990.

State of California Department of Health Services. *Epidemiologic Study of Adverse Health Effects in Children in McFarland, California, Phase II Report.* Berkeley: Epidemiological Studies and Surveillance Section, 1988a.

State of California Department of Health Services. *Pesticides: Health Aspects of Exposure and Issues Surrounding Their Use.* Continuing Education Seminar for Health Personnel Course Syllabus and Manual. Berkeley: Hazard Evaluation Section. 1988b.

State Engineers Office, State of Colorado. *Tabulation Listing all Decreed Water Rights, Division Three.* Denver: SEO, 1978.

Stewart, John Cary. *Drinking Water Hazards.* Hiram, OH: Envirographics, 1990.

Stoller, Marianne. "La merced." In Randall Tweeuwen, ed. *La cultura constante de San Luis.* San Luis, CO: San Luis Museum and Cultural Center, 1985.

Suro, Roberto. "Grass Roots Groups Show Power Battling Pollution Close to Home." *New York Times,* 2 July 1989: A1.

Swadesh, Francis. *Los Primeros Pobladores: Hispanic Americans of the Ute Frontier.* Notre Dame: University of Notre Dame Press, 1974.

Tabershaw, I.R. and Cooper, W.C. "Sequelae of acute organophosphate poisoning." *Journal of Occupational Medicine* 8 (1966): 5-20.

Tafuri, J. and Roberts, J. "Organophosphate Poisoning, Collective Review." *Annual of Emergency Medicine* 16 (1987): 193/93-102/202.

Taylor, Dorceta A. "Blacks and the Environment: Toward an Explanation of the Concern and Action Gap between Blacks and Whites." *Environment and Behavior* 21 (February 1989): 175-205.

Taylor, Ronald B. *Sweatshops in the Sun, Child Labor on the Farm.* Boston: Beacon Press, 1973.

Taylor, Ronald B. *Chavez and the Farm Workers, a Study in the Acquisition and Use of Power.* Boston: Beacon Press, 1975.

Taylor, Ronald B. "Do Environmentalists Care about the Poor." *U.S. News and World Report* 96 (April 2, 1982): 51-52.

Teltsch, Kathleen. "New Mexico Split Over Where Sheep May Graze." *New York Times,* 31 May 1990: A12.

Tinker, Jon. "Property Rights and Biotechnology." Department of Environment Seminar on "Conserving the Worlds Biological Diversity: How Can Britain Contribute?": Natural History Museum, London, 1991.

Todd, J.H. *An Analysis of the Economic Impact of Chemical Waste Management, Inc. on the Regional Economy of West Alabama and East Mississippi.* Livingston, Alabama: Livingston University, Center for Business and Economic Services, 1988.

Tomsho, Robert. "Dumping Grounds: Indian Tribes Contend with Some of the Worst of America's Pollution." *Wall Street Journal,* 29 November 1990.

Truax, Hawley. "Beyond White Environmentalism: Minorities and the Environment." *Environmental Action* 21 (1990): 19-30.

United Church of Christ Commission for Racial Justice. *Toxic Wastes and Race in the United States, A National Report on the Racial and Socio-Economic Characteristics of Communities with Hazardous Waste Sites.* New York: United Church of Christ, 1987.

United Church of Christ Commission for Racial Justice. *The First National People of Color Environmental Leadership Summit: Program Guide.* New York: United Church of Christ, 1992.

United Nations Ad Hoc Group of Experts on Community Development. *Community Development and National Development.* New York: United Nations, 1963.

U.S. Bureau of the Census. *America's Black Population: 1970 to 1982. A Statistical View.* 1983.

U.S. Bureau of the Census. *We the Mexican Americans, the Cubans, and the Hispanos from Other Countries in the Caribbean, Central and South America, and from Spain.* 1985.

U.S. Bureau of the Census. *We the Black Americans.* 1986.

U.S. Bureau of the Census. *Colorado Population Census Report: County Statistics.* Washington, D.C.: Government Printing Office, 1991.

U.S. Congress. *Migrant Farm Workers in America.* Hearings before the Subcommittee on Labor and Public Welfare. 1960.

U.S. Congress. *Migrant and Seasonal Farmworker Powerlessness.* Hearings before the Subcommittee on Labor and Public Welfare. 1970.

U.S. Department of Agriculture. *Agricultural Statistics,* 1990. Washington, D.C.: Government Printing Office, 1990.

U.S. Department of Health and Human Services, Centers for Disease Control, Atlanta. "Preventing Lead Poisoning in Children: A Statement by the Centers for Disease Control." Pub. No. 99-2230. January 1985a.

U.S. Department of Health and Human Services. *Report of the Secretary's Task Force on Black and Minority Health*. 1985b.

U.S. Department of Housing and Urban Development. *Comprehensive and Workable Plan for the Abatement of Lead-Based Paint in Privately Owned Housing: A Report to Congress*. 1990.

U.S. Department of the Interior, National Parks Service. *Environmental Handbook for Cyanide Leaching Projects*. 1986.

U.S. Environmental Protection Agency. *Environmental Progress and Challenges: An EPA Perspective*. June 1984. p. 78.

U.S. Environmental Protection Agency. "Emergency and Remedial Response Information System." May 1986a.

U.S. Environmental Protection Agency. *Heap Leach Technology and Potential Effects in the Black Hills*. Denver, CO: EPA Water Management Division, 1986b.

U.S. Environmental Protection Agency. "Parathion, re-registration document." 1986c.

U.S. Environmental Protection Agency. *Pesticide Industry Sales and Usage, 1987 Market Estimates*. 1988.

U.S. Environmental Protection Agency. *Environmental Equity: Reducing Risk for All Americans*. 1992.

U.S. Environmental Protection Agency, Water Management Division. *Heap Leach Technology and Potential Effects in the Black Hills*. Denver: EPA, 1986.

U.S. General Accounting Office. *EPA is Slow to Carry Out Its Responsibility to Control Harmful Chemicals*. GAO Report CED-81-1. 1980.

U.S. General Accounting Office. *Siting of Hazardous Waste Landfills and Their Correlation with Racial and Economic Status of Surrounding Communities*. 1983.

U.S. General Accounting Office. *Assessment of EPA's Hazardous Waste Enforcement Strategy*. 1985.

U.S. General Accounting Office. *Hazardous Waste: EPA Has Made Limited Progress in Determining the Wastes to Be Regulated*. 1986a.

U.S. General Accounting Office. *Pesticides: EPA's Formidable Task to Assess and Regulate Their Risks*. GAO Report RCED-86-125. 1986b.

U.S. General Accounting Office. *Pesticides: EPA's Use of Benefit Assessments in Regulating Pesticides*. GAO Report RCED-91-52. 1991a.

U.S. General Accounting Office. *Pesticides: Better Data Can Improve the Usefulness of EPA's Benefit Assessments.* GAO Report RCED-92-32. 1991b.

U.S. General Accounting Office. *Hired Farm Workers, Health and Well-Being at Risk.* Report to Congressional Requesters. GAO/HRD-92-46. 1992a.

U.S. General Accounting Office. *Food Safety: USDA Data Program Not Supporting Critical Pesticide Decisions.* GAO Report IMTEC-92-11. 1992b.

U.S. v. Yonkers, 837 F. 2d 1181 (2nd Cir. 1987).

U.S. National Advisory Commission on Civil Disorders. *Report of the National Advisory Commission on Civil Disorders.* New York: E.P. Dutton and Co., 1968.

Urban Environment Conference, Inc. *Taking Back Our Health: An Institute on Surviving the Threat to Minority Communities.* Washington, D.C.: Urban Environment Conference, Inc., 1985.

Vallette, Jim and Spalding, Heather. *The International Trade in Wastes: A Greenpeace Inventory.* Washington, D.C.: Greenpeace USA, 1990.

Van Liere, Kent D. and Dunlap, Riley. "The Social Bases of Environmental Concern: A Review of Hypothesis, Explanations, and Empirical Evidence." *Public Opinion Quarterly* 44 (February 1980): 181-197.

Varela, Maria. "Developing Selective Tourism Strategies for the Chama Valley." Unpublished manuscript. Santa Fe, NM: The Milagro Fund, 1989a.

Varela, Maria. "Grazing is Legitimate Method for Improving Wildlife Habitat." *Albuquerque Journal,* 28 December 1989b: A9.

Varela, Maria. "El Milagro Sheep Grazing War: Interview with Maria Varela." *CBS News Nightwatch,* 16 August 1990.

Varela, Maria. Interim Report to the Needmore Fund. Ganados' files, 16 May 1991.

Vaughan, T.L.; Daling, J.R.; and Starzyk, P.M. "Fetal death and maternal occupation: an analysis of birth records in the state of Washington." *Journal of Occupational Medicine* 26 (1984): 676-678.

Vig, Norman J. and Draft, Michael E, eds. *Environmental Policy in the 1980s: Reagan's New Era.* Washington, D.C.: Congressional Quarterly Press, 1984.

Voelker, Denise. "Political Turmoil Endangers Ecology of Canal Region." *Earth Island Institute Journal* (Winter 1988).

Wasserstrom, R.F. and Wiles, R. *Field Duty, U.S. Farm Workers and Pesticide Safety.* Washington, D.C.: World Resources Institute, 1985.

Weber, Kenneth. "Necessary but Insufficient: Land, Water, and Economic Development in Hispanic Southern Colorado." *The Journal of Ethnic Studies* 19 (1991): 127-142.

Weigle, Marta. *Hispanic Villages of Northern New Mexico: A Reprint of Volume II of the 1935 Tewa Basin Study with Supplementary Materials.* Santa Fe: The Lightening Tree, 1975.

Weisskopf, Michael. "EPA's 2 Voices on Pollution Risks to Minorities." *Washington Post,* 9 March 1992: A15.

Wellman, D.T. *Portraits of White Racism.* New York: Cambridge University Press, 1977.

Wentz, David A. "Effect of Mine Drainage on the Quality of Streams in Colorado, 1971-1972." Colorado Water Resources Research Institute, Circular No. 21, 1974.

Wenz, P. *Environmental Justice.* New York: SUNY Press, 1988.

Wernette, D.R. and Nieves, L.A. "Breathing Polluted Air." *EPA Journal* 18 (March/April 1992): 16-17.

West, Pat C.; Fly, F.; and Marans, R. "Minority Anglers and Toxic Fish Consumption: Evidence from a State-Wide Survey of Michigan." pp. 108-122. In *The Proceedings of the Michigan Conference on Race and the Incidence of Environmental Hazards,* edited by B. Bryant and P. Mohai. Ann Arbor: University of Michigan School of Natural Resources, 1989.

Westphall, Victor. *The Public Domain in New Mexico, 1854-1891.* Albuquerque, NM: University of New Mexico Press, 1965.

Westphall, Victor. *Mercedes Reales: Hispanic Land Grants of the Upper Rio Grande Region.* Albuquerque: University of New Mexico Press, 1983.

White, F.M.M.; Cohen, F.G.; Sherman, G.; and McCurdy, R. "Chemicals, birth defects and stillbirths in New Brunswick: Associations with agricultural activity." *Canadian Medical Association Journal* 138 (1988): 117-124.

Whorton, D.; Krauss, R.M.; Marshall, S.; *et al.* 1977. "Infertility in male pesticide workers." *Lancet* 2 (1977): 1259-1261.

Whorton, D. and Milby, T.H. "Recovery of testicular function among DBCP workers." *Journal of Occupational Medicine* 22 (1980): 177-179.

Whorton, D.; Milby, T.H.; Krauss, R.M., *et al.* "Testicular function in DBCP exposed pesticide workers." *Journal of Occupational Medicine* 21 (1979): 161-166.

Witt, Matthew. "An Injury to One is an Gravio A Todo: The Need for a Mexico-U.S. Health and Safety Movement." *New Solutions, A Journal of Environmental and Occupational Health Policy* 1 (March 1991): 28-33.

Wong, O.; Utidjian, H.M.D.; and Karten, V.S. "Retrospective evaluation of reproductive performance of workers exposed to ethylene dibromide." *Journal of Occupational Medicine* 21 (1979): 98-102.

Working Group on Canada-Mexico Free Trade. "Que Pasa? A Canada-Mexico 'Free' Trade Deal." *New Solutions, A Journal of Environmental and Occupational Health Policy* 2 (January 1991): 10-25.

World Commission on Environment and Development. *Our Common Future.* New York: Oxford University Press, 1987.

Worster, Donald. *Rivers of Empire: Water, Aridity, and the Rise of the American West.* New York: Pantheon, 1985.

Wright, Beverly H. and Bullard, Robert D. "Hazards in the Workplace and Black Health." *National Journal of Sociology* 4 (Spring 1990): 45-62.

Young, John. *Sustaining the Earth.* Cambridge: Harvard University Press, 1990.

Zuniga, Jo Ann. "Watchdog Keeps Tabs on Politics of Environment along Border." *Houston Chronicle,* 24 May 1992: 22A.

INDEX

A

Aborn, James, 147
ACE. *See* Alabamians for a Clean Environment
ACLU. *See* American Civil Liberties Union
ACORN, 31
Adair, Margo, 72
Adam, Nigel, 189
Adams, R. M., 167
ADECA. *See* Alabama Department of Economic and Community Affairs
Africa, 64-65, 71, 185. *See also* Global issues
African-American Black and Green Tendency, 56
African American Environmental Association, 56
African Americans, 7, 49, 50; "Cancer Alley" (Louisiana), 12-13, 27-28, 32, 35, 37; class issues, 21-22; employment patterns, 22-23, 42; and environmental planning, 94, 101; Halifax County, Virginia, 98-100; Houston, Texas, 27, 31, 33-34, 37; King and Queen County, Virginia, 95-98; lead poisoning rates, 21-22, 68, 78; Richmond, California, 29, 30, 33, 35-36, 37; and urban development, 68, 70; Warren County, North Carolina, 43, 54, 55, 198; West Dallas, Texas, 11, 27, 30, 31-32, 34, 35, 36-37. *See also* Environmental justice movement; Environmental racism; People of color; Polluting facilities siting in communities of color; Racism
African Renaissance movement, 71

Agency for Toxic Substances and Disease Registry (ATSDR), 12, 21, 77, 78, 198
Aguilar, Gregorita, 133
Air pollution, 42
Airco Industrial Gases, 29
Akesson, N. B., 165
Alabama Department of Economic and Community Affairs (ADECA), 108, 109
Alabama Environmental Coalition, 114-15
Alabamians for a Clean Environment (ACE), 114-16
Alabarado, Sonny, 27
Alexander, Edward, 93-94
Allamilla, Ileana, 187
Alliance to End Childhood Lead Poisoning, 77
Alsen, Louisiana, 27-28, 32, 35, 37
Alston, Dana, 24, 64
American Association of Blacks in Energy, 56
American Civil Liberties Union (ACLU), 24, 88
American Planning Association, 101
American Water Development, Inc. (AWDI), 155
Anderson, Bob, 13, 27
Anderson, H., 176
Anderson, Richard, 197
Anderson, Richard E., 45
Angel, Bradley, 12, 29, 201
Anger, W. K., 169
AQMD. *See* South Coast Air Quality Management District
Asian Americans, 49, 163-64
Association of Community Organizations for Reform Now. *See* ACORN

About South End Press

South End Press is a nonprofit, collectively-run book publisher with over 175 titles in print. Since our founding in 1977, we have tried to meet the needs of readers who are exploring, or are already committed to, the politics of fundamental social change.

Our goal is to publish books that encourage critical thinking and constructive action on the key social and ecological issues shaping life in the United States and around the world. In this way, we hope to give expression to a wide diversity of democratic social movements and to provide an alternative to the products of corporate publishing.

Through the Institute for Social and Cultural Change, South End Press works with other political media projects—*Z Magazine;* Speak Out!, a national speakers bureau; the Publishers Support Project; and the New Liberation News Service—to expand access to information and critical analysis. If you would like a free catalog of South End Press books or information about our membership program—which offers two free books and a 40% discount on all titles—please write to us at South End Press, 116 Saint Botolph Street, Boston, MA 02115 or call (617) 266-0629.

Other SEP Titles of Interest

The New Resource Wars
Native and Environmental Struggles
Against Multinational Corporations
Al Gedicks

The State of Native America
Genocide, Colonization, and Resistence
edited by M. Annette Jaimes

How Capitalism Underdeveloped Black America
Manning Marable

Defending the Earth
A Dialogue Between Murray Bookchin and Dave Foreman
edited with an introduction by Steve Chase